HD
29
.N4
1975

GEORGE BROWN COLLEGE
ST. JAMES CAMPUS

D1112082 /9

2-... 0491085 1994 06 10

$8.80

PAID FEB 1 1999

New Technologies
in
Organization Development: 1

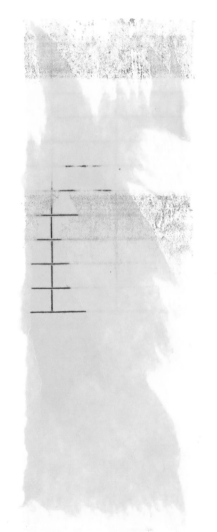

THE GEORGE BROWN COLLEGE
OE APPLIED ARTS AND TECHNOLOGY
LIBRARY

1.50

New Technologies in Organization Development: 1

(Originally Entitled
*Contemporary Organization Development:
Conceptual Orientations
and Interventions*)

Edited by

W. Warner Burke

University Associates, Inc.
7596 Eads Avenue
La Jolla, California 92037
1975

THE GEORGE BROWN COLLEGE
LIBRARY

ACCESS N. 308198

SOURCE
Univ. Assoc.

DATE
77-08-11

PRICE
7.00

CLASS NO.

CHKD.
VE

Copyright ® 1972 by NTL Institute for Applied Behavioral Science,
Arlington, Virginia 22209. All rights reserved.

ISBN: 0-88390-113-7

Library of Congress Catalog Card Number: 75-35017

Printed in the United States of America

Contents

Contributors

D. RICHARD ALBERTSON

Director, Center for
Educational Systems
NTL Institute

ROBERT R. BLAKE

Scientific Methods, Inc.
Austin, Texas

ARTHUR BLUMBERG

Professor of Education
Syracuse University

STOKES B. CARRIGAN

Manager, Employee and
Organization Development
Smith, Kline & French
    Laboratories
Philadelphia, Pennsylvania

WILLIAM G. DYER

Chairman, Department of
Organizational Behavior
Brigham Young University

CHARLES K. FERGUSON

Director, Department of
    Conferences and
    Program Consultation
UCLA

JACK R. GIBB

Consulting Psychologist
La Jolla, California

JOHN C. GLIDEWELL

Professor of Education
University of Chicago

ROBERT T.
GOLEMBIEWSKI

Research Professor and Head,
Department of Political Science
University of Georgia

JAY HALL

President
Teleometrics Int'l.
Conroe, Texas

JERRY B. HARVEY

Associate Professor of
Management Science
George Washington University

STANLEY M. HERMAN

Director, Training and
Organization Development
Systems Group of TRW, Inc.

DONALD C. KING

Professor, Administrative
Sciences and Psychology
Krannert Graduate School of
Industrial Administration
Purdue University

GEORGE F. J. LEHNER

Professor
Department of Psychology
UCLA

GORDON L. LIPPITT

Professor of Behavioral Sciences
School of Government and
Business Administration
George Washington University

ROBERT A. LUKE, JR.

Associate, National Training
and Development Service for
State and Local Government

WALTER R. MEAD

Training Director
Smith, Kline & French
Laboratories
Philadelphia, Pennsylvania

JANE S. MOUTON

Scientific Methods, Inc.
Austin, Texas

ROBERT MUNZENRIDER

Doctoral Student
University of Georgia

BARRY OSHRY

Psychologist
Boston, Massachusetts

PHILIP J. RUNKEL

Member of the Center for
the Advanced Study of
Educational Administration
and Professor of
Psychology
University of Oregon

RICHARD A. SCHMUCK

Member of the Center for
the Advanced Study of
Educational Administration
and Professor of Educational
Psychology
University of Oregon

JOHN J. SHERWOOD

Professor of Social Psychology
and Administrative Sciences
Krannert Graduate School of
Industrial Administration
Purdue University

Preface

Organization development (OD) is approximately a decade old. Although many of the elements comprising OD have existed for more than a decade, OD as a systematic body of knowledge and skill has not reached adolescence. And, like the prepuberal child, it is changing every day. In fact, the field has changed so rapidly that many persons who thought they knew yesterday are today asking the question, "What is OD anyway?" For example, OD had its genesis in human relations training, particularly the laboratory method of adult education, and in team building, but today people refer to management by objectives, career development, and structural changes in the organization as OD. Like many other practitioners and theoreticians in the field, I am still struggling with a definition. Even though continuing ambiguity regarding a definition of OD may be frustrating, I think these times are exciting—exciting to be living during the time when a dynamic area of applied behavioral science is in the process of formulation. It is also exciting to know that one is taking part in the formation itself.

A related frustration, at least for me, has been that of simply keeping up. In fact, the problem of keeping up with OD today can be described by the comment of Hercalitus about a river centuries ago: "You cannot step twice into the same river, for other waters are continually flowing in." Several years from now OD will probably be "settled," in the sense of being a lake but, today, it is a river, perhaps in search of definable banks.

What are the new approaches and interventions OD practitioners are now attempting? Some of us have been able to keep abreast of many of the new developments by attending the semi-annual meetings of the OD Network, an informal organization of approximately 750 practitioners most of whom are "internal consultants" to and full-time employees of some large organization. Other similar conferences and workshops on OD are becoming widespread. Often, however, these meetings are all too brief to allow exploration of issues and ideas in depth. To understand some new approach more time is frequently required. In an attempt to cope with my frustration about learning the latest OD activities and inventions, I decided to arrange a conference for the express purpose of gathering the latest knowledge and disseminating it as effectively as possible. I was not reacting solely to my frustration. Many others had (and still do) expressed the same feeling. Moreover such a conference seemed to fit very effectively with what I perceive to be a growing mission of the NTL Institute for Applied Behavioral Science, that of disseminating the knowledge and skill of applied behavioral science.

I began in February, 1971, by mailing a letter and simple questionnaire to two networks of practitioners, the OD Network and the network of trainers and consultants of the NTL Institute. In the letter I explained that I wanted to test with them the notion of a two-day conference on "new technology in organization development." I stated that the purposes of such a conference would be to (a) facilitate the dissemination of new OD technology more quickly and effectively, (b) stimulate more innovation in the field, and (c) help the NTL Institute launch an event of relevance in applied behavioral science which would be an activity other than laboratory training. In the questionnaire, I asked about their interest in being a presenter and requested them to describe briefly a new intervention in OD they might be using or developing.

The response was most gratifying. I received considerably more proposals than I could possibly use, so I was able to bask in the luxury of selecting what I thought would be the most interesting, appealing, and contributory proposals submitted.

At the conference itself, the presentations were designed so that (a) the conferees could participate and be involved, and (b) the presenters could receive feedback on their "new technology."

Following the conference, the presenters wrote the final version of their paper. This gave them an opportunity to incorporate any helpful reactions they might have received during the conference.

This book then is the outcome of the "New Technology in Organization Development Conference" held in New York City, October 8-9, 1971.

I would like to thank Virginia Stacy for helping me to begin the project. Patricia Walton and Bobbi Robertson were invaluable in helping me to conduct the conference. I am especially indebted to

Charlotte Rice for typing much of the Manuscript and to Bobbi Robertson for coordinating and administering the entire project. This book is special in that so many people had a hand in producing it. The presenters gave their time and effort freely and cooperatively. Their hard work and their promptness in responding to my deadlines were unusual for a "free-wheeling bunch of behavioral scientists." They have my enduring gratitude.

W. Warner Burke, Ph.D.
Washington, D. C.
September, 1972

A Look at Organization
Development Today[1]

W. WARNER BURKE

What I attempt to do in the opening chapter of this volume is take a critical snapshot of organization development. The color in my picture doesn't cover the rainbow for I am limited by my perceptions and biases. But in my role at the NTL Institute and as I serve as the "executive secretary" of the OD Network, I have been in a unique position in the past five years to see the development of what I believe will become a major arm of applied behavioral science. What follows, then, is my current perspective on organization development.

If as much organization development (OD) were occurring as is claimed by people who say they are "doing OD," we would have much more evidence of change in organizations than I believe presently exists. I have occasion to talk with a great many of the faithful in the field who are quick to affirm their commitment. As the conversation progresses, however, I inevitably discover that either (a) they do not actually believe significant change is occurring in their organization, or (b) they ask me if I know of any new techniques for really getting OD underway. In this chapter, I explore this apparent contradiction and try to account for it. First, I point to evidence that OD is a popular and growing field; then describe some of the current problems and limitations of OD. Next, I discuss some of the forces which are shaping the current practice of OD. And, in conclusion, I briefly explore the future of organization development.

OD—A GROWING FIELD

Although OD has been a part of the language less than fifteen years, there is considerable evidence that the process has made a significant impact. Several bits of evidence can be cited:

[1]. This chapter is based on a paper presented at the Annual Convention of the Academy of Management, August 17, 1971, Atlanta, Georgia.

1. Over 1,500 people currently hold membership in some organization devoted to OD. The American Society for Training and Development has an OD DIVISION which began in the summer of 1969. Starting with a charter membership of about 100, the total membership presently numbers approximately 750. The OD Network is a more informal organization which started 8 years ago with about 25 members. Currently there are approximately 700. In addition there are two OD Networks in the United Kingdom and new ones under way in Latin America and Australia. Relatively few members of these organizations would probably claim high OD competence in the field, but it is safe to say that most have considerable interest and zeal for the concept.

2. There are an increasing number of publications which are devoted to OD. Within the past four years over 15 books have been published[2] which deal with OD and a wide variety of others have recently been published or are on the way.[3]

---

2. The most recently published books which are directly related to OD:
The Addison Wesley Series (Reading, Mass.: Addison Wesley, 1969):
Beckhard, R. *Organization Development: Strategies and Models.*
Bennis, W. G. *Organizational Development: Its Nature, Origins and Prospects.*
Blake, R. R. & Mouton, Jane S. *Building a Dynamic Corporation Through Grid Organization Development.*
Lawrence, P. R. & Lorsch, J. W. *Developing Organizations: Diagnosis and Action.*
Schein, E. H. *Process Consultation.*
Walton, R. E. *Interpersonal Peacemaking, Confrontation and Third Party Consultation.*

Three other books on OD published by Addison Wesley (Reading, Mass.) are:
Argyris, C. *Intervention Theory and Method,* Reading, Mass.: Addison Wesley, 1970.
Beck, A. C. & Hillmar, E. D. *A Practical Approach to Organization Development Through MBO,* Reading, Mass.: Addison Wesley, 1972.
Fordyce, J & Weil, R. *Managing with People,* Reading, Mass.: Addison Wesley, 1971.

Other books include:
Blake, R. R. & Mouton, Jane S. *Corporate Excellence Through Grid Organization Development,* Houston: Gulf Publishing Co., 1968.
Blake, R. R. & Mouton, Jane S. *Corporate Excellence Diagnosis,* Houston, Gulf Publishing Co., 1968.
Hornstein, H. A., Bunker, B. B., Burke, W. W., Gindes, M., & Lewicki, R. J. *Social Intervention: A Behavioral Science Approach,* New York: Free Press, 1971.
Lippitt, G. L. *Organizational Renewal,* New York: Appleton-Century-Crofts, 1969.
Marrow, A. J., Bowers, D. G. & Seashore, S. E. *Management by Participation,* New York: Harper and Row, 1967.
Marrow, A. J., Bowers, D. G., & Seashore, S. E. (Eds.) *Strategies of Organizational Change,* New York: Harper and Row, 1967.
Schmidt, W. H. *Organizational Frontiers and Human Values,* Belmont, California. Wadsworth, 1970.

3. A third indication is the growth of academic programs specializing in OD. In fact, what started at Case Western Reserve a few years ago under the leadership of Herb Shepard is now found at a variety of other universities, including UCLA, Yale, MIT, the University of New Hampshire, and The George Washington University.

4. The number oι individuals seeking professional training in OD outside the universities is growing steadily. For example, in the past three years, the number of applications to the NTL Institute's Program for Specialists in Organization Development has been twice that for 1969.

5. Although I cannot support my impression with actual figures, I believe that the number of organizations interested in OD has increased significantly in the past 2 to 3 years. I do know that the number of inquiries and contacts has increased for me and for many of my colleagues across the U.S. Organizations with which I am familiar are also adding more OD personnel. Also, inquiries to me from organizations looking for OD specialists have continued to increase.

Given these indications of growth, one might conclude the chances that OD is here to stay are good. While there is no defi-

Schmuck, R. A. & Miles, M. B. *Organizational Development in Schools,* Palo Alto, California: National Press Books, 1971.
3. Examples of books in OD soon to be published include a second OD series by Addison-Wesley due in 1973; some of the more recent books published or soon to be include:
Adams, J. D. *Intentional Development of Organisations,* London: Organisational Research and Development, Ltd., 1972.
Argyris, C. *Management and Organizational Development,* New York: McGraw-Hill, 1971.
Burke, W. W. & Hornstein, H. A. (Eds.) *The Social Technology of Organization Development,* Washington, D. C.: NTL Learning Resources Corp., 1972.
French, W. & Bell, C. *Organization Development: Behavioral Science Interventions for Organization Improvement,* Englewood Cliffs, N. J.: Prentice-Hall, Inc., 1973.
Hite, A. L. (Ed.) *Organizational Development: The State of the Art,* Ann Arbor, Michigan: Foundation for Research on Human Behavior, 1971.
Kuriloff, A. H. *Organizational Development for Survival,* New York: American Association, 1972.
Margulies, N. & Raia, A. P. *Organizational Development: Values, Process and Technology,* New York: McGraw Hill, 1972.
Schmuck, R. A., Runkel, P. J., Saturen, S., Martell, R., and Derr, C. B. *Handbook of Organization Development in Schools,* Palo Alto Calif.: National Press Books 1972.
Although it is not a book, an entire issue of a new Journal was recently devoted to OD:
French, W. & Bell, C. (Eds.) Organization Development: An Overview, *Journal of Contemporary Business,* 1972, 1, No. 3, 1-74.

nitive way for me to assess the odds, I do believe the probability of success for OD as a field of knowledge will be improved if some important changes occur and certain problems and limitations are, overcome.

PROBLEMS AND LIMITATIONS

Americans have a tendency to be attracted to anything novel be it new techniques, styles, designs, or equipment. Since newness is accepted without discrimination, many new things fall into the category of fad and then fade away. For example, in the field of management, PERT and MBO have been embraced by fickle organizations only to be rejected when a new "suitor" has appeared. Organization development runs the same risk. I know some organizations that are involved in OD simply because it is the "latest thing." But if an organization has no plans for providing substance or for integrating it into the mainstream of the organization's life, then "OD" will undoubtedly fall into the historical category of superficial fad with little import.

Another problem with OD is that it is surrounded by mystique. OD is not helped by practitioners who are unclear themselves to resort to, "well, you just have to experience OD to understand it." Such explanations do not sell many hard-nosed managers on the potential of OD. Although recent publications[4] have helped to reduce the mystique, more clarity, theorizing, and research are needed.

Research efforts will also help alleviate a third problem facing OD—the difficulty of measuring results. OD is affected by many variables, both human and technical, consequently, it is extremely

4. Some of the clearest definitions of OD may be found in the following:
Beckard, R., *op.cit.*
Bennis, W. G., *op.cit.*
Burke, W. W. and Schmidt, W. G. Management and Organization Development: What Is the Target of Change? *Personnel Administration,* 1971, 34, No. 2, 44-56.
Fordyce and Weil, *op.cit.*
French, W. Organization Development: Objectives, Assumptions and Strategies. *California Management Review,* 1969, 12, No. 2, 23-34.
Hornstein, et al, *op.cit.*
Sherwood, J. J. An Introduction to Organization Development. In J. W. Pfeiffer and J. E. Jones (Eds.), *1972 Annual Handbook for Group Facilitators,* Iowa City, Iowa: University Associates Press, 1972. Pp. 153-156.
Weisbord, M. R. What, Not Again! Manage People Better? *Think Magazine,* 1970, Jan.-Feb.

difficult to evaluate the effectiveness of an OD effort. The reasons for any organizational change can be explained in a variety of ways. For example, even though the Blake, Mouton, Barnes and Greiner study (1964) provided impressive evidence in support of OD technology, Dunnette and Campbell (1968) pointed out that the results could be attributed to a variety of variables other than OD.

One of the more convincing reports evaluating OD technology has been the longitudinal study by Seashore and Bowers (1970), but such research is rare. One other piece of research, the Beckhard and Lake study (1971) provided similarly impressive results.

Although case studies do not provide "hard data," they often facilitate one's understanding of OD and give clues as to what works and what doesn't. Recent examples of OD case studies which provide such illumination include the works of Beckhard (1969), Blumberg and Wiener (1971), Davis (1967), Dyer, Maddocks, Moffitt, and Underwood (1970), Golembiewski and Carrigan (1970), Harvey and Albertson (1971), Levy (1972), and Marrow, Bowers, and Seashore (1967).

In brief, evidence in support of OD is mounting, but the process is slow and, as in most new areas, the results are not unequivocal.

The current practice of OD operates under at least four limitations:

1. It is not completely clear what the practice of OD encompasses. For example, does it include career development? Or management by objectives? What about systems analysis? Does it fit? What about advocacy consultation or sensitivity training? Are they part of OD? It may be an organization changes as a result of any one of the above events, but are such interventions a part of OD? Of course, the pragmatist might say, "OD, Shmo-D, call it what you like as long as we accomplish the objective."

To be of lasting benefit to organizations and to become what looks like a growing and developing profession, OD must move from a collection of ideas, concepts, techniques, and personalities to a systematic body of knowledge and skill. It must be more clearly defined and be able to answer the questions raised above. In response to this limitation, Harvey A. Hornstein and I (1972) have developed some general criteria which we believe define OD interventions. In brief, if an intervening activity in an organization (a) responds to a felt need for change on the part of the "client,"

(b) involves the client in the activity of planning and implementing a change event, and (c) leads to a normative change in the organization's culture,[5] then it is an organization development intervention.

According to these criteria, a student confrontation with the university administration or a strike which changes an organization would not be an *OD intervention*, while in certain circumstances a program involving management by objectives might.

2. Organization development does not deal with power dynamics very effectively. In fact, it seldom deals with power at all. Since OD practitioners seek outcomes such as collaboration, high interpersonal trust, openness, honesty, decentralization of decision making, and a sharing of authority, the technology for coping with the realities of power is rather limited. Nevertheless, OD technology to deal with power is needed. For example, it is very difficult to conduct a team building session if the team leader refuses to attend the meetings, or if he is reluctant to share power in the decision making process. Or, for another example, interdepartmental conflict can rarely be dealt with effectively if upper management reserves the right to overrule whatever problem solution the two groups might develop.

In addition, OD does not readily provide a technique or a value system for helping the disenfranchised members of organizations (e.g. Blacks, women, persons over 55) to gain such things as rapid recognition or equal promotion opportunities. OD has developed some technology for dealing with union-management problems, but the techniques usually require a redistribution of power, a step management is usually reluctant to take.

3. Most OD interventions occur over rather extended periods of time (Burke & Schmidt, 1971). Few are relevant to short-term crises, for example.[6] Since managers frequently have short time perspectives, problems are often *ad hoc* in character. Much of the current technology of OD do not appear to be relevant to many of the issues of importance to managers and their organizations.

---

5. Organizational culture is a set of learned and shared assumptions about norms or rules to which members of the organization conform.

6. A couple of exceptions are: Beckhard, R. The Confrontation Meeting, *Harvard Business Review*, 1967, 45, No. 2, 149-155; and Golembiewski, R. T. and Blumberg, A. Confrontation as a Training Design in Complex Organizations: Attitudinal Ranges in a Diversified Population of Managers. *Journal of Applied Behavioral Science*, 1967, 3, No. 4, 525-555.

Needless to say, there is a great need for more "short-term" thinking and technology.

4. Another limitation of OD is that the practice is "ahead" of the theory and conceptualization. It seems to me that many people are involved in or attempting to practice OD, but few are conceptualizing about it. The beginning that has been made toward conceptualization is certainly noteworthy. For example, Dunnette (1971) in his review of the Addison-Wesley series on OD, was quite complimentary, and added that the six volumes were "a step toward professionalizing the amorphous mass that has been known as Organizational development."

But, these volumes, and the others I mentioned in an earlier footnote, are only "a step." Considerable work has been done since 1958 but there is undoubtedly untapped information still available. I must admit that I have been somewhat surprised at the paucity of academic individuals involved in the conceptualization and research of this field. This paucity may be due to the fact that few academic persons have been in the practice.

FORCES CURRENTLY SHAPING OD

By "shaping forces" I mean those factors which are "tugging or pushing" the field of OD in various directions and will eventually mold it. I will state these forces as polarities and in the form of questions.

Will OD be incorporated within the mainstream of the management of organizations will it develop as a movement advocating nontraditional management strategies and values?

Many values underlying current OD practice are non-traditional (Burke, 1971; French, 1969) as experienced by members of an organization. For instance, it is not traditional in most organizations for people to be candid with one another and to operate on a high level of interpersonal trust (Lawler, 1971). Neither is it customary for organizational members to examine on a continuing basis their *processes* of work. Getting the job done in spite of dysfunctional processes is the more typical approach, not analyzing and improving the *way* they work. Despite these nontraditional values, some critics of OD contend that practitioners merely help the organization to do better what it already does, rather than raise fundamental questions of organizational structure, mission and values. These same critics (Bennis, 1969, for one) and others also argue that OD is based unrealistically on a model of love and trust and that practitioners to be effective, should be more confrontive and advocate certain changes such as the decentralization of decision-making. Briefly, then, the current role of the OD specialist, i.e. catalyst and facilitator, is being questioned. Some argue that the OD specialist must do more than facilitate. He should, on occasion, take stands and advocate positions even at the risk of losing clients.

Is OD a competitor of job enrichment, management (Burke & Schmidt, 1971) development, systems analysis, etc. or is OD an interdisciplinary field which encompasses some or all of these potential "competitors?"

Managers are sometimes led to believe that they must make a choice between OD and other approaches to organization improvement. This belief may be due to the tendency for persons who represent one field or the other to sell only their particular wares. However natural this may be, its consequences are sometimes undesirable. OD and "other approaches" can be seen as either/or. In these circumstances the organization may lose valuable help because one is chosen over the other. For example, it is quite possible for a program of job enrichment to fit within an overall OD effort—provided the way job enrichment is used meets the criteria for an OD intervention mentioned earlier.

There are approaches, of course, which clearly differ from OD management consultation as it is traditionally practiced is not in the same ball park with OD. For example, OD practitioners, as a rule, do not make studies of organizational problems, write reports, submit them to boards and then end the contract. As a rule, OD consultants do spend time diagnosing an organization and, based on that diagnosis, collaboratively plan with the client what action to take. At this point a variety of interventions are possible, including training, job enrichment, team building, etc. (Burke & Hornstein, 1972). The only stipulation is that the intervention meet the three basic criteria of OD interventions mentioned above, i.e. responds to the client's needs, involves the client in decision making, and leads to change in the organization's culture. The OD approach that I am advocating is interdisciplinary, involving many specialties. This leads me to the next force.

Is OD a new specialty or merely a conglomeration of many established specialties?

When hearing about OD for the first time, people respond differentially. Some think OD is a new specialty or new profession. Others believe it is just a new label[7] for many of the things that they have done in the past or a new name for sensitivity training. There are pressures, however, for OD to be a new discipline. In fact, some people (prematurely, in my opinion) are seeking to develop a means of certifying OD specialists. One viewpoint on this issue was indirectly stated by John R. Silber as he discussed "instant culture" in the U.S. in his inaugural speech May 1, 1971, as the new President of Boston University. He pointed out that "Strategies of inquiry dominated by inappropriate models of the scientific enterprise have produced specializations in the humanities, the social sciences, and even in the sciences themselves that are so narrow as to resist combination into a coherent body of knowledge." It is my opinion that theorists and practitioners in OD should resist trends of overspecialization and concentrate on establishing a coherent body of knowledge encompassing a wide variety of specialties. Of course, if OD is a new "body of knowledge and skill," even though interdisciplinary, it is a specialty of sorts, but the specialization should represent a coalescence of techniques, methods, skills, theories and principles which have heretofore been unrelated.

Does OD produce quick results or is it meant to produce long range cultural change in the organization?

As noted above, OD technology is not usually equipped to respond effectively to short-term crises. Moreover, one of the fundamental differences between OD and other approaches in organizational improvement is that OD is viewed as a continuing *process* not as an *ad hoc* time-bound program (Burke & Schmidt, 1971). But there is considerable pressure on OD practitioners to produce results in a hurry, especially in organizations where

7. There is even confusion about the label, see, for example, a brief and helpful note by Peter Vaill, OD: A Grammatical Footnote, *Journal of Applied Behavioral Science,* 1971, 7, No. 2, 264.

managers are mobile and where they (and OD consultants) must "make their mark" within a short period of time.

It may be that one of the best times to initiate an OD effort is in a time crises, disruption, or change in leadership.[8] Beckhard, for example, contends that an essential condition of an effective initiation of OD is that somebody or something in the organization is "hurting" (Beckhard, 1969). Changes can occur and problems can be solved in a short time-span. In fact, effective OD results have been documented when the process has operated for 12 months but to determine whether permanent cultural change has occurred takes much longer (Seashore & Bowers, 1970; Beckhard & Lake, 1971). As OD technology improves and newer methods are developed there will probably be better techniques for coping with a need for quick action and results.[9] But if OD continues on its current course, its efforts will be directed toward lasting cultural change and such change does not occur overnight.

THE FUTURE OF OD

Undoubtedly there are many other forces affecting the future of OD. Rather than list these individually, I will try to capture them *in toto* by making a brief and speculative prognosis of OD's future.

First, let me respond to my initial question. OD has a future if it can act in the present to avoid premature formalization and professionalization, develop strategies for coping with immediate crises and for sustaining long-term efforts, avoid being co-opted by traditional organizational pressures, and continue to develop and refine a value system that will be needed for organizational viability and renewal (Bennis, 1967; Slater & Bennis, 1964; Lawler, 1971).

Second, I believe OD will become more interdisciplinary in character. While OD will remain within the domain of applied behavioral science, it will also include more technologies such as systems analysis and/or industrial engineering, and conflict utilization methods, which are not based on a love-trust model.

Finally, the field of OD will be more "organized" in the future

---

8. See the chapter by Sherwood and Glidewell in this volume for an expansion of this notion.
9. As an example see Beckhard, R. The Confrontation Meeting, *op. cit.*

than it is today. Such organization will probably take two forms. One will center around the practitioners themselves. There will be more groups of OD specialists and they will become more professional in their orientation. For example, professional accreditation and other kinds of recognition will be more evident.

The second form of organization relates to the management of sustained OD efforts. Today, most OD is conducted by a single outside consultant or by an inside-outside consultant combination. As organizations become more complex, large systems change efforts will have to be conducted by individual teams of experts each having a variety of resources. These teams, including both external and internal consultants, will have to be managed and their activities coordinated if they are to be successful. We simply do not know much about this particular type of management, but I predict that it will be commonplace in 1980.

By definition, OD means change. As I stated at the beginning, many people say they are "doing OD," but not much organizational change attributable to OD interventions seems to be taking place. As we learn more about what we are doing and as we become clearer about the potential and limitation of OD, I believe we will become less concerned about whether OD is taking place since we shall witness change actually occurring.

REFERENCES

Beckhard, R. *Organization development: Strategies and models.* Reading, Mass.: Addison-Wesley, 1969.

Beckhard, R., & Lake, D. G. Short- and long-range effects of a team development effort. In H. A. Hornstein, B. B. Bunker, W. W. Burke, M. Gindes, and R. J. Lewicki: *Social intervention: A behavioral science approach,* New York: Free Press, 1971.

Bennis, W. G. Organizations of the future. *Personnel Administration,* 1967, Sept.-Oct., 6-19.

Bennis, W. G. Organization development: Its nature, origins and prospects. Reading, Mass., Addison-Wesley, 1969.

Blake, R. R., Mouton, J. S., Barnes, L. B. and Greiner, L. E. Breakthrough in organization development. *Harvard Business Review,* 1964, 42, 133-155.

Blumberg, A., & Wiener, W. One from two: Facilitating an organizational merger. *Journal of Applied Behavioral Science,* 1971, 7, No. 1, 87-102.

Burke, W. W. A comparison of management development and organization development. *Journal of Applied Behavioral Science,* 1971, 7, 569-579.

Burke, W. W., & Hornstein, H. A. *The social technology of organization development.* Washington, D. C., NTL Learning Resources Corporation, 1972.

Burke, W. W., & Schmidt, W. G. Management and organization development: What is the target of change? *Personnel Administration,* 1971, 34, No. 2, 44-56.

Davis, S. A. An organic problem-solving method of organizational change. *Journal of Applied Behavioral Science,* 1967, 3, No. 1, 3-21.

Dunnett, M. D. Curing the monsters. *Contemporary Psychology*, 1971, 16, No. 3, 113-115.

Dunnette, M. D., & Campbell, J. P. Laboratory education: Impact on people and organizations. *Industrial Relations*, 1968, 8, 1-45.

Dyer, W. G., Maddocks, R. F., Moffitt, J. W. & Underwood, W. J. A laboratory-consultation model for organization change. *Journal of Applied Behavioral Science*, 1970, 6, No. 2, 211-227.

French, W. Organization development: Objectives, assumptions and strategies. *California Management Review*, 1969, 12, No. 2, 22-34.

Golembiewski, R. T. & Carrigan, S. B. Planned change in organization style based on the laboratory approach. *Administrative Science Quarterly*, 1970, 15, 79-93, and The persistence of laboratory-induced changes in organization styles. *Administrative Science Quarterly*, 1970, 15, 330-340.

Harvey, J. B., & Albertson, D. R. Neurotic organizations: Causes and symptoms. *Personnel Journal*, 1971, 50, No. 9. 694-699, and Neurotic organizations: treatment. *Personnel Journal*, 1971, 60, No. 10, 770-776, 783.

Lawler, E. E. Compensating the new life-style worker. *Personnel*, 1971, 48, No. 3, 19-25.

Levy, S. The process of organizational renewal: One company's experiences. In W. W. Burke and H. A. Hornstein (Eds.) *The social technology of organization development*, Washington, D. C.: NTL Learning Resources Corp., 1972.

Marrow, A. J., Bowers, D. G., & Seashore, S. E. *Management by participation* New York: Harper & Row, 1967.

Seashore, S. E., & Bowers, D. G. Durability of organizational change. *American Psychologist*, 1970, 25, 227-233.

Slater, P. E., & Bennis, W. G. Democracy is inevitable. *Harvard Business Review*, 1964, 42, 51-55.

SECTION I

Conceptual Orientations to Organization Development

In its infancy, OD was practiced in fairly limited ways, through laboratory training (Foundation for Research on Human Behavior, 1960) team building (Blake, Mouton, & Blansfield, 1962) and occasionally intergroup confrontation (Blake, Mouton, and Sloma, 1965). Today, practitioners are not only understanding more about what they are doing, but are refining and distinguishing their particular approaches as well. The first section of this book describes some of the current practices. Some are more refined than others, some are in process, and others represent a limited approach rather than an OD strategy to some aspect of organizational change.

The fundamental assumption underlying the orientation of Harvey and Albertson is that "organizations, like individuals develop neuroses." For example, members of organizations often act contrary to information they possess for solving problems. The Harvey and Albertson treatment for organizational neurosis is to (a) confront organizational members with the myths and fantasies that exist, (b) help them differentiate reality from fantasy, and (c) assist them in developing the skills to implement realistic solutions to problems.

The Sherwood and Glidewell approach is based on Lewinian theory and emphasizes the importance of understanding and changing, through planned renegotiation, the norms that govern interpersonal and intergroup relationships. Their model of planned renegotiation has four phases—(1) sharing information and negotiating expectations, (2) commitment, (3) stability/productivity, and (4) disruption—and provides a way "to introduce controlled change by anticipating disruption and renegotiating expectations in advance."

The Sherwood and Glidewell model of planned renegotiation is based on the assumption that individuals need concepts to guide their behavior, especially if change in behavior is a part of the process. This is precisely the assumption on which Hall bases his approach. Hall argues that OD practitioners have relied too heavily on technique and not enough on theory and concepts. Like Sherwood and Glidewell, he also draws from Lewin's thinking but, more specifically, Hall looks to George A. Kelly and his psychology of personal constructs. According to Hall, the key to OD is that of individual development, specifically changing the way a person "constructs" his world—forming new ways of construing oneself, others, environmental events, cause and effect relationships, expectancies, and predictions for the future which relate more effectively with the data of experience and purpose. Change of personal constructs is a precondition to behavior change according to the theory. The "Models for Management" seminar which Hall has designed and conducted is based on this premise.

While many of us in OD have been influenced by the theories of Kurt Lewin, Stan Herman has been heavily influenced by the work of the late Fritz Perls. Thus, Herman's ideas are essentially therapeutic in nature and rely on the concepts of Gestalt therapy. Since his approach stresses individual behavior, it is unique as an approach to OD. It should be added, however, that Herman is not alone in his emphasis on individual behavior, see for example a recent article by Tannenbaum (1971). Thus, while many, if not most, OD practitioners stress that organizational members should change their behavior to something else, e.g., be 9,9 not 9,1 or be democratic not autocratic, etc., Herman would say "be more of what you are, quit trying to be something you aren't."

Lippitt's situational approach to OD is based heavily on the concept of ITORP (Implementing the Organization Renewal Process). Lippitt's schematic model of OD, or organization renewal (Lippitt, 1969) as he prefers to call it, emphasizes the need for an organization "to re-examine its goals, evaluate its performance, and renew its spirit." The ITORP program stresses diagnosis —with tools to assist in this diagnosis—the improvement of communications and teamwork, and the planning of specific action projects for renewal.

Gibb has developed an orientation to change in a system to any social system, large or small and formal or informal. The approach, called TORI (Trust, Openness, Realization and Interdependence), is based on changing interpersonal relationships in a community setting, i.e., a "community of persons" not necessarily a formal community. The major intervention of Gibb's approach is one of temporarily (as brief as a few hours or as long as several days) establishing a community of 50 to 200 persons who have maximum communication, decision-making, and interdependence opportunities. It can develop into a highly interpersonal situation as well as an intense problem solving series of sessions similar to Beckhard's "Confrontation Meeting" (1967). After he explains the theory underlying TORI, notes the goal the intervention attempts to accomplish, and provides typical TORI procedures, Gibb describes two cases where TORI has been used in actual organizations.

Using the grid model they developed about a decade ago, Blake and Mouton address themselves to the system that affects and is affected by one's organization—marriage. It is clear that family and organization, do effect one another, if not directly at least indirectly. It is only recently that managers have begun to see their organizational system as "open," that is, highly interrelated with the community, culture, society, and their families. The Marriage Grid can facilitate a manager's sensing the "wholeness" of life rather than compartmentalizing it into pieces.

REFERENCES

Beckhard, R. The confrontation meeting. *Harvard Business Review,* 1967, 45, 149-155.
Blake, R. R., Mouton. J. S., & Blansfield, M. G. The logic of team training. In I. R. Weschler and E. H. Schein (Eds.) *Issues in training,* Washington, D. C.: NTL Institute, 1962, 77-85.
Blake, R. R., Mouton, J. S., & Sloma, R. The union-management intergroup laboratory. *Journal of Applied Behavioral Science,* 1965, 1, 25-57.
Foundation for Research on Human Behavior. *An action research program for organization improvement.* Ann Arbor, Michigan: The Foundation for Research on Human Behavior, 1960.
Lippitt, G. L. *Organizational renewal.* New York: Appleton-Century-Crofts, 1969.
Tannenbaum, R. Organization change has to come through individual change. *Innovation,* 1971, No. 23, 36-43.

Neurotic Organizations: Symptoms, Causes, and Treatment

JERRY B. HARVEY and
D. RICHARD ALBERTSON

Organizations, like individuals develop neuroses. The toll on an organization's behavior, measured in terms of production, efficiency, absenteeism, turnover, overhead and morale, is tremendous. And since each of these organization variables have personal antecedents, the price paid by individual organization members, measured in terms of misery and loss of self-esteem and confidence, is inestimable. But organizations, like people, can be cured of neurotic behavior and returned to a state of healthy functioning. The purpose of this paper is to describe the symptoms of organization neurosis, to identify some of its causes, and to define a course of treatment for restoring neurotic organizations to health. Implicit throughout the paper are descriptions of the role and function of an organization consultant in the process of diagnosis and treatment.

SYMPTOMS OF ORGANIZATION NEUROSIS

Perhaps the most effective way to get a feel for the symptoms of organization neurosis is to read summaries of interviews[1] with several employees including the boss of a neurotic organization.

Interview I

Consultant: How are things going on the job?
Employee A: Terrible. I hate to come to work. And once I'm here, I don't get anything done. We just sit around and bitch. The only thing I look forward to is vacation.
Consultant: What's the problem? What's causing the trouble?
Employee A: We have a couple of problems. First, we have a lousy boss. He never holds up our end with the higher ups. He simply can't carry the flag when he deals with his boss. And second, at least two of the

---

1. All interviews and dialogues reported in the paper are annotated versions of actual interviews and discussions conducted by the authors in the course of working with neurotic organizations.

five units making up this division should not be reporting to him. Putting Sales and Research under the same man is absurd. In a lot of ways they are competitive. There is no reason for them to work together. They never have and never will.

Consultant: Have you ever confronted your boss with his failure to "carry the flag?"

Employee A: Hell, no. Do you think I'm crazy or something?

Consultant: What about the problem with Sales and Research? What are you doing to solve that?

Employee A: Just last week we met and agreed to operate under a combined budget.

Interview II

Consultant: How are things going on the job?

Employee B: Pretty bad. This is a frustrating place to work. Right now I'm looking for another job. I take as much vacation and sick leave as I can. And I don't get anything done when I'm here. Really, I'm just marking time, hoping things will get better.

Consultant: What's causing all the frustration?

Employee B: Well, for one thing our organization set-up doesn't make sense. Whoever designed it must have been drunk. Having Sales and Research report to the same man is unworkable. We spend half of our time fighting one another. In addition, our boss doesn't represent our viewpoint to the top.

Consultant: Are you taking any steps to deal with the problems you just described?

Employee B: Yes, just last week the president instructed my boss to get us together to solve the morale problem. It's beginning to cut into everyone's production. The last quarter was very poor from a profit standpoint. And two of our best researchers took jobs with another company.

Consultant: What did you do?

Employee B: We had an all day meeting and agreed to operate under a combined budget. That should force us to work together more effectively.

Consultant: One other question. What about your boss? Has he ever asked whether he is doing an adequate job of carrying the division's viewpoint to the top?

Employee B: Yes, just the other day, he said he had heard by the grapevine that we thought he wasn't giving us good representation with the president and his staff.

Consultant: What did you say?

Employee B: I said I thought he was doing a good job.

Interview III

Consultant: What problems and issues are facing your division at the present time?

Boss: Well, morale is at an all time low. We have had a couple of good people quit and go to other companies. And production is down. The heat is on me and everyone else. I've about given up.

Consultant: What's the cause of it?

Boss: One big problem is the way we are organized. My boss gave me several units that don't have any reason to work together. In fact, two of the units are actually competitive in a functional sense. With that kind of arrangement, it's impossible to build teamwork among the staff.
Consultant: What have you done about it?
Boss: Well, last week I gave a pep talk to the staff at our weekly meeting and said we had to work together more effectively. And to insure that we do, we developed a unit budget that ties each subgroup's performance into the overall performance of the division.
Consultant: Have you ever thought about telling your boss that the way you are organized does not make sense?
Boss: I've tried, but I can't seem to make him understand.
Consultant: Have you really pushed him hard?
Boss: I'm not about to do that. He might think I am not an effective manager.

As can be seen by the interviews, the neurotic organization exhibits a number of specific symptoms which are collectively expressed by its members.

Pain and Frustration

Its members complain of frustration, worry, backbiting, loss of self-esteem and a general sense of impotence. They do not feel their skills are being adequately used. As a result, they become less efficient and look for ways to avoid the job, such as taking vacation, taking sick leave, and "giving up" or "opting out" of trying to solve the problems they see as causing the pain.

Blaming Others for the Problems

Its members attempt to place much of the blame for the dilemma on others, particularly the boss. In "backroom" conversations among subordinates, he is termed as incompetent, ineffective, "out of touch" or as a candidate for transfer or early retirement. To his face nothing is said, or at best, oblique or misleading information is given concerning his impact on the organization.

Subgroup Formation

As pain and frustration becomes more intense, its members form into identifiable subgroups. These subgroups may develop on the basis of friendship ties, with trusted acquaintances meeting during coffee or over lunch to share rumors, complaints, fantasies, or strategies for dealing with the problems at hand. The most important effect of such meetings is to heighten the overall anxiety level in the organization rather than to assist in realistically coping with its problems.

Agreement as to Problems

Its members generally agree as to the character of problems causing the pain. For example, in the interviews related above, organization members agree that the organization has two basic problems: 1) The composition of the units reporting to the same superior is inappropriate, and 2) There is a failure to communicate the urgency of the composition issue to upper levels of management. The first problem reflects an important *task* issue (Benne & Muntyan, 1951), i.e., how to organize effectively. The second reflects as equally important *maintenance* concern (Benne & Muntyan, 1951), i.e., how to work together in such a way that the organization functions effectively. That agreement as to task and maintenance issues bridges both hierarchical and functional lines. Stated differently, the boss and his subordinates see the problems in the same way as do employees from Sales and Research. Although organization members may be unaware of the degree to which they agree with one another, the reality is they do agree.

Members Act Contrary to Data and Information They Possess

Perhaps the most unique characteristic of neurotic organizations is that its members act in ways contrary to data and information they possess. In analogous terms, it would be as if an outside observer viewed the following vignette involving twenty people from a neurotic organization:

Observer: (Approaching a group sitting around a camp fire.) How are things going?
Organization Members: (Who are holding their hands over an open fire.) Awful. It's too hot. We are burning up. The pain is excruciating. Our hands are too close to the coals.
Observer: What do you intend to do about it?
Organization Members: Move our hands closer to the fire, what else?

Although the analogy may sound absurd on the surface, it is certainly no more absurd than the following conversation which occurred in an actual organization.

Consultant: You say there is no possible functional relationship among the groups reporting to your boss and it is impossible to build one.
Organization Members: Yes, that's right.

Consultant: What do you propose to do about it?
Organization Members: Meet more often so we will have more opportunities to learn to work together.

It is this characteristic which really defines neurotic organization behavior the same way it defines neurotic individual behavior. The individual who consistently acts contrary to his best "internal signals" becomes neurotic, and if he acts in concert with a variety of others, the organization as an entity develops neurotic symptoms. Stated conversely, any human system must act congruently with reality if it is to function effectively.

Members Behave Differently Outside the Organization

Finally, key to the diagnosis of organization neurosis is the fact that outside the organization context members do not either suffer the pain nor demonstrate the irrational behavior (such as behaving contrary to their own views of reality) they demonstrate in their day-to-day work. Outside the organization, individual members get along better, are happier, and perform more effectively than they do within it, a fact which heightens their discomfort when living and working within the organization.

Summary

In summary, a neurotic organization is one in which:
1. Organization members feel pain, frustration, and loss of self-esteem.
2. Organization members agree among themselves as to the problems causing the pain.
3. Organization members take collective action essentially contrary to the data, information, and feelings they possess for solving the problems. That action, in turn, increases the pain, frustration, and loss of self-esteem and leads to the emergence of other symptoms.
4. Organization members do not suffer similar pain or demonstrate similar irrational behavior outside the organization.

CAUSES OF NEUROTIC ORGANIZATION BEHAVIOR

Given a description of organization neurosis, the question is then, "Why do organization members engage in behavior which is both individually and organizationally destructive?" Basically, there are two reasons.

Lack of Awareness

First, organization members are unaware of their behavior and the consequences it has for them as individuals and for the organization as an entity. Such lack of awareness may involve any of three levels. At the most superficial level, an organization member may be unaware of the degree to which the information and feelings he possesses are shared by others in the organization. Thus, a member of the organization may feel as if he is alone in his diagnosis of the organization's problems. Or, he may feel that, at most, the subgroup to which he belongs agrees as to the character of the organization's problems. He seldom realizes that his understandings and beliefs are widely shared across functional and hierarchical lines and that he is not an isolate.

Consultant: Do you think people other than yourself believe that the unit needs to be reorganized?
Employee: Well, several guys that work with me agree on that issue, but I doubt if any others do.
Consultant: What would you say if I told you that virtually everyone in the division feels the same as you do about that issue.
Employee: I'd say you must be kidding.

Since that lack of agreement reflects a simple information gap, it is the simplest form of unawareness to correct.

At a second level, organization members may be unaware of the dysfunctional group norms and standards which inhibit or prevent their coping with the problems at hand. It is at the normative level that the difference between individual and organization neurosis is most clearly articulated. Individual neurosis stems from *personal* dynamics unique to the individual. Organization neurosis stems from *collective* dynamics unique to the organization. Thus, organizations develop social norms and standards, neurotic in character, the breaking of which by individual members results in the application of social pressure to conform. For example, some organizations develop dysfunctional norms mitigating against open discussion of important organization issues.

Organization Member A: I think we ought to confront the issue of whether we are appropriately organized. I personally don't think these units belong together.

Organization Member B: Oh, knock it off! Let's not get involved in something like that.
Organization Member D: What are you trying to do? We don't need things stirred up any more than they already are.
Organization Member C: Yes, the problems aren't as bad as you crack them up to be. We really work together rather well. I move we change the subject.

As one consultant put it, "fish are the last to know that they are in water." So it is with organization members. They are frequently the last to know of the dysfunctional norms which govern and occasionally consume them. However, as Lewin (1947) has demonstrated, behavior rooted in group standards and norms is easier to change than behavior rooted in individual character structure. Because of this principle, organization neurosis is potentially more amenable to change than the individual variety.

Finally, a third level relates to the degree to which organization members are unaware of the manner in which they contribute to maintaining the problems. For example, some members may see the part others, particularly the boss, play in maintaining destructive norms and standards; but few sense their own roles in the process.

Consultant: You say your boss is at fault; that he should demand to his superior that the situation be changed.
Employee A: Absolutely. He is doing a lousy job.
Employee B: You can say that again.
Consultant: Have you or any other members of your division ever demanded of your boss that he do a better job of representing your group to the President?
Employee A: No. That's not what I'm around here for.
Employee B: Me neither.
Employee C: I think it would be foolish and disrespectful to do something like that.
Consultant: It seems to me as if you may be doing exactly the same thing you don't want your boss to do.
Employee C: (lamely) We are?

It is as if the identification with superiors, other peers, or the organization itself is so great that they lose their capacities to understand either their individual or collective contributions to the dysfunctional organization processes. Since the dynamics supporting such lack of awareness tend to be so deep within the individual and group psyche (Freud, 1951) they are the hardest to identify, make explicit, and change.

Fantasies About Consequences of Alternative Actions

Even when organization members are aware of the degree to which they agree as to the substance of the problems, are knowledgeable about the group norms and standards which prevent their coping effectively with those problems and are cognizant of their own unique ways of maintaining those dysfunctional norms and standards, they still may be unable to take effective problem-solving action. Again, the question is "Why?"

In most cases, the inaction relates to rich and varied fantasies organization members have about possible negative consequences which may befall them if they do act. The fantasies have a myth-like quality (Bradford & Harvey, 1970) which are frequently unrelated to reality.

Consultant: Each of you seems to agree this division needs to be reorganized and that the present format is unworkable. Why don't you suggest to your boss that you reorganize?

Employee A: He might fire us for treading on his territory. He's supposed to think of that, not us.

Employee B: The new organization might be worse than the present one. It's not worth taking the chance.

Employee C: I'm sure things will get better if we just wait it out. Life isn't as bad as we make it out to be.

Employee D: I've got a mortgage payment on the house. I can't afford to do anything that rocks the boat.

Consultant: Is there any possibility that things might get better if you do something other than wait?

Various Employees: We doubt it.

The fantasy-like quality comes from the fact that the projected outcomes are seldom if ever tested for reality. In general, such fantasies reflect a tremendous amount of underlying anxiety and concern that has to be taken into account in any process designed to treat the "neurosis."

TREATMENT OF ORGANIZATION NEUROSIS

Like individual neurosis, organization neurosis can be treated, and like the individual variety, the treatment is complex.

Basically, the treatment requires the following elements.

Data Collection from Organization Members

The first step is to collect data from a representative sample of organization members. It is particularly important that more than one level of the organization be represented in the data collection, since issues of hierarchy and authority are generally central to the kinds of problems identified. On the basis of their experiences with a variety of organizations, the authors have found that open-ended interviews conducted around three basic questions produces the data required. These questions are:

1. What issues and problems are facing the organization at the present time?
2. What is causing these problems?
3. What strengths are available in the organization to solve the problems?

Interviews last 45 minutes to an hour. Basic to the success of the interviews is that they be conducted by someone who can view the organization from an essentially objective standpoint. Although it is possible that an inside consultant with enough functional autonomy can achieve and maintain the kind of objective detachment required, an outside consultant is generally preferred. An outsider is less likely to be caught up in the dysfunctional processes underlying the neurosis and, therefore, is less likely to have distorted perspectives of the organization and its problems.

Essentially, verbatim notes are taken by the consultant. When all interviews are completed, the data from interviewees are sorted into themes[2] which are identified with non-evaluative titles. Actual statements of organization members are grouped under each theme. A typical set of themes and supporting statements are shown in Exhibit I.

EXHIBIT I
EXAMPLES OF THEMES, SUPPORTING DATA
AND SUMMARY STATEMENTS

Theme 1: Division Composition
1. The composition of this division does not make sense.
2. This division is a group of independent units operating under an umbrella.
3. It is not a group. It is a collection of units just thrown together.
4. Research does not belong in the division.
5. The way the division is constituted is inappropriate.
6. The division needs to be subdivided.

2. A theme is arbitrarily defined as an issue or concern which is spontaneously mentioned by at least 50% of the organization members interviewed.

7. It is a mixture of apples and oranges.
8. The division is made up of remnants of an earlier era. There is not much logic to it.
9. What we have is a variety of sub-groups.
10. Units do not have much in common.
11. It is not a group in any sense.

Summary Statement

The present composition and/or structure of the division is inappropriate, out of step with the opportunity to accomplish our purposes, and should be changed.

Theme 2: Collaboration within the Division

1. Some staff members do not communicate with anyone.
2. No communication within division.
3. Staff share few common goals—the exception is survival.
4. There's no relationship between some units, like Sales and Research.
5. There's too much time talking as a group. The subjects talked about are not perceived as making much difference.
6. There is no support. I occasionally feel close to harassment. We frequently talk to other staff members rather than confronting the person we should talk to.
7. Within the division some are more willing to jump unit lines than others.
8. Other units in the division fight each other for stature.
9. Some units in the division are pro-active while others sit around waiting to be told what to do.
10. Each unit is a kingdom unto itself.

Summary Statement

In general, units within the division do not work together.

Theme 3: Top Leadership

1. The boss is too nice and that causes people to take advantage of him.
2. His style keeps us from confronting problems even when conflict is there.
3. The boss is unable to carry the "flag." I don't know why.
4. He has not been able to change or get the attention of top management.
5. He spends a lot of time telling the group that everything is okay—all is right with the world—but that is not true.
6. His style is not congruent with the confrontation style that works in the organization today.
7. He sometimes has to support positions that he does not believe in and that makes him ineffective in dealing with top management.
8. His inability to be defensive and hostile get him in trouble.

Summary Statement

The boss's style is not of a confronting nature.

Theme 4: Pain

1. We are suffering from . . .
2. I feel no support and occasionally feel close to harassment.
3. People who are committed are frustrated as well.
4. Nothing feeds failure like failure.
5. Creativity is squelched.
6. Joe Smith is being stiffled.
7. We want to contribute in a positive way, but can't.
8. There is a lot of insecurity and morale is very low.
9. The division is not conducive to good mental health and working conditions.

Summary Statement

Most division personnel are frustrated, worried, and feel insecure; morale is low.

It should be stressed that the data must be verbatim accounts of what the organization members said relative to each theme. The data must not be a summary of what the consultant would like organization members to say or believe. Throughout the process of consultation, the actual data contributed by organization members, not the consultant's biases and prejudices, must be the topic of exploration.

Data Feedback to Organizatibn Members

After data are collected and sorted into themes, the consultant presents both the themes and supporting statements to the interviewees in a modified version of a confrontation session (Beckhard, 1967). During this session, which usually requires several hours, organization members are encouraged to discuss, clarify and, modify both the themes and the supporting statements. Whenever organization members are satisfied that the themes and the supporting data are accurate reflections of their own feelings and knowledge, they are asked to develop a single summary statement which adequately summarizes the data contributed under each theme. Examples of summary statements are also contained in Exhibit I.

After each theme has been discussed and a summary statement developed, organization members are asked to vote publicly as to whether they agree or disagree with the content of the summary statement.

Votes are counted and if a clear majority do not agree with a summary statement, the consultant works with the group to clarify the reasons for the disagreement. Discussion continues until the statement is modified so that most organization members can agree with it, or until the statement is eliminated because it does not actually reflect their feelings and attitudes.

Taking a public vote is important because it transfers ownership of the themes and the supporting data from the consultant to the organization members themselves. Stated differently, the vote forces the organization members to accept responsibility for the validity or lack of validity of the data they contributed.

Once the data are identified as belonging to organization members rather than the consultants, the next step is to ask each member to "own up" (Argyris, 1962) to his individual contribution to each issue represented by the various themes.

Thus, each organization member is asked to produce a series of written statements according to the following directions:

For each of the summary statements, write a few sentences describing the way in which you contribute to the issue which is summarized. Your descriptions will belong to you. Although you may want to share your thoughts with others later on, there will be no requirement to do so.

Here, the purpose is to help each organization member focus on his possible contribution to maintaining the processes causing the problems. It also helps to set a norm of examining one's own contribution to the organization's problems rather than blaming others.

Sharing the Theory

One of the most important steps in the treatment process involves the sharing of the consultant's theory with organization members. Again, organization members' own views of reality, which they have affirmed through a public vote, is central to the presentation process. The rationale for presenting the model is that theory itself is a powerful intervention. In brief, it helps organization members to diagnose and understand organization problems and to plan action steps which do not foster the continuation of these problems.

Basically, the theory is presented by the consultant as follows:
When organization members:

1. Experience pain and frustration,
2. Agree with one another as to the problems and causes, and
3. Act in ways contrary to their own thoughts, feelings, and information;

the following assumptions should be tested:

1. Organization members are implicitly or explicitly collaborating with one another to maintain the status quo,
2. Organization members have fantasies about the disastrous consequences of confronting those issues and concerns they know and agree cause the pain and frustration.

At this point, the consultant helps organization members apply the model to their own lives by "walking them through" an actual case involving their own organization.

Consultant: In this organization you agree that you are unhappy and frustrated (Theme 4), that the organization is inappropriately constituted (Theme 1), and that units do not work well together (Theme 2). Yet, when asked by top management to make a proposal for solving the problems of the organization, what happened?
Organization Member: We made a proposal.
Consultant: What did you say in the proposal?
Organization Member: That we develop a matrix organization and operate under a combined budget.
Consultant: What will that decision require?
Organization Member: Well, for one thing, a lot more teamwork.
Consultant: Is that decision congruent with the reality that everyone feels the organization is inappropriately constituted and that the various sub parts do not work well together?
Organization Member: Oh, hell! We've done it again, haven't we?

Using members' own data forces them to become aware of the discrepancy between their own views of reality (We don't work well together) and the actions they take which, in effect, deny that reality (making decisions which require working more closely together). This new awareness confronts them with the necessity of making a conscious choice to explore alternatives based on their views of reality (for example, dissolving the division and reorganizing, a solution which may require painful shifts in job, status, and location) or continuing to act on the basis of irrational fantasies which are individually and organizationally destructive (organizing in a way that denies their beliefs that the composition of the division is inappropriate).

If the consultant is to be effective in helping the organization alter its destructive patterns, he must continue to help members confront the basic discrepancy which exists between their views of reality and the decisions they make. The ways in which he assists in this confrontation process are discussed in the following sections.

Consultant Functions in Change Process

Throughout the data feedback session, and in other encounters within the organization, events occur which mirror the problems organization members have in working during their day-to-day activities. In these encounters, the consultant has a variety of functions all of which require his being sensitive to underlying emotional and process issues. Examples of the consultant's functions include:

Building Awareness of Dysfunctional Group Standards and Norms.

The process of presenting data to the persons who contribute it helps organization members become aware of the degree to which they agree with one another about the character of the organization's problems. In effect, the sharing of data assists in solving problems stemming from an "information gap." However, the consultant must also help organization members become aware of dysfunctional norms and group standards which inhibit their capacity to cope with problems identified in the data sharing stage.

Organization Member: (to consultant) I did not like being forced by you to fill out the questionnaire regarding my contribution to maintaining the problems. When you asked me to do that, I felt very manipulated. I didn't think the process would lead to anything and still don't. I just filled it out to suit you. It sure as hell didn't suit any need of mine.
Consultant: I wonder how many others felt that way.
Various Members: I did.
Consultant: In some ways, that is similar to the tendency of members of this organization to act contrary to their own best views of reality.
Organization Member: I don't understand that either. We just did as we were told. What's wrong with that?
Consultant: Well, it looks as if most of you did not want to respond to the questionnaire because you didn't think it was relevant. Yet everyone responded and nothing was said at the time. That's very similar to not confronting the problem of reorganization even though there is uniform agreement that reorganization is needed.
Organization Member: Damn it. You got us again.
Consultant: I didn't get you.

Organization Member: Yeah. We got ourselves. We contributed to the problem again.
Previous Member: Yes, but he still makes me mad, catching us.

Coping with Feelings.

As the previous vignette indicates, the members of a neurotic organization, like neurotic individuals, demonstrate extreme difficulty in the area of learning new behavior. They find it difficult to appraise the past in the light of the present. As a consequence, they find it hard to assimilate and utilize new knowledge, although it may be all around them and clearly apparent to an outsider. They seem to be restricted to coping responses rooted in history. Although these responses may be inadequate and dysfunctional, organization members persist in using them and even exert a tremendous amount of collective energy in trying to maintain them.

Much of that energy in a change process may be directed against the consultant in the form of anger and resentment or lavish praise.

Organization Member: He makes me mad, catching us that way.
Organization Member: He doesn't make me mad. He sees things none of the rest of us see. He's doing a great job.

The feelings of ambivalence are understandable for the consultant, in ways similar to the individual therapist, represents both a threat and a promise to organization members.

It is important for the change process that the consultant understand this and be prepared to cope with such feelings when they arise, because in any organization change process, as in an individual therapeutic process, there is an initial period of disorganization, pain and anxiety before new, more functional norms and standards are developed.

The coping can take two forms. One is to help members learn from their feelings.

Consultant: Both comments may reflect some reality and some fantasy. For example, I don't think I "caught" anyone. And I also doubt that I'm the only one who sees what I reported. I would like to check that out with others here.

The other form of coping is more pragmatic. The authors suspect that it is around this issue that many organization change processes are terminated. Thus, organization members must be informed in advance of the possible turmoil they may feel and of the potential positive consequences. Otherwise, a change process may be stopped at the very time constructive change takes place. In short, just as it is with a neurotic individual, the neurotic organization is its own worst enemy.

Encouraging Fantasy and Reality Testing.

One of the basic reasons for acting contrary to one's own view of reality are fantasies about the consequences for alternative actions. Again, underlying these fantasies is a great deal of emotionality and concern that must be dealt with if organization members are to clearly differentiate fantasy and reality. One way to facilitate the process of clarification is to encourage the process of fantasizing.

Consultant: One of the reasons people sometimes act contrary to what they really know is that they have notions about what will happen if they really do what needs to be done.
Organization Member: What do you mean?
Consultant: Well, one of the reasons people may not want to question whether Jim (the boss) is confronting enough in upholding the viewpoint of this organization to top management is that they don't know what he might do to those who question his actions.
Organization Member: Damn right. He might fire me. (nervous laughter)
Another Member: Or send me back to the production line.
Another Member: Or get back at me when annual reviews come along.
Interviewer: Has anyone in this group ever questioned Jim's actions before?
Organization Member: I have.
Consultant: What did he say?
Organization Member: He said "thanks" and that he was unaware of what he was doing.
Another Member: Same thing happened to me.
Consultant: I wonder if all of the worries you have voiced are justified? Do they have any reality?
Organization Member: It doesn't sound like they do.

Coaching.

Although organization members may (a) have full access to information, (b) be aware of dysfunctional norms and standards, (c) understand the way they contribute to maintaining those norms, and (d) be able to distinguish between fantasized consequences and reality, they still may not be able to develop new ways of coping. Therefore, a third function of a consultant in a change process is to "coach" organization members in new behaviors. Such coaching can take place in group meetings, in private conversations, and in various sub group configurations.

Organization Member: Okay, I want to tell Jim (the boss) that I don't think he is holding up our end with the President. What do I say? Do I say "Jim, you are a lousy manager." That doesn't seem to make much sense.

Consultant: One alternative would be to admit your own feelings about Jim and what he is doing.

Organization Member: What do you mean?

Consultant: Well, you might say, "When I don't feel you represent us at the top it makes it a lot harder for me to do my job in addition to making me downright angry." That way you're not saying that Jim is personally incompetent. You're saying what his actions do to you.

Organization Member: Hmm. I've never thought of that approach before.

Other Functions.

Obviously, organizations cannot be "cured" of neurotic behavior in a single session. About all that can be expected in a brief meeting is that organization members may develop some awareness of the degree to which they agree with one another on important issues and of the manner to which they contribute to maintaining dysfunctional organization processes. They may also become aware of the degree of discomfort they feel with the situation and of their motivation and readiness to change it. In addition, in one meeting organization members may decide whether the consultant and his approach might be helpful to them in coping with their problems.

Assuming that the decision is affirmative, there are several additional roles that the consultant may play in continuing the treatment process, all of which involve building awareness, coping with feelings, encouraging fantasy, and coaching in new behavior. These roles include:

1. Attending regular work meetings of various organization units to serve as an observer, confronter, reality tester.

2. Individual coaching sessions with key organization members concerning their roles in the process. Since the role of the superior of the unit is always central to the underlying problems of an organization (Crockett, 1970), coaching sessions with him can have an unequal impact on the organization's operations.

3. Working with the organization to develop acceptable measures of progress and improvement. Sometimes individually tailored measures are developed and sometimes "packaged" research materials such as Likert scales (1967) are em-

ployed. Whatever measures are used, they must be acceptable and agreed upon collaboratively by both the organization members and the consultant. If such agreement is reached, it is far more likely that organization members will accept measures of progress or regression as valid and as reflecting reality. Collaborating in the development of such measures also helps members to learn to act on the basis of their own view of reality. Thus, such measures do not contribute to maintaining the very norms and standards which are the targets of change.

4. Helping develop reasonable expectations about speed of change. As can be understood from the preceding discussions, the processes supporting organization neurosis are complex, and the skills needed to change those processes cannot be learned quickly. As a consequence, the "do-it-tomorrow" perspective, frequently characteristic of organization members, is unrealistic. However, to the extent that there are ways of measuring progress which are agreeable to organization members and the consultant, periodic assessment of results can be made. Time, thus, becomes less important as an absolute variable in the evaluation process, since it may be viewed in the light of whatever positive or negative results are achieved.

SUMMARY

Organizations, like people develop self-defeating neuroses. Such organization neuroses produce a variety of symptoms which are easily identifiable. The treatment of organization neurosis involves the use of consultants who help members (a) collect reality centered information about the organization, (b) gain understanding of the dysfunctional norms and standards which keep them from using whatever information which is available, (c) help them in differentiating reality from fantasy when assessing alternative solutions to the problems which are identified, and (d) assist them in developing the skills necessary to implement realistic alternatives. Although organization neurosis involves complex long-term treatment, change is possible and well worth the effort in terms of both economic and humanistic savings.

REFERENCES

Argyris, C. *Organizations and innovation,* Richard Irwin, Homewood, Illinois, 1965.

Beckhard, R. The confrontation meeting. *Harvard Business Review,* Harvard University, March-April 1967, Vol. 45, No. 2, pp. 149-154.

Benne, K. and Muntyan, B. *Human relations in curriculum change,* Dryden Press, 1951.

Bradford, L. P. and Harvey, J. B. Dealing with dysfunctional organization myths, *Training and Development Journal,* Vol. 24, No. 9, 2-6, 1970.

Crockett, W. J. Team building—one approach to organization development. *Journal of Applied Behavioral Science,* Vol. 6, No. 3, 1970, 291-306.

Freud, S. *Group psychology and the analysis of the ego.* Liveright Publishing Corporation, New York, 1951.

Lewin, K. *Field theory in social science.* Harper and Co., New York, 1951.

Likert, R. *The human organization.* McGraw Hill, New York, 1967.

Planned Renegotiation:
A Norm-setting OD Intervention

JOHN J. SHERWOOD and

JOHN C. GLIDEWELL

Organization development has been described as "an educa. tional process by which human resources are continuously identified, allocated, and expanded in ways that make these resources more available to the organization, and therefore, improve the organization's problem-solving capabilities" (Sherwood, 1971). The concept of planned renegotiation describes a procedure by which controlled change can enter an organization in such a way that resources become more available to the organization. It is derived from a clear and simple theory of how roles are established and changed (Glidewell, 1971).

The theory itself is a norm-setting intervention because it is intended to become part of the normative structure of an organization, and as such to become part of the language, rhetoric, and expectations of members of the organization. Furthermore, the use of these concepts in successful problem-solving leads to the learning of behavioral skills by insight, reinforcement, and imitation. As we often like to hear Lewin (1951) say, there is nothing as practical as a good theory. Where the concept of planned renegotiation becomes part of the norms of an organization, it can constitute the heart of an OD effort.

THE MODEL

The model describes how social systems—that is, relations between persons and relations between groups—are established and become stabilized so that work can get done, and how change can enter the system. The model is cyclical and it includes four phases:

(1) *Sharing information and negotiating expectations.* When

Copyright © 1971 by John J. Sherwood and John C. Glidewell.

THE GEORGE BROWN COLLEGE
OF APPLIED ARTS AND TECHNOLOGY
LIBRARY

persons begin to establish a relationship which they expect may endure over some period of time—as brief as a pre-employment interview or as long lasting as a marriage or an appointment to the U. S. Supreme Court—they first exchange information. They share information about themselves and they exchange expectations, which are usually implicit and unspecified, about how each is to behave with the other(s). They are essentially trading information and establishing expectations about how a "member" of this relationship, or a member of this group, is going to behave (see Goffman, 1956, p. 162, 1961, pp. 105-132; Thibaut & Kelley, 1959, pp. 21-25; Blau, 1960).

Once a sufficient exchange of information occurs, so that uncertainty is reduced to an acceptable level and the behaviors of the parties are more or less predictable, and if the relationship is seen as enduring sometime into the future, then commitment to these shared expectations takes place.

(2) *Commitment.* Once commitment to a set of shared expectations takes place, then each member's role is defined, and each member knows for the most part what is expected of him and for the most part what he can expect from the others. The strength of each individual's commitment and the range of his behavior encompassed by his role are both measures of the importance or centrality to him of this particular relationship. The more important the relationship, the more evidence of commitment is required and the more behaviors—including attitudes, values, and perceptions—are embraced by the role expectations. With commitment comes stability.

(3) *Stability and productivity.* When there is commitment to a set of shared expectations, these expectations govern the behavior of group members and provide stability within the relationships—that is, for the most part you do what I expect of you and for the most part I do what you expect of me. This stability in the relationships leads to the possibility that work can now get done. While stability does not guarantee productivity, it is necessary for productive work to occur. The energy of the principals is now available for other things, since their relationships are sufficiently predictable that they no longer required sustained attention.

Commitment to a set of shared expectations then governs behavior during a period of stability—but invariably, sooner or later, disruption occurs (Blau, 1967; Homans, 1961).

(4) *Disruption.* Disruption occurs because of a violation of expectations by the principals or because of external intrusion into the system. It is assumed that disruption is inevitable, only the duration of the period of stability varies, because (a) information is never completely shared during the initial period when expectations are negotiated; and (b) individuals, groups, and organizations are viewed as open systems (Katz & Kahn, 1966)—i.e., they change as a consequence of transactions with their environment (Glidewell, 1971).

Disruptions may be external in origin, such as a new person assigned to a work group, a loss of personnel, an assignment of a new task or higher quota, a budgetary cut and reallocation of resources, or reorganization of personnel and subsequent reassignment of duties. The first child born into a marriage is an example of a new input into the relationship which is likely to lead to the violation of previously established expectations. Disruptions may also be internal in origin, such as, the sharing of information which was not made available earlier when expectations were being negotiated. Persons also change as a consequence of new experiences, training, and education. When the changed person returns to the unchanged role, expectations may be violated leading to a disruption,of the relationship.

It is at the point of disruption that change can enter the system, for it is at this time that expectations are no longer fixed. New information can now enter the system, and the renegotiation of expectations can occur. Once again the system recycles through: (1) sharing information and renegotiating expectations, then (2) commitment to a set of expectations, which governs behavior during a period (3) of stability and productivity, when, for the most part, you do what I expect of you and I do what you expect of me, until (4) disruption once again occurs, because of a violation of expectations by the principals or because of external intrusion into the system. With disruption change can once again enter the system, as it cycles from renegotiation through disruption, and yet another opportunity for renegotiation (see Figure 1).

The paradox is that the very moment the system is most open to change there are strong inhibiting forces working to return things "to the way they used to be," because of anxiety accompanying the uncertainty which characterizes the system at the time it is in a state of disruption (Lanzetta, 1955; Korchin *et al.,* 1957).

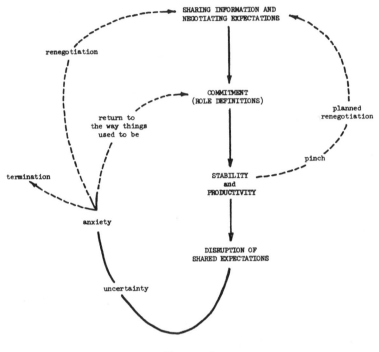

FIGURE 1

When a disruption of expectations occurs, uncertainty follows—
because I can no longer depend on your doing what I expect of
you, and my own role is also unclear to me—and with uncertainty
the principals become anxious. The anxiety is uncomfortable. The
quickest and surest way to reduce that anxiety is for the relationship to return once again "to the way things used to be." This is
often a ritualized commitment to prior expectations, such as a
perfunctory apology, handshake, or embrace, without admitting
the new information into the system, which is now available since
it gave rise to the disruption. This new information would form
the basis for renegotiating the expectations governing the relationship. The relationship remains closed to change, when the parties
deal with the uncertainty and anxiety produced by disruption by
returning to the original level of sharing expectations without
renegotiation—for example, the pledge, "it won't happen again,"
or the admonition, "don't let it happen again," or the reaffirma-

tion of the way things used to be, "let's be gentlemen" or "I'm sorry, I was wrong, everything is now okay. . . . nothing is changed!" (Postman & Bruner, 1948; Hermann, 1963).

It is during the period of disruption, when the parties are uncertain about their roles and the future of the relationship and are therefore anxious, that the system must be held open if change is to enter. If new information is allowed to enter the relationship and is treated in a problem-solving way, it can provide the basis for renegotiating the expectations governing the relationship. The newly renegotiated expectations are therefore more likely to be in line with the current realities of the situation, and once commitment occurs, the period of stability is likely to be more enduring before the next ensuing disruption.

If the parties share this model as a part of their language and their mutual expectations, these concepts are likely to help them by increasing their tolerance for the uncertainty and the accompanying anxiety which surround their relationship while expectations are held open during renegotiation. Through continued use of these concepts, the behavioral skills of the parties also increase, thereby facilitating the renegotiation process.

The theory predicts that disruption without renegotiation leads to an increasing frequency and intensity of disruptions. When each disruption is not treated as a new source of information and a new opportunity for adjustment of expectations and change, but rather as a disagreeable state that cannot be tolerated due to the urgency to return "to the way things used to be," then the source of the disruption is never satisfactorily remedied, improved, or even ameliorated. If the problem or difficulty in the relationship is never addressed directly, it is likely to persist and add to the intensity of future disruptions precipitated by new problems entering the relationship.[1] The more inflexible the system—a two-person relationship, a group, an organization, or a community—the more likely a final disruptive event will be explosive and destructive. Such a relationship is likely to be terminated in a manner which is destructive to the parties involved.

---

1. The intensity of future disruptions is not likely to be increased where problems or difficulties in a relationship are handled by reducing commitment to the relationship. In this case, an apparent "return to the way things used to be" is actually a withdrawal of commitment. Over time such a strategy leads to an atrophied relationship. (In the *Marriage Grid* (1971) by Mouton and Blake, this is a 1,1 orientation, e.g., "Home is where I eat, sleep, and keep my things.")

Whenever disruption occurs the possibility of terminating the relationship is always an alternative solution. Termination is more likely to be a constructive, problem-solving solution, when it is a consequence of renegotiation. Termination is more likely to result in the destructive loss of resources, when one or more of the following are present: (1) the disruption is unplanned and explosive, (2) the system is rigid and inflexible, or (3) the parties have little or no prior experience in renegotiating adjustments to changing conditions.

PLANNED RENEGOTIATION

The model states that relationships cycle through (1) the sharing of information and negotiation of expectations, through (2) commitment to (3) stability and productivity to (4) disruption and the possibility of renegotiation and therefore change. It has also been assumed that it is difficult to hold the system open for renegotiation because of the uncertainty and anxiety that prevails at that time. These concepts then provide a way to introduce controlled change by *anticipating* disruption and renegotiating expectations *in advance*. This is known as planned renegotiation.

Where this simple model of how roles are established and how they change is available to the parties and where they have skills in sharing their reactions, feelings, and perceptions about their relationship, change can be introduced in a controlled and systematic way through planned renegotiation. This is less stressful than renegotiation under conditions of disruption. Both the model and the concept of planned renegotiation thus become parts of the relationship—so that "whenever I feel a pinch," that pinch is shared and the possibility of renegotiation is raised. A *pinch* is a signal of the possibility of an impending disruption and it describes a sense of loss of freedom within one's current role (see Figure 1). The felt loss of freedom may be due to a sense of expanded resources or to subtle constriction of expectations by others. In either case, there is the possibility of resources lost to the system.

Some examples of pinches which raise the possibility of renegotiation are:

—"I think I am now ready to go to New York on a buying trip without you."

—"I find that I am defensive with you, because you judge others so harshly. I don't want you judging me that way."

—"While I will continue to do all the drafting work, I would like to do some engineering work on this project."

—"I think that I somehow have to know all the answers, because no one in this group ever admits that they don't know something. I therefore bluff my way along."

—"We are always talking about how bright we all are, and as a consequence I am becoming more and more cautious about the ideas I choose to share lest they appear anything but brilliant."

—"I have to begin saying, 'no' to you or you have to stop adding to my workload. I will be unable to meet the commitments I have already made unless something is changed."

—"I like you a lot, and I suddenly realize that I am very hesitant to disagree with you for fear that you will then dislike me."

When the question of renegotiation of expectations is raised "when I feel a pinch," the parties have more *choice* and more control over change. They are subject to fewer negotiations "under fire," and they are less often victims of crises and pressures to return to the way things used to be.

Implications and Discussion

Planned renegotiation is likely to be a successful norm-setting intervention in an organization where there is some prior commitment to the concept of organization development, so that persons are neither so closed that differences are ignored and inappropriately smoothed over nor so competitive that differences are exploited by subversive rivalry.

On the other hand, people need concepts to guide their behavior. Organization development efforts often involve skill training in interpersonal relations, or process consultation, or prescriptions to do things differently—such as, "be open"—with training in interpersonal skills, but without an adequate theoretical framework that provides concepts to guide behavior. The tools of Gestalt therapy[2] help people expand their own awareness of themselves

2. See Stanley M. Herman's "A Gestalt Orientation to Organization Development," in this volume.

and make more data available to the system. But what to do with data once it becomes more available? The planned renegotiation model supplies a framework for building more productive working relationships with information generated through organization development efforts.

Similarly, participative management systems need more information from all levels of supervision in order to function effectively. But once the information is generated, how is it to be handled? The planned renegotiation model provides a framework for allowing new information to change the system, where such change is agreeable to all parties involved.

The theory underlying the concept of planned renegotiation is clear and simple and straightforward. Theoretical elaborations have been purposedly avoided. It is intended that the concepts become part of the language of organizational life. Persons can be trained in the skills of planned renegotiation. It is important that people learn to detect pinches before disruptions develop. A pinch is felt by an individual, whereas a disruption is experienced by all parties involved in the relationship. It is therefore incumbent upon an individual who feels a pinch also to take responsibility for raising the question of renegotiation with the other(s), rather than asserting that it is someone else's problem or responsibility. At the same time, it is important he understand that when he experiences a pinch, this is going to make him anxious. When a pinch is shared and renegotiation considered, then others become anxious as well. People get anxious both because of the uncertainty which is introduced into the relationship, and because they are never sure whether they will personally be better off after the renegotiation is completed than they were before. When people work with this model, they learn that anxiety becomes controlled and tolerable, when there is a commitment to problem-solving. There remains nevertheless a risk each time the relationship is opened for examination and renegotiation.

In the first few attempts at renegotiation within the model, people are simultaneously working on two problems: (1) trying out a problem-solving model and developing skills and procedures for its use; and (2) working on the pinch that gave rise to the renegotiation. Over time both skills and procedures develop, as does confirmation of the model and its usefulness to the parties involved (or its lack of usefulness).

Based on the assumption that "most people in organizations prefer a fair negotiated settlement to a state of unresolved conflict," Harrison (1971) has developed a very sound procedure for changing role relationships. It should be useful to those who would like to try planned renegotiation in a formally structured and specifically programmed way. Harrison calls his procedure "role negotiation." It is a detailed program for exchanging expectations and demands for the behavior of others in terms of what each wants others (a) to do more or do better, (b) to do less, or (c) to remain unchanged. These expectations are written, so as to be clearly understood by both sender and receiver. When one person makes a request or demand for changed behavior on the part of another, he must specify a *quid pro quo* he is willing to give in order to get what he wants. The process is complete when an agreement is written which specifies the agreed upon changes in behavior and makes clear what each party is expected to give in return, including a discussion of possible sanctions for noncompliance. The procedures are clear and simple, if a bit mechanical, and they require a consultant in the early stages to establish the rules and to moderate their use.

There are various other ways organizations might make use of the concept of planned renegotiation. An organization might design a "renegotiating arena," where the principals commit themselves not to leave the field until a satisfactory set of mutual expectations is established.[3] A skilled third party consultant might be available to them (see Walton, 1969).

The question is sometimes raised, if planned renegotiation is encouraged, won't this lead to the termination of some relationships that would not otherwise terminate? Yes, it probably will. Where relationships are terminated by choice, this is likely to be an outcome which is more healthy for the individuals and more productive for the organization over the long run, than to retain members who are essentially "captive."

While the theory of how roles are established and changed

---

3. The method, "Meetings for Two" in Fordyce & Weil (1971, pp. 114-116), is a highly structured session designed to provide the opportunity to renegotiate expectations in a two-person relationship without the benefit of a theoretical model. While a third party is not required, the procedure is so highly structured that the presence of a third person seems almost essential.

seems to be interpersonal in focus and appears to concentrate on the modification of behavior in one-to-one situations, the concepts also describe the relation of a person to a group and the relations of all members of a group to one another—e.g., task group, committee, subordinates reporting to one supervisor, family, etc. Relations between groups are also subject to disruption and renegotiation as well—e.g., relations between departments, branch offices, or project teams.[4]

Rather than a theory of interpersonal affairs, the theory is better described as a description of the establishment and change of *relations* between elements of a social system—persons or groups. The theory is more encompassing than it first might seem, it can include some of the major realities of organizational life, such as the power of economics and legitimate authority and the competition between persons or groups for scarce resources. A subordinate can certainly raise the question of renegotiation with his supervisor, and can help his supervisor learn to use the model. Issues of authority can be subjects of renegotiation. Where individuals or groups are highly competitive, renegotiation can take the form of more open bargaining rather than secretive, and sometimes subversive, rivalry.

While all of us need concepts to guide our behavior, it would seem that the model of how roles are established and changed and the concept of planned renegotiation would be particularly useful for those who frequently enter and work with temporary systems (Bennis & Slater, 1968). The more fluid and changing the system, the more important it is to be able to develop means of producing information rapidly which then permits people to appropriately influence one another and to accept appropriate influence. Furthermore, working within this model even within an enduring and established relationship is likely to help a person develop those behavioral skills which are effective in life in temporary systems. These concepts are also probably useful to those who play a mediating role as a third party consultant to others in conflict.

---

4. Several persons have reported that this model is also useful for negotiating change in the behavior of a single person (intrapersonal change). Persons have talked to themselves about themselves and held dialogs in a Gestalt fashion between "how I am now" and "how I would like to be," followed by commitment to a new set of expectations, stability, disruption, and renegotiation.

SUMMARY

This paper is based on the assumption that people need concepts to guide their behavior. A clear and simple model of how roles are established and changed is presented—relationships cycle through (1) the sharing of information and the negotiation of expectations, then (2) commitment to a set of expectations, which governs behavior during a period (3) of stability and productivity, when, for the most part you do what I expect of you and I do what you expect of me, until (4) disruption occurs and the possibility of change enters the system. This theory itself is a norm-setting intervention into an organization when it becomes a part of the normative structure, language, and expectations of members of the organization.

The concept of planned renegotiation is derived from this model and represents a procedure by which controlled change can enter an organization, thereby freeing and expanding resources for problem-solving. This enhances an organization's internal flexibility which is one important criterion of organizational effectiveness (Schein, 1965).

With a statement such as planned renegotiation, people have more choice in their lives and are less likely to be victims "of the way things used to be. . . ."

REFERENCES

Bennis, W. G., & Slater, P. E. *The temporary society.* New York: Harper, 1968.

Blau, P. M. *Exchange and power in social life.* New York: Wiley, 1967.

Blau, P. M. A theory of social integration. *American Journal of Sociology,* 1960, *65,* 550-553.

Fordyce, J. K., & Weil, R. *Managing with people: A manager's handbook of organization development methods.* Reading, Massachusetts: Addison-Wesley, 1971.

Glidewell, J. C. System linkage and distress at school. In M. J. Feldman (Ed.), *Studies in psychotherapy and behavior change,* Buffalo, New York: State University of New York at Buffalo, 1971. Pp. 25-44.

Goffman, E. *The presentation of self in everyday life.* Edinburgh, Scotland: University of Edinburgh, 1956.

Goffman, E. *Encounters.* Indianapolis: Bobbs-Merrill, 1961.

Harrison, R. Role negotiation: A tough-minded approach to team development. In W. W. Burke & H. A. Hornstein (Eds.), *The social technology of organization development,* Washington, D. C.: NTL Learning Resources Corporation, 1972.

Hermann, C. F. Some consequences of crisis which limit the viability of organizations. *Administrative Science Quarterly,* 1963, *8,* 61-82.

Homans, G. C. *Social behavior: Its elementary forms.* New York: Harcourt, Brace & World, 1961.

Katz, D. & Kahn, R. L. *The social psychology of organizations.* New York: Wiley, 1966.

Korchin, S. J. et. al. Visual discrimination and the decision process in anxiety. *AMA Archives of Neurology and Psychiatry*, 1957, *78*, 424-438.

Lanzetta, J. T. Group behavior under stress. *Human Relations*, 1955, *8*, 29-52.

Lewin, K. *Field theory in social science.* D. Cartwright (Ed.) New York: Harper, 1951.

Mouton, J. S., & Blake, R. R. *The marriage grid.* New York: McGraw-Hill, 1971.

Postman, L., & Bruner, J. S. Perception under stress. *Psychological Review*, 1948, *55*, 314-323.

Schein, E. H. *Organizational psychology.* Englewood Cliffs, New Jersey: Prentice-Hall, 1965.

Sherwood, J. J. An introduction to organization development. *Experimental Publication System, Washington*, D. C.: American Psychological Association, No. *11* (April, 1971), Ms. No. 396-1. Also appears in J. W. Pfeiffer & J. E. Jones (Eds.), *1972 annual handbook for group facilitators.* Iowa City, Iowa: University Associates Press, 1972.

Thibaut, J. W., & Kelley, H. H. *Social psychology of groups.* New York: Wiley, 1959.

Walton, R. E. *Interpersonal peacemaking: Confrontations and third party consultation.* Reading, Massachusetts: Addison-Wesley, 1969.

Models for Management: An Alternative to Technocentric Atheoretical OD Interventions

JAY HALL

Technology: Literally defined, the branch of knowledge which deals with arts, crafts, and techniques. For many years, while the behavioral science approach to organizational life still amounted to a weak voice crying in the wilderness, technology was the sworn enemy of practitioners. A common tack employed by many practitioners to illustrate the need for behavioral science intervention was that of citing the disproportionate growth of technological expertise *vis a vis* effectiveness in the management of human resources. Today we are faced with a peculiar paradox; for we are becoming the victims of our own technologies. In a manner of speaking, as practitioners in applied behavioral science, we have become preoccupied with our own special arts, crafts, and techniques. Nowhere is this preoccupation more apparent than in the area of organization development; indeed, many tend to define OD in terms of the techniques which can be applied. How often, for example, has OD been described as a confrontation meeting, or as an ongoing series of T-group encounters aimed at and involving the total system, or as a planned program of change involving six phases? In our zeal to intervene, impact, and effect change in ongoing human systems we risk becoming so enamored with our intervention techniques that we frequently lose sight of the reasons why we intervene at all.

The problem is compounded by an unhealthy kind of advocacy on the part of behavioral science practitioners. It is almost as if we have split ourselves into philosophical camps; camps differentiated according to the arts, crafts, and techniques embraced. In a word, it would appear that we have become *technocentric*. And as technocentricity flourishes, we have become increasingly atheoretical in our approaches, adopting on a purely pragmatic basis those techniques, arts, and crafts which either seem best to accomplish unarticulated goals or, more often the case, which individual practitioners seem best able to handle and apply. In this sense, the same dysfunctional effects of technology often cited as the *raison d'etre* for behavioral science interventions might be said to exist as well among those who would intervene. It would seem to me that in our zeal to protect and advance the technologies to which we owe allegiance, we have lost touch with the *sine qua non* of any technology: namely, a basic theory underlying the utility and application of technique. Moreover, the atheoretical and technocentric preoccupations which I have observed among practitioners seem best described as some form of latterday sophistry; as such, it would appear to be a symptom of the immaturity of our professional stance.

The "Models for Management" design might best be thought of, therefore, as a reaction to atheoretical technocentric approaches to OD interventions. In and of itself, the design amounts to little more than yet another technique for stimulating and creating conditions for organization development. In this respect, the design is relatively less important than the theory upon which it is based. For this reason, the present discussion will focus not on the elements of the intervention design, but rather on the rationale underlying the development and application of the design. The present paper addresses in some detail the theoretical basis upon which the "Models for Management" seminar experience, along with all of the Teleometrics materials, is based. The significance of the presentation, I would suggest, lies not so much in its explication of a new technological twist, as suggested by the present conference context, but rather in its focus on a theory of human learning and the relationship between individual values and thought processes and the quality of organizational and systemic affairs. In short, the paper constitutes an attempt to avoid technocentricity by emphasizing theoretical antecedants.

AN UNDERLYING RATIONALE OF LEARNING AND ITS APPLICATION TO INDIVIDUAL AND ORGANIZATIONAL PRACTICES

The working assumption of the Teleometrics approach to both laboratory learning in general and to organization development specifically is that *awareness precedes choice, and choice should precede change*. This working assumption has its roots in the work of many theorists and researchers in the behavioral sciences. The

condition of awareness becomes the major objective of the learning experience in the "Models for Management" seminar; and, as
such, it evokes a concern on the part of the practitioner with those
conditions and steps most required in the achievement of that kind
of awareness which leads, in turn, to enlightened decision making
among choices: Awareness buttressed by feelings of commitment
and responsibility of the type which lead to the action steps of
change. The objective of awareness, when defined operationally in
this way, may be seen to be quite consistent with the general objectives of organization development. Consider the issue of awareness
and its significance for programs of individual and organizational
change.

Issues In Awareness Training

The concept of awareness—either personal or collective—as
used in the Teleometrics formula for learning is based primarily in
the work of George A. Kelly on the psychology of personal constructs. According to Kelly, underlying, structuring, and controlling most behavior is the manner in which individuals, groups, and
cultures *construe* the world and make predictions regarding it. The
constructs which individuals rely upon as a basis for interpreting,
predicting and forming expectancies regarding the significance of
internal and external events, the implications that these have for
the roles one is required to play in the service of effective adaptation, and the whole series of cause-and-effect relationships upon
which one relies in the day-to-day coping are the critical dimensions of awareness constructs. These constructs, Kelly is quick to
point out, may differ from individual to individual; and they do not
necessarily coincide with either objective reality or any kind of
factual data. Yet, from a phenomenological standpoint, they are
the real stuff of which perceived life and one's behaving in life are
made. It might be said that one's constructions of himself and
others and the relationships which exist between these and the
external environment serve as an internal gyroscope for directing
the individual, keeping him on course, and pointed toward the
achievement of some purpose. Not all of the constructs on which
individuals rely are consciously experienced, nor are they all capable of articulation. Yet, according to Kelly, they lie at the core of
his behavior and from an experiential point of view determine both
what he is and what he will be. The task of change—or in Kelly's

terms that of reconstruction—may best be thought of as one of creating new constructs or new kinds of awarenesses which yield new ways of interpreting and responding to the data all about. To the extent that one's way of construing the world and his place in the world can be thought of as a deterministic influence on his behavior, then the focal point of change efforts must be personal constructs themselves. By extension, we can think of the culture of an organization—and all that this implies in the way of values, practices, and purposes to be attained—as simply reflecting, much as a decision product, the collective constructs of its individuals which have been brought to bear on corporate issues. Again, the influence of individual construct systems, as parts of corporate systems, may not proceed as a conscious process; yet, nevertheless, organizations are composed of and do reflect, however indirectly, the contributions, idiosyncrasies, predilections, capacities and intentions of their various members. Thus the key to organization development would seem ultimately to lie with individual development; and, in the words of Kelly, individual development entails reconstruction of existing individual constructs: The forming of new ways of construing onself, others, environmental events, cause-and-effect relationships, expectancies, and predictions for the future which better jive with the data of experience and purpose. In terms of the objectives of OD, reconstruction might best be described as creating conditions for contemplating the possible, however these conditions might fail to coincide with those previously held constructions upon which individuals relied in their organizational pursuits. A major motivational dynamic to be seized upon is the fact that individuals desire the most reliable and valid construct systems available, and are motivated to update their constructs when the need for this can be recognized. Awareness or reconstruction, therefore, constitutes the major objective to be served in any kind of OD intervention under the Teleometrics approach.

The Nature of Constructs and Construct Systems

In order to better understand just why construct systems and awareness are the major focus of interventions, some consideration of the unique and oftentimes ubiquitous attributes of construct systems might prove beneficial. While a lengthy discourse on the basic provisions of construct theory are beyond the scope of the present discussion, some of the salient features and assumptions might be touched upon.

Constructs channel behavior, feelings, and thought. First of all, under construct theory, a major postulate is that a person's processes—that is, behavior, feelings and intellectual dispositions—are psychologically channelized by the ways in which he anticipates events. Thus, the traditional points of focus of behavioral science training such as cognition, affect and skill are all thought of as being by-products of the manner in which one anticipates events or, put differently, by what he expects to happen in a given situation. The channelization notion addresses the fact that a person's cognitions, affect, and psychomotor practices do not occur randomly in a vast emptiness, but rather proceed through a network of pathways. Although the network is thought to be flexible and frequently modified, it is structured in its facilities and, as a result, restricts the individual's range of action or the options he perceives as available to him.

Not only do individuals differ greatly in their construction of events, but they also differ in the manner in which they seek to relate their various constructs. In general, each individual attempts, characteristically, to organize his construct system so that a more coherent and comprehensive system of constructions becomes available to him as a basis for anticipating events and for purposes of constructing or interpreting the meaning of experienced events. The building of relationships between constructs is an evolutionary process which takes place as a function of one's need to elaborate on his system. Herein lie the seeds for self-consistency, on one hand, and for the rudiments of inflexibility and protection of the system, on the other hand. As Kelly points out, the likely result of a disconfirmed construction system is anxiety, and most people work quite hard to avoid the anxiety associated with disconfirmation. Thus, many behaviors take on a self-fulfilling prophetic quality which serves to replicate and reaffirm the utility of the evolved system of personal constructions. Thus, one of the major barriers to effective change and reconstruction is the very human tendency to avoid the discomfort and anxiety associated with reality testing and the possibility of disconfirming a comfortable and erstwhile useful system of personal constructs.

Constructs are dichotomized dimensions of thought: If not A, then B! A major facet of construct theory may be found in the postulate that a person's construction system is composed of a finite number of dichotomous constructs. The elements within such a construct system constitute bipolar conceptions which are cross referenced in a tightly interwoven system of mutually supportive relationships. The tendency to deal in dichotomized constructs not only has implications for the range of movement—that is, the number of options which the individual perceives as available to him—but it also has significance for the degree of comfort which the individual experiences as he moves within the bipolar range imposed by his construct system. Kelly points out that the dichotomization of data does not necessarily follow logically from the manner in which data present themselves, but that the tendency nevertheless has become one of dealing in unidimensional bipolar constructions of events. Numerous examples of the tendency to dichotomize may be found from basic research in both the physical and social sciences. For example, in the field of electromagnetism we often encounter the construct of negative versus positive poles; in the field of genetics we frequently speak of dominant versus recessive characteristics; and in studies of person perception, the goodness-badness dimension has accounted for a major portion of perceiver variance. The same tendency may be found among behavioral science practitioners, who as part of their jargon frequently think and talk in terms of content versus process, structured versus free-form, authoritarian versus permissive, cognitive versus affective, lecture versus group discussion, and theoretical versus heuristic. As Kelly has observed, none of these necessarily constitute *logical* bipolar anchorages of the same dimension; but so long as they are construed as such, behaviors based upon them will continue to reflect the imposed dichotomization.

Of significance for this latter point, is another facet of construct theory; namely, that a person chooses for himself that alternative in a dichotomized construct through which he anticipates the greater possibility for extension and definition of his system. Put differently, this says that individuals develop preference for and predispositions to cluster additional constructs around one or the other of the dichotomized positions in a construct system. In defense of the system, individuals tend to become judgemental and interpret events in an "all or none" manner: A vs. B; if not A, then B! Thus we find advocates for free-form to the exclusion of structure in many OD interventions, or an aversion to cognitive emphases as opposed to focusing on affective events in training. Kelly observes that it is only when the individual is willing to tolerate some day-by-day uncertainties that he may broaden his field of vision and thus hope to extend the predictive range of his system. He may, in Kelly's terms, opt for constricted certainty or for broadened understanding, but in either event his decision is essentially one of elaborative choice; that is, a decision to elaborate further on the nexus of personal constructs comprising his basis for interpreting the world. Choice remains a very definite and live option for the individual; but, depending upon his particular need for certainty and consistency in responding to demands of both internal and external events, his choices, more often than not, will be for extension, definition, and further elaboration of his system. He will tend to choose those alternatives which afford the greater possibility of reinforcing existing constructions, laying the groundwork for a closed system.

By way of summary, constructs are two-way streets along which one may travel to reach conclusions; or, in teleological terms, they may be thought of as the controls that one places upon life: the life within himself, as well as the life which is external to him. The forming of constructs may be considered to be a binding of sets of events into convenient bundles which are handy for the person to carry around. These events, in turn, when so bound, render the world more predictable, manageable, and controllable. The two-ended pathway of movement provides the individual with choice, choice which is channelized by the construct of interest. As an individual makes choices and perhaps reconstrues the world, he may construct new pathways across areas which were not previously accessible; or he may choose to simply move back and forth in the old constructural slots. When he is under pressure, it is not likely that he will develop new channels, but rather will tend to reverse himself along dimensional lines already established. This latter point may have implications for training experiences in which we send individuals rambling back and forth along dimensional lines because of the stress we create as part of the learning experience.

Change of constructs as a precondition to behavior change: Validation as the key. As previously mentioned, a person's construction system varies as he successfully or unsuccessfully construes the replications of events. All kinds of experiential learnings are assumed into the structure of personal constructs; and herein lies the possibility of modulation and modification of construct systems. Obviously, the degree to which a system may be either modulated or modified is to a great extent dependent upon the utility of the constructs within whose range of convenience the variants lie.

It is thought further that, to the extent one person employs a construction of experience which is similar to that employed by another, his psychological processes will be similar to those of the other person as well; and very likely he will be more attracted to such individuals. Similar others serve to reinforce one's preferred construction systems. Thus similarity of construct systems becomes a basis for the formation of interpersonal groupings; and these, in turn, perhaps underlie cultural entities not unlike those described earlier among practitioners as being differentiated according to their philosophic devotion to OD technologies.

Finally, it follows, from Kelly's position, that if the individual is to change—either in his cognition, affect, or psychomotor dispositions—needed will be a change in his construct system. This may amount to a reconstruction based on the addition of new constructs, the deletion of current constructs, or perhaps the discovery of new pathways and linkage among constructs. Premature or forced movement should be guarded against, according to Kelly, because of the threat that can be generated when one's construct system is attacked by external agents. Personal security is greatest in consistent and more concrete construct systems. It is these which will tend to be defended and most protected against outside assault. Insensitivity to the significance of the construct system for the individual's ability to cope and his own sense of comfort most often will result in erratic, compensatory behavior which Kelly has described as running back and forth in dimensional slots between the bipolar anchorages of the construct.

The direction of movement for most people, and hence their motivation, is toward better understanding of what will happen. Thus individuals have the choice of withdrawing into a more and more predictable world, or moving out toward making more and more of the world predictable. It is toward the latter choice that awareness training and OD interventions are most likely pointed; for the former case constitutes a condition of individual or corporate neurosis which is less amenable to reconstruction. The key to reconstruction, and by inference the success of individual or OD interventions, may be found in the concept of validation.

If, as Kelly suggests, a person's construction system varies as he successfully construes the replication of events, validation points out the successive cycles in his construing. If a person makes only vague commitments and/or predictions regarding the future, he receives in return only vague validational experience. By the same token, if his commitments and predictions are far reaching and have sweeping significance, his validations may, in themselves, be far reaching and with sweeping significance. Thus, the provision of validating experiences becomes the key for the introduction, reinforcement, and perhaps reaffirmation of constructs regarding the individual's construct system. By the same token, it becomes necessary and desirable to pull out from the individual his commitments and predictions regarding the future so that they might be submitted for validation or invalidation according to the provisions and limitations of the learning experience per se. In this way, by designing validating and invalidating experiences it becomes possible to reinforce and/or to weaken or disconfirm those constructs of significance to the goals of behavioral science intervention. Validation becomes the key to reconstruction and, within the terms of the Teleometrics formula, validation in the service of reconstruction becomes the key to awareness.

The conditions for validation and construct change. Kelly has also given considerable thought to the conditions deemed favorable to the formation of new constructs. The first of these concerns the use of *fresh elements;* that is, the construction of an artificial learning situation which constitutes an analog to the real world of the individual and into which new constructs may be designed for consideration. Such situations should be designed, according to Kelly, in such a way that the individual is only gradually involved, and the new constructs which are developed are allowed to replace only gradually those undesirable role constructs which, although currently exercising control in the individual's life, have outlived their validity. It would seem that the new elements facet of reconstructing parallels, in a number of ways, the learning laboratory typically employed by behavioral science practitioners.

The second element of reconstruction cited by Kelly is that of *experimentation;* and, again, a number of parallels exist between his essentially therapeutic approach and that found in behavioral science laboratories in that an atmosphere of experimentation is created in which the consequences of one's experimental acts are seen as limited. One does not, in a manner of speaking, play for keeps. New constructs are seen as being tried on for size; they are propositional and, as proposed representations of reality, they constitute less threatening entites for personal choice. Finally, the availability of *validating data* becomes a significant aspect in the formation of new constructs. If, again, a construct is thought of as a framework for making predictions, it follows that if the construct does not work, a tendency will arise to alter it; particularly so within the more permeable aspects of the construct system. If valdiation, or return on the predictions made, is unavailable or unduly delayed, one is likely to postpone changing the construct under which the prediction was made. Therefore, validating data must be immediately available if new constructs are to be formed; and this is essentially an issue of design. Those interventions which do not provide in their designs for immediate and germane validating or invalidating data are interventions which, within Kelly's scope at least, are self-defeating from the standpoint of new construct formations. It is interesting that it is in this area particularly that our OD technologies are perhaps most different one from another.

Summary

Thus by way of summary, the awareness objective of Teleometrics materials reflects most directly the work of George Kelly and the significance for behaving that personal construct systems are presumed to have. These systems define both the object targets of interventions and, at the same time, give insight into the manner in which they might best be changed or reconstructed. This reconstruction amounts to the improvement of personal and organizational functioning by virtue of an assumption into existing construct systems of new constructs with greater predictive validities. The provision of new constructs and opportunities for validating experiences becomes the underlying objective of the technology of the Teleometrics approach, derived, as should be obvious, from a theoretical perspective, rather than from any particular sense of advocacy regarding technique. The question to be addressed next, therefore, is the conditions necessary for the achievement of awareness; awareness characterized by such a level of commitment that it will be followed upon by the making of choice decisions and the undertaking of acts in the service of greater construct validity and predictability.

Awareness Requires Involvement, Feedback, and Perspective

Kelly, in his treatment of the modification and modulation of construct systems through validation, provided insight into the conditions under which a change in construct systems might best be achieved. Essentially, the creation of conditions necessary for construct change constitutes the action components of the Teleometrics approach to laboratory learning and organization development. The issue, again, is one of enumerating those conditions and steps which are most required in the achievement of awareness. Extrapolating from Kelly's construct theory, the achievement of awareness might be put into a formula for learning:

$$\text{INVOLVEMENT} + \text{FEEDBACK} \times \text{DAMPENING}$$
$$= \text{AWARENESS}$$

The above formula underlies the development of all Teleometrics materials in general, and influenced the design of the "Models for Management" seminar experience in particular. As the formula suggests, the attempt has been one of providing learner involvement, following this involvement immediately with feedback on attributes of the involvement process, and then providing an opportunity for obtained feedback to be dampened. The rationale and objectives to be served by each of these steps are briefly explained below:

The Involvement Process: A Mechanism for the Experimental Generation of Fresh Elements

Perhaps the most unique characteristic of behavioral science interventions is that they have tended to rely on experiential learning formats. The impetus for this approach may be traced to the early work of Kurt Lewin on the relative effectiveness of lecture versus group discussion approaches to attitude change. Out of the work of Lewin and his colleagues grew a conviction on the part of applied behavioral scientists that individuals learned best and became most committed to learnings under conditions of learner participation. Essentially, the dynamic that is harnessed by a group discussion or some other form of experiential learning is that of ego involvement. This means that the *self* of the learner is acti-vated. Because of opportunities for active participation by join-ing in the discussions, thinking through implications, the solving of problems, and the like, or by simply contemplating one's own internal processes, the experience resulting becomes a highly per-sonal one with implications for maintenance and enhancement of one's self image. The work of Muzafer Sherif and his colleagues on the dynamics of ego involvement are quite consistent from an explanatory standpoint with the action results obtained by Lewin in his early research. The findings from various pieces of research on the efficacy of learner involvement seem to converge on the net effect that learners are more committed, more attentive, experience greater satisfactions, feel that they have influenced the direction of events and retained more personal fate control—and hence are more likely to follow up on acquired learnings—when some in-volvement technique is employed. For this reason, involvement has become not only a key ingredient of the laboratory approach to learning, but it is a key ingredient in the Teleometrics approach to the achievement of awareness.

The Teleometrics approach differs, perhaps, in its recognition of the fact that there are many kinds of involvement. Because of tech-nocentricity among practitioners, it is many times felt that free-form agendaless discussion is the only involvement mechanism available. Others feel that involvement is equated with the examination and exploration of affectual issues to the exclusion of cognitive inputs or considerations of any type. We at Teleometrics feel that such positions simply reflect the operation of dichotomized constructs among our behavioral practitioner colleagues. Indeed, it would seem that anything, be it group discussion, an action exercise, a meaningful theory input, or participation only as an outside ob-server, might be found involving if the issues at hand are pertinent to the construct system of the individual involved. The point is that it is not the technique of involvement which is important under the Teleomerics approach, but rather the relationship of the involving experience to the construct system of the individual learner and the utility that the two have for his ability to predict and interpret the world around him in a more effective manner. Thus, the involve-ment component of the steps required for the achievement of awareness may take many forms; and the major criterion for what is or what is not involving lies with the objectives of awareness. These may be either cognitive, affectual, or psychomotor in kind. Involvement in and of itself, however, is not enough, notwithstanding the practices of many devotees of the pure involvement intervention approach.

Feedback As A Key to Validating Involvement-Induced Constructs

As Kelly has made explicit, and as the follow-up research of Lewin's protege, Bennett, has suggested, involvement per se is not enough to insure either the new awareness or the degree of commitment necessary for sustained change. Behaviors which take place in a vacuum without apparent purpose are behaviors which are difficult to reinforce through validation or to disconfirm through invalidation. From a design standpoint, therefore, they are relatively weak ingredients for a learning process aimed at greater awareness and ultimate change based on incorporation of new elements into one's construct system. The need for information concerning the *efficacy* of one's practices, the *utility* of one's approaches, or the *significance* of one's attitudes, has been evident since the early work in learning theory of E. L. Thorndike. The key ingredient in such information is that it serves to tell the individual when he is off course with respect to his desired objectives. Thus, negative feedback is perhaps the most important kind of information for the modification of construct systems. While information to the effect that one is doing well may serve to reinforce desired practices, because of the self deception that so often characterizes one's attempts to protect existing constructs, such reinforcement may also have the effect of simply strengthening dysfunctional construct systems. At best, reinforcement is a subtle mechanism for learning "approved" behaviors.

Far more information may be obtained from feedback which tells the learner that what he thought to be an effective construct is falling short of his goals and is, therefore, a less than optimal component of his construct system. The seeds for reconstruction may, therefore, not only be sown by feedback in general, but particularly by invalidating feedback. Thus, means for harnessing feedback information in such a way that it is objective and communicates clearly the amount of discrepancy between desired or predicted outcomes based on the use of a given construct and actual outcomes based on the use of that construct should be designed into learning experiences aimed at the modification of construct systems. The working assumption of objective and reliable feedback of this type is that discrepancies bother people. They will begin to open up to and search out alternative constructs, as a rule, in direct proportion to the extent to which they are bothered by discrepancies. If their construct systems are such that feedback data reveal no discrepancies, then individuals are in a position of simply trying to gain reinforcement for an already viable construct system. It is those individuals and organizations employing construct systems which run counter to the tenets of good behavioral science practice who are perhaps the more significant targets for behavioral science interventions. Again, feedback of a disconfirming, discrepancy-identifying type is an essential ingredient in the Teleometrics approach to achieving reconstructed awareness. Feedback, too, however, has its limitations and its undesirable side effects.

Dampening

Because of the dichotomized nature of constructs, and the tendency of individuals to think in black and white, A versus B, terms, the impact of feedback may often be other than intended. Given, for example, the individual's tendency to construe the world as "if not A, then B" the message of feedback should be such that it does more than simply send the individual back and forth in what Kelly called "dimensional slots." Too often, this is precisely what feedback does. We have all, I am sure, had experience with over-reactive compensatory behaviors resulting from one's reception of well-intentioned feedback. The dominant member of a group, for example, who upon being told that he is talking too much frequently construes the message in terms of his "talk versus no talk" construct system; and decides that if he is not to talk as much this means that he is not to talk at all! Dysfunctional over-reactive silence becomes the net effect of his feedback. By the same token, we have all known of managers who construe their practices in terms of an autocratic versus permissive bipolarization. These individuals upon learning that they are seen as autocratic frequently see only a permissive option available to them and react to feedback accordingly.

Not only are such over-reactions to feedback other than those desired or intended from the introduction of feedback, they tend

not to sustain themselves. The talkative person has already revealed his preference for talking and will find silence unendurable
beyond some point. The autocratic manager, by the same token,
has already revealed where his "predictions for effectiveness" lie
and will be quick to pick up the fact that his trial run of permis-
siveness was not effective in the pursuit of those goals desired by
him. Thus, conditions are frequently created for boomerang effect;
feedback alters behavior initially, but ends up strengthening the
original behavior in the long run because the extreme alternative to
it perceived is not feasible or has been invalidated during an experimental trying out. The seeds for recycling and reaffirmation of
more preferred behaviors are sown and the system becomes more
closed and more self reinforcing. Elaboration upon existing constructs occurs—now defensively—and new attempts at reconstruction are likely to fall on deaf ears.

These and related points have been made most eloquently by
Rosenblueth, Wiener, and Bigelow in their classic article *Behavior,
Purpose and Teleology*. Needed, to avoid the pitfalls associated
with raw feedback, is some *dampening* device; means for relating
feedback to the purposes of the individual and his predictions are
required. According to Rosenblueth *et al,* when feedback is dampened it tends to stay more on target and to avoid the over-oscilla-
tory effect described above. Such teleological feedback takes on
more predictive or extrapolative value for the individual. Dampening may be achieved by several methods. The Teleometrics approach relies upon three different dampening techniques:

(1) *Modular dampening.* A type of dampening feedback con-
    cerns, for want of a better word, modular comparisons.
    When an individual completes a personal feedback instru-
    ment on himself or behaves in an action exercise, whether
    he realizes it or not, he is building up a score favoring
    several different approaches or practices regarding organi-
    zational events. These practices and their related scores
    may be thought of as being passed through a modular filter
    such that the end product reflects the individual's assess-
    ment of personal practices and beliefs relative to the dimen-
    sions of the behavioral model upon which the instrument
    or exercise is based. Thus, the feedback one receives tells
    him something about the utility of his practices for achiev-
    ing the goals specified in the instrument as these practices

are evaluated relative to the normative provisions of the
behavioral model. Both effective tendencies and notable
discrepancies from effective tendencies may be identified,
oftentimes in a plottable way so that graphic information
may be achieved by the individual. This information is
dampened by being referenced to the provisions of accepted
behavioral models for personal functioning. It is perhaps in
this case that the dampening of feedback yields the most
objective, reliable, and clearcut facets of one's practices
and how these are discrepant from what is thought to be
more effective practices. Thus, dampened negative feedback
becomes the major learning dynamic in the use of modular
dampening techniques.

(2) *Normative dampening.* Normative dampening pertains primarily to the results of feedback from self appraisal instruments. The practices which one reveals through completion of a personal feedback instrument yield numerical
ratings which, in turn, allow an individual some insight
into the discrepancy between his practices and those perhaps more effective under the provisions of a behavioral
model. Such raw data, however, constitutes raw, undamp-
ened feedback and is in need of being placed in a proper
context or "corrected for culture." Thus, in many of the
Teleometrics materials the individual is provided an opportunity for comparing his own self-assessment with the self-
assessments of several hundred other individuals similar to
himself. In this way, his raw data become dampened relative to contextual factors. An example would be that of an
individual who scores 135 on an IQ test. Given only that
information, he may or may not feel particularly good
about his performance. Given normative information—or
dampened feedback in the present language—that the average score in his culture on the IQ test was 100, the individual might then begin to feel quite good and more
confident about his superior score of 135. Another example
might be in terms of one's use of exposure and feedback-
solicitation in interpersonal affairs. If an individual on the
Personnel Relations Survey were to achieve an exposure
usage score of 30 and a feedback score of 35 out of a
possible 50, he might feel that his interpersonal style was

in a pretty good state of effectiveness. If the style revealed by these scores, however, were assessed against a back-drop of the culture in which the individual operates, the picture may not be quite the same. For the sake of argu-ment, let us assume that the culture score on exposure is 40 and the feedback score for that culture is 20. The in-dividual would come across to others within that culture as fairly closed and underexposing, while being overly pre-occupied with the solicitation of feedback. Thus, there is a need for additional feedback; information considered to be second order in nature which will serve to dampen raw feedback and put it into a realistic perspective. This is one way in which over-reactive compensatory behaviors might be avoided.

(3) *Self-other dampening: Systems linkage.* A third and final type of dampened feedback may be achieved through the use of self-other comparisons. Again, with the use of per-sonal feedback instruments, one may achieve information regarding the manner in which he perceives his own prac-tices. Not only may these data be referenced against the practices of others like him and against the provisions of a behavioral model, but they may also be compared with the manner in which he is perceived by significant others from the real world of work. For example, an individual may complete a personal feedback instrument in which he ap-praises his own managerial practices: the data which he will receive may be quite valuable and thought provoking to him; but when he receives information from his sub-ordinates, according to the same dimensions upon which he has rated himself, the picture may change drastically. He may find that they concur with his own personal assess-ment, and his underlying constructs may be reinforced; or he may find that they view him quite differently than he views himself, and uderlying constructs may be invalidated. The upshot of either reinforcement or discrepancy dampen-ing is that the individual is frequently motivated—cer-tainly he is encouraged—to join with those who have made assessments of his practices for purposes of discussing and critiquing his practices and the effect these have had on the relationhip among all parties. Such discussions, critiques,

and plans for future practices which come out of these self-other comparisons are fully consistent with the goals of OD. The self-other dampening provision constitutes a catalyst and serves as a springboard to opening up for discussion and review much of what has transpired among people in the past and what should desirably transpire in the future. Thus, other individuals and their comments and suggestions may be harnassed as feedback and may be used to further dampen laboratory-based feedback information. It is through such dampening techniques that new pathways and linkages become available for testing by the individual so that construct systems may be opened up for the assumption of new constructs along with the deletion of those constructs found wanting in predictive validity.

Summary

Thus, by way of summary, the Teleometrics approach to laboratory learning—particularly with respect to the design of the "Models for Management" seminar—is one in which involvement coupled with dampened feedback is thought to be the key to reconstructed awareness. Reconstructed awarenesses, in turn, are thought to be the key to individual, cultural, and organizational change.

THE AWARENESS MODEL AS A BASIS FOR DESIGNING OD INTERVENTIONS

It is perhaps noteworthy that the major influences on both the purposes and designs of OD interventions have been those which address the construct systems of individual managers and organizations. The classic work of Douglas McGregor on the articulation of managerial value systems is a case in point: Theory X and Theory Y conceptions of the nature of working man simply represent two construct systems found among managers, the first well developed and elaborated upon and the second in need of elaboration. We are all familiar with the impact of McGregor's approach on management thinking; to many, McGregor is the father of organization development. In much the same vein, the work of Herzberg may be considered to address construct systems pertaining to issues of job satisfaction. Herzberg's major contribution, it would appear, has been that of invalidating the bipolarity of a traditionally dichotomized construct: namely that of satisfaction versus dissatisfaction with one's work. The suggestion, supported by research, by Herberg that feelings of satisfaction and feelings of dissatisfaction do not represent two ends of a morale continuum, but rather reflect feeling states, each due to unique factors and worthy of investigation in its own right, has had a significant impact on current management thought. Further, the work of Likert and Blake and Mouton on integrating perennially dichotomized management values—production versus people—has laid the groundwork for some of the major OD interventions to date. By exploring new pathways, introducing fresh elements, and affording opportunities for either the confirmation or disconfirmation of managerial predictions, these investigators have infused new awarenesses into organizations. The upshot has been an increased recognition of the possibility of complementarity among the achievement goals of an organization and the needs and potentials of its human resources. All of the elegant, spontaneous, and creative technologies which have been developed for intervening notwithstanding, it would seem that no single technique has approached in its impact on an ongoing human system any of the construct oriented contributions just cited. This fact should be instructive to behavioral science practitioners.

Organizational Construct Systems: The Targets of OD Interventions

Whether they have done so wittingly or not, most behavioral science practitioners have concerned themselves with the construct systems existing in organizations. We are all familiar with the oft stated objectives of organization development. There is little need to repeat these systemic goals here; rather, it may prove helpful to concern ourselves with their opposites. Assuming that there is needed some movement toward the objectives stated under organization development values, there is implied a movement away from some current existing construct systems. Implicit in the stated goals of OD is the notion that organizations currently are characterized by the following constructions of systemic events and potentials:

1. Individuals within organizations construe the world in such a way that they are basically distrustful and expect others to be untrustworthy, particularly members of other groups and individuals in different levels of the authority hierarchy.

2. The constructions of individuals in organizations are such that they perceive little utility or possibility for open and candid relationships; and, as a result, tend to magnify differences both within and between groups, leading to a construction of problem situations according to a win-lose dichotomized construct system in which the range of movement and its attendant options are extremely limited.

3. The prevailing construct system of organizations is such that decision making and problem solving responsibilities are best located in particular roles or levels of authority, and this very likely reflects a policy level attempt to embellish and elaborate upon traditional construct systems in a more formal way.

4. The conception of managerial role is that of planner, director, and controller, such that goals and objectives and their attendant decision steps must be articulated by managers per se and passed on to those in non-management positions whose roles are construed according to different expectations and dimensions. Issues of ownership and commitment do not fit comfortably into such construct systems.

5. The current constructs pertaining to relationships among individuals and groups typically reflect values associated with the competitive ethic. The construct used is an extension of win-lose bipolarization, elaborated upon to incorporate the anticipation that competitiveness energizes individuals, groups and organizations. There is little room for collaborative values and their attendant pathways in such a construct system as it exists.

6. The prevailing construct systems of individuals and the organizations to which they belong have been captured by technological and task concerns reflecting a content preoccupation; the major focal point of such constructions is intellectual mastery and technological achievement. Reflecting but a single end of the content-process bipolarization, existing construct systems extend themselves and their predictive utility to the exclusion of any consideration with individual, interpersonal and intergroup processes.

If this opposite-state description of currently existing construct systems makes sense, then an important issue becomes that of the efficacy of our technologies in effecting change. We might ask ourselves to what extent our favorite techniques do in fact move from current constructural states toward the building of trust, the creation of open problem solving climates, the location of decision making and problem solving responsibilities close to information resources, increased sense of ownership of organizational goals, and more collaborative and creative relationships among interdependent groups in such a way that an increased awareness of group and individual processes and their performance consequences prevail? It is my opinion that most technocentric approaches have failed massively in the large proportion of cases; more often than not, only one or two OD objectives are served by steadfast devotion to a single art, craft or technique.

Levels of Awareness and Their Significance for Organization Development Strategies

Practitioners, like their client groups, have tended to deal in dichotomized construct systems; the result has been intervention technologies addressing only limited facets of awareness. These are, as it turns out, at least three major awareness levels of importance to organizational construct systems. These are intellectual, affective, and psychomotor or skill levels. Too often, because of the tendency to view the world of intervention in terms of cognitive versus affective, structured versus free-form, theoretical versus heuristic, and the like, interventionists have construed as possible only certain intervention strategies. Thus, we are confronted with a proliferation of affect-oriented interventions; skill training interventions abound; and the quasi-problem solving "discover it for yourself" technique is found in wild profusion. Much of our organizational time is being spent in rediscovering the wheel so that we may be more committed to its roundness, rather than in any consideration of the utility that wheels might have for the achievement of organizational movement. And yet we wonder why members of organizations fail to see the practicality of our objectives and are instead resistant to our attempts to "help" them.

Eric Berne has pointed out perhaps most clearly that any intervention attempt which focuses primarily on intellectual issues runs the risk of closing off and isolating equally important affectual dynamics. By the same token, he hastens to add interventions which focus primarily on affectual issues tend to close off and isolate intellectual dynamics; both are important and necessary ingredients for the kind of awareness which leads to change! Atheoretical technocentric approaches have obscured this basic fact. Needed, it would appear, is a construction of intervention awarenesses if we, as behavioral science practitioners, are to really serve the goals of organization development. New pathways and alternatives to what might now be labeled a theory versus technique construction are to be desired. Theories are of only limited utility without techniques of application; but technique has never been able to replace theory in the evolutional scheme of things. The effective integration of the two is the sign of the master craftsman, and I would suggest that it is time for us to address this integration.

A Gestalt Orientation to Organization Development[1]

STANLEY M. HERMAN

ABSTRACT

This paper describes the application of Gestalt therapy principles to organization development. These approaches differ from many conventional OD practices in their emphasis on developing self-supports for individuals rather than environmental (team or group) supports. Authenticity is stressed as a key value—even when this involves "authoritarism" and other seemingly negative behaviors. The author believes that the most effective and fulfilled manager (and subordinate) is one who can experience and be what he now is; *not* one who tries to conform to a prescribed model of managership (whether it be Theory Y or some other).

Herman further suggests that many OD practitioners too often fall short of identifying and facilitating the resolution of real issues by attempting to solve problems prematurely. There is a need for us to improve our capacity to become aware of core issues rather than symptoms by: 1) helping clients to fully experience extremes (polarization); 2) helping them to become more aware of how they stop themselves from getting what they want (truncating their power); and 3) encouraging them to stay with difficult intra and inter-personal transactions until they have truly finished each piece of business (closure).

A few months ago a psychotherapist friend of mine asked me to join him in consulting with one of his patients. The patient, a highly successful general manager of a building supply company, had just been offered the presidency of a very large retail chain organization. Taking over the new assignment would, as he saw it, require drastic changes in the company's way of doing business, and likely the "reformation" or replacement of several high level people. That was the dilemma. This energetic, talented and essentially tough-minded general manager had about a year or so before attended a sensitivity training laboratory, had been deeply touched by his experience of warmth, affection and support in the group and had attempted subsequently to expand his knowledge

1. A number of people were very helpful in reviewing and commenting on drafts of this paper. I would like to express my appreciation especially to Sheldon A. Davis, Vice President, Industrial Relations, TRW Systems and Robert N. Philips, M.D., a psychiatrist with whom I have worked in developing and applying Gestalt methodology in organization development.

by readings in organization development. Then, he had tried to apply the principles he had learned to his own and other's relationships in his organization. The results of his attempts had been mixed. Some subordinates had responded well to his openness and participative style. Others had used the greater leeway he gave them as an opportunity to become lax and ineffective. Nevertheless, the general manager stayed devotedly with his perceptions of what good human relations ought to be, and in fact his hesitancy about accepting the new job offer had to do with his doubt that his management approach would work with his new subordinates. And as he put it: "I would rather quit managing altogether than go back to my old authoritarian ways."

After some exploratory discussion it became clear that a certain amount of misinterpretation had occurred in this man's understanding of sound human relations practice (as most experienced O.D. people will have guessed). But in a larger sense a great deal of what was troubling this manager I recognized as a common theme among many people who have been influenced by the sensitivity training derived theories of O.D. He had come to regard his own power—both his organizational position and his personal force—as something uncomfortable, even bad. And so he worked diligently to restrain that power for the sake of others whom he saw as less powerful. I believe that this discomfort with the overt exercise of directive authority is quite common among many people involved in O.D. theory and practice.[2]

For some time the main thrust of organization development efforts has been directed at changing organization environments in ways that will make them more supportive and facilitative to people. For example, we frequently speak of the requirement to change an organization culture in ways that will support such

2. To provide closure on the incident; the manager, my friend and I discussed the issue he raised, and he did some "Gestalt work" on his decision to accept or not accept the new job. I also later sent him an earlier draft of this paper and a related one and got the following response:
"Dear Stan:
I cannot thank you enough for taking an evening to help out a troubled person with some good, sound organizational development advice.
I read your two articles. Funny thing, it seemed as though these articles were written especially for me and it seems as though there is a common thread between the problem I am incurring when I attempt to fit myself into the mold of the prototype leader. I am quite sure I am much more effective just being myself. You point this out rather dramatically. The application of Gestalt techniques to organizations is an exciting idea . . ."

values as openness, participation, inter-dependence, etc. I believe
that emphasis has been useful but not sufficient. In this paper I
want to suggest an additional approach, one that is largely derived
from the theory and practice of Gestalt therapy.

In the following pages I intend to emphasize the "ungentle"
aspects of organizational behavior, those that have generally received less attention and have frequently been regarded with less
comfort by many O.D. theoreticians and practitioners.[3] My objective here is not to provide instruction on making the organization
culture safer, more pleasant or easier for the individual, but rather
to help the individual recognize, develop and experience his own
potency and ability to cope with his organization world, whatever
its present condition. Further, I would like to encourage him to
discover for himself his own unique wants of that environment
and his capacity to influence and shape it in ways that get him
more of what he wants.

The most formidable barrier to the person and his free expression of himself in the organization setting is probably fear. Fear
of others, and how they might affect him and his life, and even
more importantly fear of himself and how he might make mistakes,
do the wrong thing, and so imperil "his future" and/or his image
of himself as a modern manager, specialist, or whatever.

One of the most crucial areas of study in examining organization behavior is the manager—subordinate relationship. In this
relationship, probably more than any other, both managers and
subordinates frequently constrict the potential range of their interaction (and their potential capacity to enjoy each other). In the
sections below I will discuss currently prevalent patterns of relationships and some alternatives, first from the perspective of the
manager and then the subordinate.

THE MYTH OF OMNIPOTENCE

For many years an important focus for theories of management has been the area of power and control. Even before Douglas McGregor postulated his X and Y theories of management
many other theorists advocated caution in the manager's use of

3. I do want to note that recently there has been increased attention to the
power aspects of organization life by some O.D. people and I believe this is a
hopeful sign.

power and control. Cases were made for participative permissive or otherwise moderated styles of supervision. By now it has become clear to almost every manager or supervisor who sees himself as "beyond the dark ages" that bosses are not supposed to be domineering and authoritarian, or, at least if they are, they are not supposed to seem that way to their subordinates. This was a heavy self-imposed requirement of the building supply company general manager in my earlier case example.

It is clearly true that a dictatorial or oppressive style of management is no longer generally acceptable in the United States. But I believe that the real basis for this truth is not found in philosophical images of theoretical democracy; rather, it stems from the high probability that most people who work in present day organizations are unwilling to tolerated oppression. They will find a way of rising up against it, either overtly or covertly, through sabotage.

For many managers though, the image of "democratic leadership" has not served as a useful model. Their attempts to regulate their own behavior to make it "fit the image" have been strained and unnatural, and frequently received with discomfort and suspicion by their subordinates. A man is a man, and if his behavior is authentic it must reflect his own internal personal realities at any given point in time, not a prescribed external ideal. In the Gestalt context, forced or deliberately planned "corrections" in behavior—even when they are ostensibly voluntary— produce exhibitionistic rather than genuine change. Such change is very difficult to sustain and the effort to sustain it is usually at great cost to the individual. *Genuine growth requires that a person first recognize and acknowledge his present qualities before he can proceed with his own natural development.*

Withheld Thrust

In the practice of psychotherapy, therapists repeatedly encounter the guilt and anxiety-ridden patient who tortures himself with fantasies of how he has abused or injured others. In this way he brings himself to a state of such self-mistrust or self-hate that he becomes unable to encounter people around him and can only turn inward. His vitality and excitement are lost as he spends his energy in restraining and punishing himself.

In an organization culture where the exercise of direct authoritarian power is ostensibly disapproved by the established norms of the organization, many people in positions of authority may experience a comparable (though, of course, less extreme) pattern. They may become vaguely uncomfortable or even terribly concerned about the "awesome force" they have over other people. I call this syndrome the myth of Omnipotence.

The myth of omnipotence is a specter that can paralyze potency. The manager who believes too much in his own power to harm begins to withhold or divert his energy, his spontaneity and his thrust in order to avoid hurting others. This withheld thrust has adverse affects both on the withholder and on those from whom he withholds. In the course of my organization consulting I have encountered many cases in which the manager of an organization struggles painfully within himself to try to force his behavior to conform to an image of managership in which he is continually benign, non-authoritarian, encouraging and facilitative toward his subordinates. And at the same time within himself he feels but holds back his own wants, convictions, and desires to move things ahead. He also experiences "negative" emotions toward his subordinates, such as irritation, criticism, impatience, and so on and yet withholds these because a "good manager" (like a "good parent") is not supposed to express such things to those who are below him (his children).

Believing the myth of his own omnipotence might have some consolation for a manager if he could, at least subjectively, feel himself stronger and more capable in comparison to his subordinates. But the typical manager seldom enjoys that feeling of superiority even at a subjective level, instead he struggles with intermittent ambivalence and lack of fulfillment.

Perhaps more important, his subordinates may also suffer from the ambiguity of the signals the manager sends out. On the one hand the manager's words are encouraging, patient, and reasonable, but on the other hand the expressions on his face, his tone, his body signs (e.g. fidgeting, tension, etc.) almost invariably also show through, and these too are perceived by his subordinates. The disparities, however, are seldom if ever dealt with.

Full Expression

It would be far healthier for the manager to fully express his feelings, negative as well as positive, and to allow himself fuller expression of his authoritarian-directive impulses as well. With their full expression his subordinates can more completely experience the totality of the manager's reality. Then they can accept or contest it (and him) as they see fit. From this interchange of full expression and full reaction both the manager and his subordinates can grow in a more meaningful way. Their growth follows at least two dimensions. First, in the interpersonal and intrapersonal sense they learn to really know each other more richly and authentically, and through a heightened awareness of their own feelings, they learn to know themselves better as well. Secondly, with repeated practice and greater familiarity between each other, the substance of their ideas can also be more adequately tested and new, more effective ways of working together developed.

In one organization I worked with the high level manager of a large staff who had developed a strong, indeed passionate, commitment to "OD values." Included in these values, as he saw them, was the requirement for a manager to be fair, rational and helpful to those who reported to him. Most of the time he conformed to these requirements quite easily and naturally. He was, however, an individual of great personal force, with strong emotions and subject to occasional moodiness. Those who reported to him recognized these qualities and had gradually grown accustomed to them, though as might be expected, comfort with his style differed among them.

Over a considerable period of time this strong, able manager grew increasingly discontent and unhappy in his relationships with several members of his staff and staff members, in turn, were also troubled. The "problem" can best be illustrated by the patterns of interaction in the manager's staff meetings. These were generally conducted in a fairly free-flowing and participative style with the floor pretty much available to anyone who wanted it. Sometimes the meetings were quite business-like and at other times they consisted mostly of a series of rambling discourses punctuated occasionally by concise irrelevancies.

For the most part the manager and his staff were fairly satisfied with both the focused and the "non-productive" discussions. From time to time, however, and for no very apparent reason except his mood at the moment, the manager would suddenly jump into the discussion with all the force of a safe dropped from a ten story window, usually landing on one of about three or four members of his staff. Frequently, though not always, his "attack" was logically sound, it was not so much the substance as the vehemence and unexpectedness that seemed to most affect those who were its targets.

The responses of those who were "attacked" by the boss varied, but few were completely unresponsive. This was clearly not an oppressive environment. Some replied by defending their position with counter-logic. One used humor, including self-depreciating comments to "reduce the tension." Still another acted out and sometimes verbally expressed his feelings of being "punished" by the boss. Whatever the response though, what most frequently seemed to happen was that after a round or two of exchange the boss would cease to respond, frequently settling into a glum, silent posture. When that happened the entire group would experience a long awkward pause, with no explicit resolution of the issue, if indeed an issue was even identifiable from the brief exchange.

After working with the group for some period of time, I found myself face-to-face with their classic syndrome. An important proposal for a change of policy had been made by one of the staff, and tentatively supported by two others. The manager's reaction was quick and strongly negative. He accused all the proponents of being panicky, unrealistic, and out of touch with the organizations needs. After the typical pattern of responses from these staff members and another round or two of exchange the manager lapsed into grim silence.

The alternatives for me as a consultant then were: (1) I could intervene in such a way as to focus even more sharply on the disruptive, inhibiting effects on his staff of the manager's outbursts, possibly I could analyze or encourage the group to analyze the reasons for and consequences of the interaction pattern; or (2) I could intervene in a way that *encouraged the fight to continue* (without having any clear idea of what consequences might come out the other end). With some anxiety I made the latter choice, primarily by allowing my own emotions of resentment and antagonism to come out. I challenged the manager to follow through on his punishing behavior—in fact to really get into it more fully.

After some hesitation the manager began, at first with some awkwardness, but soon with great enthusiasm, to blast a number of his staff. At the same time the people he attacked were encouraged to respond, even counter-attack if they felt like it. Soon other members of the staff also joined the fray, usually on the side of their colleague. This free-for-all style was allowed to develop into a room full of shouting people that more resembled a disorderly convention of longshoremen than a staff meeting of high level managers of a major corporation. And the outcome was marvelous.

As the group re-examined its processes some time later, members recognized that this turbulent meeting (and a few others since) had produced for the entire group a greater sense of vitality, excitement and relatedness than they had felt for many months, and that this feeling had carried over into subsequent staff meetings as well. In addition, the manager reported that their fights had brought him a new sense of respect for the staff members who stood up to him. In subsequent encounters other staff members also began to stand their ground more readily.

What was the theoretical basis for my choice of intervention? First, I need to say that the choice was mostly intuitive rather than theoretical. It came out of my immediate feelings and my willingness to risk making a mistake. (Since I've mostly gotten over my own myth of omnipotence I'm less worried about making *catastrophic* mistakes. As a consultant, I'm just not that crucial to my clients.) Nevertheless, in looking back on the incident for an ex-post-facto theorization I recognize the following.

As I worked with the group over some period of time it became clear to me that the manager was quite aware of the effect of his "attacks" on his staff members, *perhaps too aware*. Why then did he, an enlightened, devoted, "Theory Y" manager, continue this behavior?

The answer is because the feelings behind his behavior were part of him—part of the whole of his humanness, power and emotionality—those same qualities for which his staff and many others respected and trusted him. What then could be done? To preach self control or even temperance to this manager hardly seemed worthwhile (whether the preaching was overt and direct or through the more subtle use of group "feedback.") Even if he resolved to stop his verbal interruptions his feelings would still be sensed by others and would float like a pervasive phantom among them all. No, the answer was not for this manager to back away from his impulsive behavior, but rather, again, in the Gestalt framework, *to go further into it.* The point was not to cut himself off with his guilt feelings about abusing his subordinates after an exchange or two and then settle into melancholy self-blame. Rather it was to stay engaged with them in "the battle" until it reached its natural conclusion—until he and they had the opportunity to fully experience and possibly to finish the unfinished business between them.

Over time some major positive effects came from this new style of engagement for the group: The entire staff became more comfortable with the boss and each other, and the manager began to *enjoy* his relations with his people more than he had before. I believe that the experience the manager had in allowing himself to follow through on his aggressive impulse rather than holding back was a significant one in his own growth. He discovered that, lo-and-behold, his "victims" did not perish from his onslaught, but rather seemed to grow stronger. Conversely, I suspect a similar positive effect in the subordinates discovery that they were able to handle whatever the boss threw at them and to come back swinging.

I have seen several high level managers, long inhibited by their images of the good "participative manager," finally able to fully and spontaneously release their pent up feelings. When the breakthrough comes out in strong expressions of anger, affection, dislike or whatever, there may well be an initial shock that is uncomfortable to everyone, including the consultant. But with time and courage to stay engaged, those involved work it through. They are able to deal with each other's strong emotions much better than they can handle the avoidance and phantom expressions, and eventually they may achieve a vital, robust and mutually satisfying relationship in which both manager and subordinates are far freer and energetic than in the past.

It is, of course possible that some managers, if encouraged to fully express themselves, would turn out to be intolerable tyrants. I believe there are few such people. In the context of Gestalt theory the "intolerable tyrant" is likely to be an individual suffering the myth of his own personal total helplessness. Thus he defends himself by trying to control completely all those around him. In the therapy for such individuals, as they are able to confront their feelings of helplessness and come to recognize for themselves that they are not as totally helpless as they feel the tyrannical behavior begins to disappear. At any rate I suspect that a straightforward undisguised tyrant is easier and better to deal with than a disguised one.

Consultant's Focus

In most organizations the interaction style just described would not be an easy one for people to initiate and pursue without help. Generally most organizations have too much of an overlay of historical norms and traditions of "appropriate behavior." Here, I believe is where organization development and the third party consultant can be of great help. The consultant can concentrate on assisting managers and subordinates to fully experience and express "where they are" both on issues and in relationships with each other. He can highlight their interpersonal process, help them to discover their own vitality, and the satisfaction and excitement of full expression. He can help them to become aware of *how they stop themselves* from completing their experiences. He can help them become aware of their own predictive (and usually catastropic) fantasies, i.e. the manager imagines: "If I really let myself go I would oppress, overpower, do terrible damage to my subordinates." The subordinate thinks, "I must be very careful because this is a very dangerous environment." And when these murky catastrophic expectations have been surfaced the consultant can help the people explore and test them against reality, and finally work out individual arrangements between people that will allow them greater self expression and fulfillment.[4]

While many of the processes I am describing, I'm sure, seem quite similar to typical O.D. consultation theory, in practice there are important differences of execution. "Confrontation," and "owning feelings" are of course, common concepts in O.D. In my experience, however many O.D. consultants facilitate confrontation only to the point of emergence of an identifiable problem (e.g. manager A does not listen to subordinate B, or the manager of one organization repeatedly fails to solicit the advice and involvement of other managers with whom he "ought" to be interdependent, etc.) In some organizations the surfacing of such complaints—the fact that they have finally been brought out into the open and acknowledged—can be a major step, but frequently the consultant then moves too rapidly to the task of problem solving.

---

4. In a later paper detailed approaches and techniques for these purposes as well as other Gestalt oriented OD applications will be outlined.

Thus with the consultants help, the manager acknowledges his fault and resolves to "listen more carefully" to his subordinate; or action items are prepared and task groups formed to develop new processes to assure better coordination between the various organization sub-units, etc. The trouble is that this premature movement into problem solving may be addressing symptoms rather than causes and may produce solutions that are superficial and temporary at best.

The Gestalt mode encourages stronger, deeper, and more concrete (as contrasted to abstract or generalized) interactions. Most importantly we emphasize *staying with* the transaction until both parties have *completed* their business with each other. The individual or contesting parties are encouraged to dramatize and even exaggerate their behavior—to become fully aware of what they are doing and how they are doing it (not why). The manager who does not listen is encouraged to go further into his non listening mode, to discover and be explicit about what he is doing instead of listening, how he keeps himself from listening, and to complete whatever it is he needs to complete before he can give his attention to listening. The subordinate who is not listened to may be encouraged to discover how he keeps himself from being heard (i.e., from talking louder or more forcefully—from *demanding* attention). The managers of the non-interacting organizations are encouraged to state clearly what each wants (or even demands) of the other, with emphasis on meeting his own selfish needs rather than because it would be good organizational practice. And each manager is encouraged to respond "yes" or "no" to each demand.[5] Interdependence is not an automatically presumed virtue in every case (though it may be a real operating requirement) and when consensual decisions cannot be reached within a reasonable time-power based decisions are not considered disreputable.

THE TYRANNY OF THE UNDERDOG

The other side of the myth of managerial omnipotence is the tyranny of the underdog. O.D. theory has for most of its relatively

5. The reaction to this "selfish," demand oriented process is frequently quite remarkable. Paradoxically these heated exchanges generate more respect and positive feeling between the contesting parties than a raft of cool, rational, for-the-good-of-the-company, sessions. The ultimate decisions also seem to be more viable.

brief history stressed the support of "the underdog"—the subordinate, the reticent team member, etc.—and the solution of disagreement through rational processes. In the context of our national culture and traditions this is not surprising nor can I object to the general underlying philosophy. Unfortunately, however, some of our approaches have attempted to "help" the underdog by providing an easier world for him through advocating the restraint (usually by "self control" and under the moral pressure of "human relations rightness") of the powerful manager or team member. I believe this approach is wrong. Not only does it foster the inhibiting omnipotence myth and guilt feelings of the manager discussed earlier, it can also be experienced as a *confirmation of his own inferiority or invalidism by the individual who is granted the so called benefits of other people holding themselves for his sake.* Better by far to help the underdog to discover, use and rejoice in his strength and ability to move forward for himself than to have others take turns pushing his wheelchair for him.

Robert W. Resnick (1970), a Gestalt-oriented psychotherapist, makes the point this way in his paper, "Chicken Soup is Poison:"

"Many therapists see themselves as members of the "helping professions" engaged in the helping relationship." Beware! Such people are dangerous If successful they kill the humanness in their patients by preventing their growth. This insidious process is somehow worse realizing such therapists typically want the reverse. They want their patients to grow, to live, and to be, and they guarantee the antithesis with their "help." The distinction between true support and "help" is clear: To do for the other what he is capable of doing for himself insures his not becoming aware that he can stand on his own two feet . . ."

Polarities

An important part of Gestalt therapy is the concept of polarities, the extremes within each of us; i.e., weakness-strength, activism-passivity, etc., that together comprise our full natures. One of the manifestations of polarity is the "top-dog" vs. "underdog." The top-dog is that part of us that mostly serves the function of director and disciplinarian, that part of our personalities that tells us what we *should do.* The underdog is the resistive part of us, that part that balks at the bossiness of top-dog and attempts to subvert or derail his directives.

Our underdog may work at his mission by pleading that we are unable to do what the top-dog demands, or he may delay and promise to do it tomorrow, or he may divert the top-dog's directions, and so on. Fritz Perls in his development of Gestalt therapy believed that the underdog in each individual almost always triumphed in the long run over the top-dog. This phenomenon, incidentally, may well explain why in organizations as well as elsewhere so many plans and vows to change seem to fare no better than most people's New Year's resolutions.

Great energy is frequently bottled up in the conflict between these two conflicting drives within an individual, energy that is therefore not available for other more satisfying purposes. Further, the conflict between the top-dog and the underdog frequently produces unhappiness and a sense of lack of fulfillment for the person.

Relationships between some individuals within organizations have many of the same characteristics as this top-dog/underdog conflict. The apparently powerful, assertive person makes demands on the ostensibly weaker underdog, but somehow, the demands are never quite met. And while the top-dog's pressure may be great, the underdog's ability to divert, deflect, or delay is often greater. So-called weak parties in a variety of relationships may have very great, though not immediately apparent, advantages in their ability to resist without attacking and to use, like a judo expert, the strong person's own strength against him. I have worked with a number of teams in which one or two members, undoubtedly without conscious intent, skillfully manipulated the apparently stronger members of the group, including the boss into "helping" them. This helping takes many forms. It can be protecting the quiet member, taking his side in a competitive situation, being more sympathetic to his problems and inabilities to meet his commitments than would be the case for other members of the team, etc. One of the most harmful accommodations to the "weak party" involves others holding back their forcefulness and vitality in order to keep from offending or upsetting the underdog.

Ogre Building

A variation of the underdog game is ogre building. Almost all of us in organizations have the capacity to build ogres fearsome enough to scare ourselves half to death. The ogre may be a supervisor, especially one at a higher level than those we are accustomed to dealing with, another organization, or, perhaps most insidious of all, "the system." Ogres can be very useful sometimes in helping us to avoid doing what we don't really want to do anyway. I do not object to the use of the ogre for that purpose if indeed we are conscious of what we are doing and that we *want* to do it. More frequently, however, we are not aware of what we are doing and our ogres are not so clearly useful. They are compounded of some degree of organizational reality plus our own projections and predictions of dire consequences. Organization development methodology is frequently useful in dealing with ogres, especially the mutual ogres dreamed up by internally competitive organizations for each other. I believe more can be done, especially in working with individuals in helping them to discover their courage and capacity to confront and deal with their own ogres.

In the therapeutic process that addresses top-dog/underdog conflicts the first step involves heightening polarization. The patient increases his awareness of both forces within himself; especially, he becomes aware of *the power inherent in his underdog position*. With this new awareness grows a sense of excitement, pride and energy. Later, when he has well experienced his own extremes he may move naturally to an "integration" i.e. he is able to regain his access to those parts of himself he had submerged or renounced and so eventually he becomes able to utilize as the situation requires, a more complete spectrum of his behavioral potential.

Consultant's Focus

In the organization consulting process, especially when dealing with "complaining people"—those who see others and/or their environment as oppressive and preventing them from doing what they want to do—it is a good idea for the consultant to begin working with his client in a way that concentrates on identifying the client's strength. That may not be easy, the complainer's strength is not readily apparent. On the contrary he usually spends much of his time denying he has any strength at all. All power belongs to "the others"—his boss, his more influential, articulate, or aggressive co-workers, or most oppressive of all to "the company."

As a consultant I begin by being suspicious of these complaints.

This is not to say that I think the complainer is intentionally deceptive, nor do I doubt that widespread inequalities of power and opportunity for certain classes of organization citizens do exist. Rather, I have found that most people do possess some form of power even if that power is passive, resistive, or a withholding kind that is used to manipulate others, often by triggering feelings of guilt among the more active and assertive people with whom they deal.

A case that illustrates the subtleties of power distribution involved a large government agency I worked with. We began with a team-building session between the top management group (including the chief and his central staff) and about a dozen field supervisors, each of whom headed a local service office. The pattern of complaints, and there were many from each side, were clear and repeated. For the central staff it was that those in the field seldom seemed to be able to respond to the requests for new informaion that they were asked to provide, nor did they often try out proposed new methods developed by the central staff for use in the field. When they occasionally did try out the recommended procedures, it was in a most cursory way that practically assured the failure of the new approach. Finally, after repeated efforts, the central staff people had quietly abandoned their efforts to direct the field supervisors and adopted what they felt to be the more modern management approach of asking the field people to submit their own ideas for innovation and improvement. This approach fared no better.

What I noticed as I heard the presentation of this information from the central staff people was their almost complete lack of emotion. This pattern of relationships which had been going on for about a year must have produced frustration for the agency chief and his staff, yet in listening to the presenters I heard only careful neutrality, infinite patience, and dispassionate though devoted interest in objective "problem-solving."

It took considerably longer for the case of the field supervisors to emerge. Their first responses to the complaints of the central staff were rather desultory and almost apologetic. They had very heavy work loads, many new people to train, spent a great deal of time on public relations, and so on. All of which limited their ability to concentrate on new approaches. Besides, they felt it was quite unlikely that they could develop any new methods that would really satisfy the central staff, since the central staff people were obviously so much better informed about the latest trends in their specialized field. Similarly, the information emerged that in the past year a few of the field supervisors felt they had attempted to institute some of the recommended new approaches of the central staff but had not done well at it. And while they had not been overtly criticized by the staff they had "felt" disapproved of.

As a consultant here I again experienced myself at a decision point. I could try to help the field supervisors by encouraging the central staff to examine their olympian posture and how their cool paternalism put down the supervisors. They could then examine ways they might change this pattern into a more encouraging one. Secondly, I could pursue the problem solving approach by helping the total group to recognize specific areas of weakness in the supervisors' skills and then to develop training programs for building those skills. Thirdly, I could encourage the field supervisors to (in the Gastalt sense) go even further into their complaints. I chose the third.

I requested that the supervisors (in a "fish-bowl" arrangement) elaborate further on their grievances against the staff. The result, after some initial hesitancy, was a varitable river of complaints, many of which went back for years. In essence, the field supervisors reported they felt like second class citizens, without influence or power in their dealings with the staff. They didn't know what the staff meant by "innovation," and what's more they didn't much care. (They did, however, have some good ideas from time-to-time which they put into effect without fanfare, seldom telling the staff anything about them.)

When the venting had subsided I asked the field supervisors to talk about how they characteristically dealt with the staff. After a slow start the supervisors rolled out a substantial list of "passive-resistance" and "playing stupid" techniques. In a little while they were enjoying their catalogue immensely, as were the central staff people, who prior to this time had perceived themselves in the superior position, and so very much "responsible" for the oppressed feelings of the supervisors.

Sometime later, after the supervisors had become aware of the way in which they exerted their own resistive power in their dealings with the staff, we were able to turn successfully to the possibilities of developing different modes of interaction between the groups. Now, however, they were able to do so, not as impotent sufferers, but as equals. Interestingly, one of their demands was that the staff be more clearly demanding. Their experience in the past, they reported, had been confusing. Since the staff (in their efforts to be "understanding") had been so tactful in making requests, it was almost impossible to tell what was really important to them and what wasn't.

Many other aspects of this case emerged and were dealt with in this and subsequent meetings, including our attention to the operating styles of the agency chief and the central staff members, the identification of real developmental needs for both staff and field personnel, and so on. I believe we were able to deal with these other problems better, later on, because we started where we did.

CONCLUSION

In the model of the consultant's role I advocate the primary step is not to help people embark on self-improvement programs. Rather, it is to encourage them to recognize and appreciate where they are now. Then the consultant may help them find their own unique paths forward to change and growth. It is also important to recognize that this change and growth, at best, will occur naturally rather than being forced either by external pressure or internalized models. Paradoxically, natural change in an individual does not preclude his boss or others from exerting power or expressing their wants strongly and explicitly. *What is explicit and up-front is seldom harmful, though it may be difficult to deal with.* Covert, withheld or truncated expression is harmful. In most circumstances the consultant will do best to encourage in both individuals and organizations the full recognition and completion of their negative feelings rather than a premature objectivity or problem-solving approach. The consultant will also do best in setting an example through his own clear and explicit statement of what *he* wants and how *he* feels.

We in the field of behavioral science have placed great emphasis on the negative consequences of authoritarian management for both organizations and individuals. In voices sometimes gentle and sometimes determined, we have addressed the power figures in organizations and called upon them to depart from old patterns, to risk a new approach and allow greater and more meaningful participation in the organization's affairs by those below them in the hierarchy. Many of us have made substantial contributions in helping managers to recognize and exercise their responsibilities toward their subordinates. This has in the main been good and worthwhile. The time has come though, I believe, for us to begin to address subordinates as well. We need to help manager and subordinate become aware of alienating and vitality-sapping consequences of both "playing helpless" and "playing helpful." We must question ourselves and encourage others to question unthinking acceptance of and adaptation to someone else's rules of good human relations, without regard to how those feel inside.

I believe it is worthwhile to urge ourselves and others to take new risks—risks of greater self assertion, more spontaneity, and more willingness to experiment with power and aggression as well as trust and love. If we in O.D. do indeed believe in a wider distribution of power it would be well for us to stop trying to deny power's existence, muffle it, wish it away, or disguise it under velvet wrappings. Rather we can encourage as many people as possible at *all* levels of the organization from highest manager to lowest subordinate to discover his own power and use it.

POST SCRIPT

What follows says what I have to say in a somewhat different way.

OBJECTIVITY

I am not cool anymore
Dispassionate calm no longer moves
    me to admiring nods
I do not smile appreciatively
    at the neatly disciplined point
Nor at neatly checked restraint
Nor neatly channeled moderation

I am more messy now
And I like it better

The smoothly quiet logic that purrs
Like a Detroit built engine from
the smoothly quiet throats of
    practiced men impresses me not
I suspect the emissions of those throats
    as much as I suspect the emissions of those
    engines

Pure reason is not pure
It is the product of an isolated head
And no head can be isolated
    yet still alive.

A man is a total of all of himself
    plus probably more
And his reason issues from him—
    all of him
What is isolated is distorted or
    dead
It is no real message and not
    worth my hearing.

Objectivity is a concept
And if I take it to mean my best attempt
To hold my prejudice in check
    for just a moment as I hear
It seems a decent thing to try
But if I make of it a more
    pretentious thing than that
I will only frown
And grow enmeshed in guards,
    and counter guards, and
    counter, counter guards
In senseless toiling to balance
    off the balances
To assure the fairness for all
    view
Until, like some over sterilized
    laboratory culture
I am no fitting host for any
    viable position to take hold.

Fairness is a virtue I still find
But it is only one of many
And I would choose to find my fairness
In the clashes of
    expressions that allow
Life space
    for passions as well as reasons
Rather than in the noiseless mausoleums
    of disconnected minds.

SYMPATHY

My friend, it may pain you to hear
And probably pain me even more
    to say, but
You give me nothing very good
    when you give me your sympathy

Love and gentleness are other
    matters
But even those are best for us both,
    giver and receiver
If they are firmly handed
    and firmly held between us
Soft and yielding pity will not
    support my sorrow or me

When all is truly said
Only I can support myself
And only you can support yourself
Not in isolation
We may touch and hold each other
But we ought not suffer for
    each other

For that only confuses my grief
    or yours
And keeps it from full feeling
    and clean completion
And if it is not full felt
    and cleanly completed
Mourning never ends

No. Suffer not for me and ask
    me not to suffer for you
Let us not cloud or dilute sorrow
Do not give me sympathy
Rather, in my time of need
    grant me better than that
Your hand and heart to hold to while
    I feel my pain
And your smile and joy with me
    when I am done with it.

I WILL DO YOU NO FAVOR

If I withhold my voice of anger from you
  for your sake
You, in listening too hard to me,
Will hear more anger than ever any
  real voice of mine would have held

If I curb my raucous ribald
  pleasure voice for anticipation of your
  sensibilities
You will know I have curbed and
  pleasure will be dimmed and
  overlaid with grimy speculation
  as to why.
(What else than pleasure was there that
  he did not say?)

If I damp my robust affection for you
  and keep my arms that want to
  hug you bound at my sides
(As would seem more appropriate
  for men of our station and trade)
Your arms, or perhaps only fingers,
  will twitch too, stifled and pinched
  off meanly
And perhaps in spite against their
  mind-formed shackles
  will tense to fists

All that I withhold diminishes me
  and cheats you
All that you withhold diminishes you
  and cheats me
When we hold back ourselves
  for each others sake
That is no service to us either one
We only collude in the weakening
  of us both.

Implementing the Organization Renewal Process (ITORP)
... A Situational Approach to OD

GORDON L. LIPPITT

The turbulence faced today by organizations is caused as much by the increased complexity of their functions as by revolutions in our contemporary society. In addition, predictable strains are being exerted on organizations by more dynamic interrelations and increased interdependence among government, industry, communities, and education. These multiple forces must be met with a process of organization renewal, adaptation, and planning for change.

As stated by John Gardner in *TIME,* April 11, 1969:

> "The true task is to design a society (and institutions) capable of continuous change, renewal, and responsiveness. We can less and less afford to limit ourselves to routine repair of breakdowns in our institutions. Unless we are willing to see a final confrontation between institutions that refuse to change and critics bent on destruction, we had better get on with the business of redesigning our society."

Recognizing that renewal is a requirement is not the same as having the capability to initiate such a process. The challenge for organization executives today is whether or not they have the capability, the resources and the skills to bring about the renewal in their organizations that will be required if they are going to meet the challenge of the 70's.

During the past three years, the author has tested a model and a method for helping organizations in this respect—and we have called it Implementing The Organization Renewal Process or ITORP. The program consists of five sessions of one half day in length which will be explained later in this paper.

I feel that the key element in organization renewal is the ability to respond appropriately to *situations*. Such response meets the criteria for being appropriate if the action taken results in all four of the following:

1. Optimizes the effective utilization and development of the *human resources* in the organization;
2. Improves the *interfacing* process in the organization;
3. Contributes to the maturation of *the organization;*
4. Is *responsive to the environment* in which the organization exists.

In a very real sense their criteria provide a frame of references to assess whether one is really doing organization development rather than a temporary change intervention that may not affect the total organization system. Such criteria are necessary so that those of us who advocate a "situational" approach to OD are not perceived as indicating that any or all situational interventions are valid.

In "Practice Theories in Organization Development" Peter Vaill (1971) is concerned about the increasing inability of the formal theories of OD to explain or predict the situations in which the practitioner finds himself. Formal OD theories, says Vaill, are rigid, inflexible and based on an objective view of organizational life. Current OD theories consist of behavioral models which the practitioner should adopt, thus ignoring the situational and highly subjective needs of the practitioner. Furthermore, the OD theorist/researcher, since he views organizational problems categorically, frequently doesn't *want* to know about the mind-set of the client system.

"Formal theories run the risk of gross impracticality unless they take account of the situation in which the OD practitioner finds himself" (Vaill, 1971). Vaill's thesis is that OD theory must be tempered by the perception of reality as viewed by the client system and change agent. He describes the frame of reference of the practitioner in terms of a "practice theory" or "a personal theory in the mind of the practitioner." A practice theory is a conglomeration of perceptions, attitudes, beliefs, and prejudices—a world view—that influences the behavior of the practitioner. Vaill's twelve characteristics of a practice theory seem to boil down to the notion that anything the practitioner does is, ipso facto, a function of his practice theory. It has no predictive or explicative ability.

It is completely subjective and therefore impossible to evaluate in a normative sense. It cannot be verified scientifically; for that matter, it is not based on scientific inquiry or rigorous empirical constructs.

The key point however, that Vaill is trying to make is that reality in organizational life, as perceived by its management, is a highly subjective matter. Any formal theory is bound to be impractical if it fails to take into account the unique situational factors that bear on organizational problems and the unique perceptions of those factors that take place in the mind of the O. D. practitioner.

What the O. D. theorist/researcher should offer is not a set of rules, values, or assumptions for the practitioner to follow but a science-based form, a structure, a model through which the organization can be viewed, analyzed, and needed planned change implemented. It is for this reason that I feel a conceptual model is essential to any planned O. D. effort.

The model to depict the rationale behind the ITORP program is provided in Figure 1.

In using the word "situations" as the focal point in this circular model of organization renewal, it is intended that the multiple and complex nature of such words as "problem-solving," "confrontation," "crisis," and "everyday decision" be included. There will be differences in the various degrees of situational intensity, but let it suffice in this conceptual model for us to recognize that "situations" may refer to such things as the death of the leader of the organization, inadequate cash flow to maintain financial stability, an embarrassing error in an annual report, or the pickets at the main gate when a strike is in progress.

Decisions are made with respect to situations, rather than situations creating decision. A situation is not always a problem, but problems are always caused by situations. Situations will test whether individuals and groups in the organization are really able to meet many kinds of needs. It is through working on situations and examining the subsequent failures and successes that organizational systems discover the worth of their selection procedure, interfacing process, training program, communication efforts, and organization development activities.

It is relatively foolish, even in theory, to believe that all responses to situations can be based on predetermined plans, con-

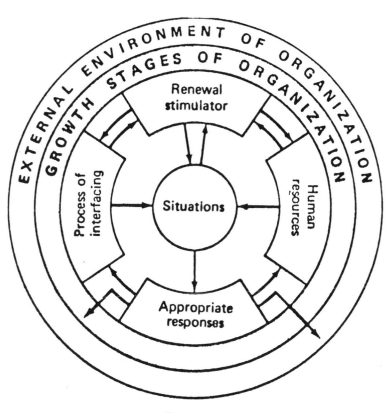

FIGURE 1

scious strategy, or objective action. There are occasions when a situation calls for and effectively produces unplanned response. While a great deal of the recent writing on behavioral science and organizational theory has focused on planned change, there is a place for spontaneous action, the seemingly instinctive response, or emotional reaction. It would seem that some of the experts in organizational management wish that all situations could be approached with the kind of rational and unemotional behavior once advocated by a founder or organizational theory—Max Weber.

It might be helpful to define some of the key concepts in this model:

Human resources refers to the individuals, pairs, groups, and larger units of persons in the organization that need to interrelate to achieve multiple goals and human potential.

Interfacing is primarily a process by which human beings confront common areas of concern, engage in meaningfully related dialogue, actively search for solutions to mutual problems, and purposefully cope with these solutions. Interfacing may also involve the confrontation between human beings and machine processes or technological systems.

Organizational growth refers to the concept that organizations are complex organisms that have a life cycle, with stages of development commencing with birth and progressing through survival to later stages of maturity.

Environmental response refers to the relevance of a situational response to external forces, factors, and influences that are affecting the existence and growth of the organization.

Renewal stimulator is the name this author is using for that individual or group in or across line or staff functioning that has the skill and courage to initiate action, plans, and processes that might lead to organization renewal.

Success in organization renewal will not come about by good intentions, platitudes, or even frenetic activity. It will come about when there is an understanding of where an organization is at the present and what it wants to become—*and an understanding of how to get there.*

"Organization renewal requires that change be preceded by a self-study process relating present functions and potential resources to the needs and characteristics of the people who operate the organization as well as to those who the organization will service. It also requires that those affected by the change be involved in the self-study process. They must believe that their views will have representation and that management intends to follow its study by changing existing parts of the organization, as well as extending beyond current organization boundaries" (Culbert, 1969, p. 3).

The design of the ITORP program is to help the leaders of an organization, through films, instruments, and group learning to confront the five key aspects of organizational life depicted in the model that impinge on appropriate response to situations.

EXAMINING ENVIRONMENTAL FORCES

In session one of the ITORP program the participants examine some of the key revolutions impacting on their organizatiuns.

We have little or no influence over some of modern environmental forces. They affect organizations in dramatic ways. Government officials, industrial managers, financial executives, voluntary agencies leaders, and professional men and women are well aware that our society is now involved in multiple *revolutions*. This word—revolution—should not and is not used loosely here.

By revolution, I do not mean change brought about by violence, but rather, bringing about change at a considerably more rapid rate than might normally be expected. The youth "revolution" is not a fad. There is a technological, economic, consumer, knowledge, and a moral revolution. Undergirding all these and causing many of us to find it difficult to initiate change in our organization, is one which we call the anti-authority revolution. People, young and old, are no longer accepting direction, advice, wisdom, or guidance from others just because they are older or more educated, or because they have college degrees, or are in managerial positions. People are more independent of, and impatient with, any form of authoritarianism.

Such lessening of the acceptance of authority of organization managers, leaders, and professionals is creating a need to understand the *process of organization renewal.*

This suggests that the responsibilities of those having authority are partially rooted in being responsive to the need for change. Every organization, as it grows larger and matures, has to take on a form and structure for purposes of perpetuation, standardization, predictability, and efficiency.

Our choice in organizations today is to plan in advance for the impact of these revolutions, or to wait until they force us to react. Organization renewal allows us to plan for these changes and the others that will follow. It allows us to go past reaction to anticipation. It allows us to influence the course of these revolutions.

Organization renewal is the process of initiating, creating and confronting needed changes so as to make it possible for organizations to become or remain viable, to adapt to new conditions, to solve problems, to learn from experiences, and to move toward greater organizational maturity. In short, organization renewal is a process which enables us to make our organizations—business or non-profit, government or private—and more relevant to the age of change in which we live. But organizations change slowly and reluctantly *because* they tend to get locked into form and structure.

Meanwhile, within and without the organization, values, feelings, dynamics, and forces are changing. If these are multiple and pronounced, a large gap exists between the organization's form, structure, policies, products, and services—and its changing internal and external world.

If the gap is too great, more or less violent attempts are made by some to tear down the form and structure. The problem for organizations is how to stay "in tune with" the changing internal and external forces so as to lessen the dissonance. If successful, the organization is flexible and viable, and responsive to its environment and to its times.

We should always start the process of change as soon as possible. Why wait for pickets, lawsuits by citizens, high turnover of professionals, rejection by the youth of an organization or community, and other manifestations of crisis? Why not begin the essential process of evaluating and revising the form, values, structures, technology, and human processes of organizations?

Often we hear our employees, associates, and ourselves commenting:

—"You know, we don't have the spirit of excitement we used to have when we first started the organization."

—"Why can't managers be creative and be more interested in our success?"

—"Why are our employees so apathetic?"

—"Why can't the different work units in this organization work together?"

—"This organization just doesn't seem to be relevant to the problems of today's society."

Such sentiments are an expression of the feelings of people today relative to their desire either to be a part of an organization that is "with it"—dynamic and renewing. If not met, they will take their interest, money, and motivation somewhere else.

In the first ITORP session the examination of the revolutions and their effect on the organization are realistically examined.

In the ITORP sessions conducted with organizations, I have

found it imperative that the people involved have a frame of reference by which to analyze their goals and needs, as they are affected by environmental forces. Relating the basic management processes to the different stages of organizational growth is an essential step in the initiation of organization renewal, as we conclude Session I. Most organizations have the potentiality of moving from creation to maturity. Let us examine those stages.

Understanding the Growth Potential of An Organization

If renewal is to become a reality, organization leaders must confront their present stage of functioning. It is essential that they analyze the stages of growth through which their organizations have passed and that they relate these six stages to fundamental management functions.[1]

The first stage of growth is the *creation* of a new organization. Many organization leaders have lived through the birth of their organizations. It took some risks and frustrations to get an organization started in a new field.

Soon after comes the second stage—*survival*. Everyone had to sacrifice to make it possible for the organization to continue to exist. New services and employees were needed. A set of guidelines were developed. The first Board of Directors were elected. The organization hired its first professional specialists.

Many organizations are in their stage of development—*stabilization*. At this stage, management must know how to organize—how to set up job functions, prepare organization charts, establish effective communication networks with employees, creatively compose boards of directors, and all the other things necessary to maintain an organization. Many organizations stay at this level of growth. At this stage many executives spend most of their time immersed in administrative details—personnel problems, reports, job descriptions, and so forth. Their organizations have not moved on to the fourth stage—*gaining a reputation and developing pride* —because they have not had the courage to review and evaluate what they have been doing.

The fifth stage—*the achievement of uniqueness and adaptability*—is rarely reached by an organization, because this requires the leadership to see whether or not it needs to change plans, pro-

1. For fuller treatment see Chapter II of Lippitt, G., *Organization Renewal*, New York: Appleton-Century-Croft, 1969.

grams, products, services, and activities to become unique. Most organizations do not take the time or effort to accomplish this objective.

Finally, we come to a sixth and final stage—*contribution* to society, to the industry or profession of which the organization is a part, to the community and nation of which it is a part. This stage is the epitome of the challenge of being relevant today. It involves social responsibility.

Related to this stage of growth is a recent study of 1,800 graduates from Wharton Business School. It was found that the first and most important reason these young M.B.A.'s gave for working in their present organizations was whether or not that organization was relevant to the society of which it was a part. It is my thesis that any organization that reaches maturity will have as a key element in that maturity the ability to be socially responsible and to contribute to the larger society of which it is a part.

These six stages of growth do not come about automatically, nor does it mean that once the organization has achieved a particular stage it might not slip back into an earlier stage. For example, an organization at the fifth stage can slip back to the need to survive, the second stage, if a competing organization comes into existence or a crisis hits a particular industry.

Developing Open Communications for Improved
Organizational Effectiveness

Implementing organization renewal requires the development of skills in confrontation by those *inside* an organization. Organization change can best be brought about by internal confrontation of situations by those in the organization, rather than awaiting external confrontation by those who may have little concern for the long range growth of the organization. This is where the *process of Interface* indicated in the model is important to see whether this aspect of situational improvement is present.

In the second session of the ITORP program, it recognizes that this process of organization renewal will require: (1) confrontation, (2) search, and (3) coping. One hears a great deal today about confrontation. Students are confronting the university; civil rights leaders are confronting local communities. But housewives also confront the lack of a stop light near a school. People confront the chopping down of precious trees in parks. Confrontation today is part and parcel of our way of life. Organization leaders should not expect these confrontations to go away. They probably will increase.

Nevertheless, confrontation can be a very valuable thing. A manager cannot change his organization or his way of doing his job unless he confronts the present inadequacy of the organization and his own personal need to improve.

The process of renewal requires awareness, self-development, and organizational change. Each of these, in turn, require confrontation. Leaders must confront the fact that they are not always aware of the needs of employees, operating situations, youth groups, clients, environments, and external forces.

Organization renewal does not occur unless the manager also confronts his own need to improve as a leader of others. Confrontation means facing up to reality. It means "saying it as it is." It means looking at things through clear glasses rather than either rose-tinted or dark-tinted glasses. But confrontation is not enough to bring about awareness, self-development, or change. It is only a beginning.

Many leaders, however, feel that if they have *confronted,* their problem is solved—and that they have *coped.* This is not necessarily true. It usually is necessary for people to *search* for ways to work on the process of understanding each other, communicating with each other, solving problems, making decisions, planning new activities and new programs, and new ways to get people appropriately involved. It is the search for unique and innovative ways to solve organizational problems. Search is the key to whether or not coping will take place, because coping means something more than just decision-making or problem-solving. Coping means confronting a problem and searching for ways of working on it—and from working upon it, learning how to solve similar problems, more problems, and new problems. In the second session of the ITORP program the participants are given an opportunity to confront their own need to further their skills in individual, group and organizational situations. Each individual fills out a "Self Growth Multiple Role Inventory" following the viewing of the BNA film entitled "Confrontation, Search, and Coping." In groups of three, the participants dialogue with each other about their own personal goals for improved skills in confrontation. In addition, the reality of intergroup confrontation is experienced in a competitive group task situation.

OPTIMIZING ORGANIZATIONAL HUMAN RESOURCES

Organization renewal, then, comes about through the process of confrontation, search, and coping. But with whom do we start? One place to start is by building a network of effectively functioning groups in the organization. In session three of the ITORP program the emphasis is on the need for team work. The participants view the film "Individuality and Teamwork" and measure key factors in teamwork. In workgroup sessions they are given an opportunity to analyze teamwork factors and introduce the element of teamwork for further development throughout the organization.

In addition to the top executive group of the organization it is desirable to build throughout the organization the kind of teamwork that will make it possible for all functional groups to work effectively together, for project groups to relate effectively, and for professional specialists to build a cohesive work unit that will contribute to the growth and goals of the organization.

There are ten key elements of teamwork. These elements of teamwork are not easily arrived at, but they are excellent targets for any manager to work toward as he develops the various suborganizations, including committees, staff, and task forces that are set up to get work done:

1. Teamwork requires an understanding and commitment to the goals of the group.
2. Teamwork requires the maximum utilization of the different resources of individuals within the group.
3. Teamwork is achieved when flexibility, sensitivity to the needs of others, and creativity are encouraged.
4. Teamwork is most effective where participative leadership is practiced.
5. Teamwork requires a group to develop procedures to meet the particular problem or situation.
6. Teamwork is characterized by the group's ability to examine its process so as to constantly improve itself as a team.

7. Teamwork will best take place when the climate of the organization is encouraging and defense-reducing.
8. Teamwork utilizes the appropriate steps and guidelines for decision-making in the solution of a problem.
9. Teamwork requires trust and openness in communication and relationships.
10. Teamwork is achieved when the group members have a strong sense of belonging to the group.

The human resources of an organization are the essential element in organization change. People constitute "sub-systems" of the larger organizational system. They solve situational problems and contribute to the growth stages of the organization of which they are a part.

The reality of social systems is well annotated in behavioral science research on organization. Besides the typical superior-subordinate relationship, the work group behavioral phenomena with the powerful effects of group norms and cohesion, and inter-group conflict between one group and another, there is the well-known reality of informal structures in any modern organization. In addition, organizations are finding it necessary to utilize temporary human sub-systems to achieve goals. These "task forces" or "project groups" are providing new ways of linking appropriate human resources together to achieve results. Such organizational forms will become more prevalent as organizations strive to adapt to new needs and responses in our changing society.

It has been found that in implementing organization renewal, effective group action at *all* levels in the organization will help strengthen the *"psychological contract"* of the individual and the organization. In the face-to-face work unit the individual can still be important and influence change in the organization. This then is the fourth part of the model in Figure #1 that is part of the ITORP program.

COPING WITH CHANGE BY RENEWAL STIMULATORS

The fifth important area for implementation of the organization renewal process, as depicted in Figure #1, is the skill and courage of persons in the organization to analyze, initiate, and cope with change. In less than two decades, modern technology has leaped from conventional to nuclear power, from the piston age to the jet age, from "earth men" to "space men."

As we examine the needs of organizations to cope with change, it is evident that there are two basic categories. One type is *unplanned change* which will happen to and in all organizations. A tornado that blows down a warehouse, a new interest rate on bank loans, a power failure—these are situations to which the organization *must react*.

A second category of change is *planned change*—the type of change which is involved in the process of organization renewal. It can be defined as a conscious, deliberate, and collaborative effort to improve the operations of a system—whether it be self-system, social system, or cultural system—through the utilization of knowledge. It usually involves both a renewal stimulator and the elements of an organization, which are brought together to solve a problem or to plan and attain an improved state of functioning by being *pro-active*. A person, a group, or an organization can be a renewal stimulator.

The manager, consultant, or social scientist engaged in planned or inventive change has some social *"goals"* (objectives) and he has a well-structured *"design"* (means) for achieving these ends. Planned change, therefore, involved *inventing a future,* and creating conditions and resources for realizing that future.

Changes, planned or unplanned, are ubiquitous aspects of modern organizations. Unplanned changes occur because of such factors as maturation, depression, accidents, death, or loss of resources. Planned changes may occur because of the need for improved technology, new organizational structure, of new procedures. The changes that can be observed in an organization are of endless variety. Examples are changes in tools, in procedures, in values, in the structure of the organization, or in its policies.

In general terms, such changes imply, for each of us, uncertainty about our future role and our behavior in that role. These changes also imply uncertainty about the roles of others and our relationships with them. Such ambiguity is unsettling; it generates a need to give meaning to the situation, to try to understand it. It also generates a tendency to react in terms of the meaning we discover, whether or not that meaning is correct.

In the fourth session of the ITORP program we assume that each person is a responsible member in an organization where organization renewal involving change occurs or is contemplated.

What might you do? How could you start? The group views the film "Coping with Change" and then develops a change goal and plan to implement following the ITORP program.

In developing plans for change it is important that the participant know how to *diagnose* the forces in the planned change effort as a first step to initiate action.

A useful concept, theory, and method for thinking about change, was developed by social scientist Kurt Lewin. He looked upon a level or phase of behavior within an institutional setting not as a static habit or custom, but as a dynamic balance between forces working in opposite directions within the social-psychological space of the institution. He indicated that we should think diagnostically about any change situation, in terms of the factors against change (restraining forces). These forces may originate inside the organization, in the environment, or in the behavior of the renewal stimulator.

We can think of the present state of affairs in an organization as an equilibrium which is being maintained by a variety of factors that *"keep things the way they are"* or *"keep us behaving in our customary ways."* The renewal stimulator must assess the change potential and resistance, and try to change the balance of forces so there will be movement toward an improved learning processes that focus on the themes that I have outlined. Each ITORP participant uses the Force Field Analysis method in diagnosing his change project.

As Dr. Culbert (1969) states: "Organizations frequently are blocked from renewing their public relevance by a reluctance to address internal conflicts surfaced at times of external demands for change. Coping with internal conflicts not only may free the organization to respond externally but provides those within the organization an opportunity to learn substantively about issues which are present in their organization's interface with the public."

Every organizational system has within it the potentiality for either bringing about its own death, maintaining the status quo, or growing into maturity. The leadership of its management or concern of employees expressed in action will be the key factor. The challenge for today's organization leaders is whether or not they have the capability, the resources and the skills to bring about the renewal in their organizations that will be required if they are going to meet the challenge of the 70's. As John W. Gardner (1966, p. 48) suggests:

"What may be most in need of innovation is the corporation itself. Perhaps what every corporation (and every other organization) needs is a department of continuous renewal that could view the whole organization as a system in need of continuing innovation."

In our ITORP design we see each participant or group of participants as renewal agents to assist the organization to initiate the needed changes to improve its functioning.

SPREADING THE ORGANIZATION RENEWAL EFFORT

Lewin pointed out that the effect of change will be maintained if the initial set of forces is unfrozen, change initiated and then the change refrozen at the new level. In many situations, however, such change is only temporary. Even significant changes in organizations are often followed by a regression toward an older pattern after the pressures effecting change are relaxed. This creates the need for planned change to affect the total system and not just one individual or group. In the *fifth* session of an ITORP program we find it desirable to help organization leaders to examine ways to spread, reinforce, and secure multiple commitments to planned change efforts. If this is not done, organization renewal normally will not take place. Further, we believe it desirable to produce concentrated and continuing efforts to relate the organization's people, technology, structure and resources to the problems confronting the organization as it relates to its changing environment. Each ITORP program participant has a chance to secure help on the role he should take in planning change.

Almost all organizations are caught up in the massive forces that are changing the political, social economic and religious life of the world today. To ignore these forces would be folly. To respond to them by executing the same old programs and services would be to ignore a responsibility. To rush into illconceived programs is wasteful and to be opportunistic is shallow.

SUMMARY

My reason for categorizing the ITORP program as a "situational" approach to OD is based on the fact that the underlying conceptual model of the five-session ITORP program is designed to use real issues, problems, and situations as the foci for initiating renewal. These situational confrontations can be examined through multiple learning processes that focus on the themes that have been described.

Normally an apparently appropriate action will solve a problem by eliminating or altering a situation. But not always. It can happen that insufficient information has caused misjudgment of the situation. And sometimes—perhaps just to prove the case for human inconsistency—apparently inappropriate action surprises us by somehow dealing with a situation satisfactorily, although it may not contribute to organizational growth.

At the beginning of this paper the author suggested that one way to measure the appropriateness of an action is to assess the way it relates to the external environment within which the organization exists. Most attempts to examine organizational dynamics tend to ignore the interrelationship between environmental forces and organizational responses. Every organization is embedded in a total environment that conditions its form, decision-making process, and the way it utilizes the resources of the organization. In appropriately responding to situations, an organization should manifest an awareness of its responsibility to the larger external environment.

An example of the relationship between environment and organizational response is the work of P. Lawrence and J. Lorsch (1967) who examine the effects on organizations of an environment which is characterized by rapid rates of technological and market change, and a high degree of uncertainty and unpredictability. The ways the managers in a quickly changing environment (such as an electronics industry) will respond is quite different from the way those in the more stable environment of a public utility will. Joan Woodward (1965) found in her studies that the nature of ones products related to whether the organization functioned in a mechanistic or organic manner.

An industry may be in a quasi-governmental partnership where controls on wages, profits, and processes are important factors in the environment. On the other hand, a new and highly competitive field (such as the plastics industry) is confronted with the need to keep costs at a minimum, react quickly to changing markets, and be constantly alert to the cash flow balance in the corporate budget. This is equally applicable to a volunteer agency (such as the

YMCA) which finds its services to a middle-class suburban area not completely relevant to an economically stunted and culturally deprived urban area. If it wants to remain relevant to its constituency and viable as a system, sensitivity and adaptation to its wider environment should be a prime consideration for any organization.

Appropriate response, therefore, is defined as those actions which will contribute to improve interfacing in the organization and effective utilization of human resources, and result in growth of the organization and positive adaptation to the environment.

This schematic model of organizational renewal emphasizes the need for the organizational system to re-examine its goals, evaluate its performance, and renew its spirit; and it demonstrates that the ability of the sociotechnical system to cope is an essential element. The quality of situational coping, therefore, may be aided by a renewal stimulator—an organizational development office, training director, group manager, or some other kind of change agent.

The ITORP program is designed to help people in organizations to initiate and implement Organization Renewal in their organization by analyzing their organizational system, improving communications, developing teamwork, and planning specific action projects.

This training program is increasingly being used in civic, industrial, governmental, health, business, and educational institutions. It has led to numerous experiences in which this five session program has been integrated with on-going individual and organization development processes.

It has always been the intention of the creators of the ITORP training program that it *not* be a complete organization renewal effort. Rather, it serves an initiating and fact-finding function that can be made available to line and staff managers to help further improve organizational functioning. It always needs to be related to other processes in the organization and to be reinforced by the continuing leadership of renewal stimulators with appropriate management support and follow-through task forces.

As with all efforts leading toward change, ITORP has on occasion produced minimal results. It has been our observation, however, that this usually occurs where organization renewal does not really have the support of management, where there is inadequate follow-up by internal or external consultants, or when the training program is not properly interrelated to the other processes of organization renewal, change and development.

Some examples of success would be in a large government agency in Canada where approximately 415 managers went through the ITORP training program as a part of a successful change from a government agency to a quasi-private agency. In a telephone company, some 100 ITORP trained managers in a large division later identified cost-savings valued at $300,000.00 and a representative of each of the ITORP groups became a part of a standing organization renewal task force. In a third example, a group of 25 community college presidents identified during an ITORP session a number of follow-up steps with students and faculty that led to increased relevance of these colleges to their communities.

As further evaluation studies take place, additional revisions of the design and data collection instruments will occur. The ITORP program, however, might best be seen as developing in organization the awareness that change starts from within the system.

Success in organizational renewal starts with awareness. If organization leaders are not aware of the need for renewal, it is foolish to think that the process will ever be carried out or achieved. Organization renewal also starts when the individual begins to recognize the need for his own improvement as a leader, manager and a motivator of others.

Organization renewal is a process, not a technique or a gimmick. It is a way by which each person can begin to make his organization grow toward a state of maturity that is required if it is going to meet the needs of its employees and the society of which it is a part. This is not an easy task.

The hope and challenge of organization renewal is to bring out of the past experiences of people in organizations effective comprehension of confrontation and coping for the growth of ourselves, our organizations and our society.

REFERENCES

Culbert, Samuel A. Organization renewal: Using internal conflicts to solve external problems. Research Paper No. 26, Division of Research, Graduate School of Business Administration, UCLA, 1969.
Gardner, John W. *Self renewal*. McGraw-Hill Inc., 1966.

108   CONTEMPORARY ORGANIZATION DEVELOPMENT

Lawrence, P., & Lorsch, J. *Organization and environment: Managing differentia-tion and integration.* Boston: Harvard Business School, 1967.
Vaill, Peter B. *Practice theories in organizational development.* School of Busi-ness Administration. University of Connecticut, August, 1971. (An earlier version of this paper was read before the Annual Meeting of the Academy of Management, Atlanta, Georgia, August, 1971).
Woodward, Joan. *Industrial organization.* London: Oxford Univ. Press, 1965.

The TORI Community Experience as an Organizational Change Intervention

JACK R. GIBB

The TORI theory is a general theory of social systems developed by Jack R. and Lorraine M. Gibb and their associates. The TORI community experience, to be described here, is an example of one organizational intervention that is derived from the general body of theory. The theory is described in detail elsewhere (Gibb, 1965, 1971a; Gibb, J.R. & Gibb, L. M., 1967, 1968a, 1969).

The theory has been stated in a form that is directly applicable to the change processes in social systems. It is a unitary theory that applies to all formal or informal social systems, of any size: families (Gibb, 1965; Gibb, J. R. & Gibb, L. M., 1971), counselling and therapy groups or communities (Gibb, 1968a, Gibb, J. R. & Gibb, L. M., 1968a), business organizations (Gibb, 1964b, 1969a, 1971c; Gibb, J. R. & Gibb, L. M., 1968b), neighborhoods and natural communities (Gibb, 1968b; Gibb, J. R. & Gibb, L. M., 1971), learning communities and school systems (Gibb, 1965; Gibb, J. R. & Gibb, L. M., 1968b, 1971), religious organizations (Gibb, 1965), and training groups (Gibb, 1971a; Gibb, J. R. & Gibb, L. M., 1968b, 1969).

THEORY UNDERLYING THE COMMUNITY EXPERIENCE

The community experience is derived from the several following general assumptions embodied in the theory.

1. Any social system—a group, person, community, nation, or organization—is best understood and improved most effectively by focusing upon system characteristics of a living, growing organism.

2. The primary and leverage variables in system growth are the antithetical processes of fear and trust and their correlates.

3. Growth occurs as a movement from fear towards increasing trust. The primary correlates of this central process are the following four: movement from depersonalization and role towards greater personalization; from a closed system towards a more open system; from impositional motivation towards greater self-determination; and from dependency or counter-dependency towards greater interdependence (Gibb, J. R. and Gibb, L. M., 1971). TORI is a convenient acronym for these four factors in the growth of living systems: *t*rust, *o*penness, *r*ealization, and *i*nterdependence.

4. Fear-defense levels are thus manifested in systems in four ways: depersonalization and role living; facade building and covert strategies; impositions and persuasions; and high control and dependency (Gibb, 1961a, 1971c).

5. Trust and low defense levels are manifested in systems in four ways: personal, intimate and non-role behavior; open and transparent behavior; self-determining, assertive, and actualizing behavior; reciprocally-fulfilling, interdependent, and "with" behavior.

6. An efficient way of optimizing growth and the trust factors in growth is to focus upon the macro-environmental forces that impinge upon participants in the system. This environment may then nurture and sustain growth behaviors, which are associated with classic and desired system outcomes: productivity, creativity, and organismic vitality.

From these and related assumptions, and from a number of experimental and field studies, we have designed several interventions as part of our theory and practice of organizational development. It is the purpose of this chapter to describe one of these interventions, the TORI community experience.

We make the following set of assumptions about community living. These come from experimentation with either natural (business systems, congregations, school faculties, conventions, etc.) or contrived (gathered together for the purposes of experimentation) communities.

1. Systems at any level of complexity or size are analogues for systems at other levels of complexity or size. Thus, a "community" of 150 people, when it becomes aware of itself as a social system, develops a personality style, characteristic ways of defending against internal and external threat, and characteristic and

unique styles of coping with classic "concerns": inclusion, decision making, communicating, organizing, building goal structures,
etc.

2. Systems tend towards disintegration or stagnation when system styles are predominantly impersonal and in-role, strategic
and closed, persuasive and coercive, and dependent-controlling.
Systems tend towards self-sustaining growth when system styles
are predominantly personal, open, allowing, and interdependent.

3. Systems "learn" actualizing styles of coping when the environment is low-defense. Persons, groups, communities, and na-
tions create functional styles under high-trust environments and
create dysfunctional life styles under fear-distrust-defense environments.

4. Functional behaviors or styles (personal, open, self-determining, and interdependent behavior and attitudes) are intrinsically rewarding and self-perpetuating if the immediate system environment is a high-trust and low-defense environment.

5. The flow of perceptual and feeling data in high-defense communities and organizations is so low that raising these data to
visibility in the system is a powerful force in creating more functional styles of coping and relating. Functional feedback is apparently a powerful variable, as is indicated in a number of recent
studies.

Later in the paper specific ways of translating these assumptions into actions in the community settings are discussed.

WHAT THE TORI COMMUNITY IS DESIGNED
TO ACCOMPLISH

The TORI community experience is designed to accomplish
the following specific aims:

1. Create a low-defense community of 50 to 200 people who
see each other as a community.

2. Optimize the feelings of "ownership" of the community.
When the community experience has occurred we hope that members will feel that the community belongs to them, that the community is important to their lives, that they are significant members of the community, that they can influence it, and that they
are "members" in a full sense. We see some evidence that when
a member comes to own the community he takes constructive

community-centered actions, is concerned about other members and their welfare, works hard to contribute to community goals, and perceives the community as a unit and as a living organism that is changing and changeable.

3. Optimize the visibility of resources within the community to the members of the community. We see some evidence that this visibility of resources creates forces toward interdependence in the system. We see interdependence as the primary leverage variable in the effective community. In interdependent systems individuals see each other as sources of affective support, as project and task help, and as aid in all of the hourly and daily activities in the community. Members come to learn that others are *motivated* to be helpful and that they are *capable* of giving significant help. Perceived willingness to offer help, and perceived competence to provide help are both increased in high-trust environments.

4. Create an experience that is long enough and intense enough to be perceived by participants as rewarding, successful, and worth the input of time and effort. The frequent experiences of "community" in most organizations are less than rewarding. Company picnics, Christmas parties, sales conferences, official parties and receptions, retirement banquets, weekend retreats, conventions, cocktails, and even management training programs are seldom seen by organizational members as fulfilling and rewarding corporate or organizational activities.

5. Visibility of member fears and trusts, how these fears and trusts influence coping behavior in specific ways, and how fears and trusts change with environmental forces and internal states.

6. Visibility of the clusters of behaviors that are directly related to fear and trust, both in self and others, and in the total community. Personal learning and community building are each enhanced when members are increasingly attuned to the major polarity clusters and their effects: personal and role behaviors, open and strategic behaviors; allowing and persuasive behaviors; and interdependent and controlling behaviors. These behaviors are the significant leverage points in the system, determine effective interpersonal relationships, and determine productivity and creativity in the system.

7. Create a positive and effective experience with what is likely to be the organization of the immediate future: flow, emergence, transcince, high lateral mobility, movement less around power

and more around information and task systems, less pyramidal and more temporary and function-related systems, and less fear-defense. Functional organization emerges and flows with a wide range of people and systems in an impressive way, at least under the conditions used in our experimental communities and in our organizational development efforts.

8. Create conditions under which persons are better able to grow, learn, and develop behaviors and attitudes that are uniquely functional for them as persons. The TORI community experience has been developed as an intervention in the development of organizations, but we have found it to be a major innovation in human relations training as well.

COMMUNITY PROCEDURES

The community experience, to have optimal effect, must be an integral part of the overall organization development effort. The planning group must represent wide segments of the organization. The community experience is best when it flows from other activities that create a demand for greater intimacy, greater community participation, or greater unity and interdependence. The community experience cannot be "sold" to the organization. It happens best when some organizational members have experienced the TORI community as part of another organization to which they belong.

The TORI community has greatest effect upon the organization when all or nearly all members of the organizational unit participate in the experience. The experience is very powerful and creates feelings of deprivation in members who were left out. We have had most experience with "natural" and interdependent organizational units that number 50 to 200. We have used the design successfully with as many as 5,000, but this size requires special physical facilities and considerable leader skill. The TORI experience is designed for a group that sees itself as interrelated or wishes to build greater interdependence. The unit may be the members of a college faculty, management of a division, all members of a small company, all members of a department together with their wives, all occupants of a company building, all residents of a dormitory, or all residents of a neighborhood.

The initial experience must provide sufficient time for the feeling of community to emerge. This emergence cannot be forced or "induced." The emergence may take from 10 hours on a given day to two full days of interaction, depending upon a number of conditions the nature of which are unclear, but about which we have a number of hypotheses. We have used as much time as is available, up to five full days of intensive interaction. An evening followed by two days is a successful format for most groups. It is possible to use a weekend for the purpose, but it is more powerful if the organization sanctions the experience by using paid work time during the work week. The experience is then seen by all as having direct, economic, and not tangential relevance to important organizational goals.

Physical facilities are of central importance. It is best if all participants can see all others at most times, so that opportunities for contagion, confrontation, intermingling, and structural flow are as frequent as possible. Open space is essential. Possible locations are a large studio or ballroom, a level field, a gymnasium, a conference center, or a stadium. Open space is necessary to allow a high degree of physical movement, large group games or projects, subgrouping of various planned or spontaneous activities, and high visibility. Movement and flow are important aspects of emergent organization. We have found that if activities are vital, exciting, and relevant the group has little need for snacks, coffee, time breaks, or "rest." Participants are only aawre of needs to snack, smoke and rest when they are bored, threatened, or otherwise disengaged. Comfort is good but not vital or necessary. Carpeting, mats, or flat pillows may help. No furniture is needed.

The community may have one person who acts as convener, and who may provide initial structure. He or she may suggest at the beginning some activities that have been found in previous groups to meet as many of the following criteria as possible.

1. High visibility to each person and to the total community of the dynamics of fear and trust.

2. A high incidence of non-verbal, and someitmes non-visual activities. Words often get in the way of communication in depth. Non-verbal activities can be structured so as to be highly visible to the total community. These activities provide a continuing source of important data to community members, useful in decision making and in flow.

3. A high degree of involvement of the total community in

interdependent activities: community planning sessions, total group lifting, community feeling census, community projects, etc.

4. Multiple options for the individual so that he can look at his choices, the effects of his choices, and come to take full responsibility for them. Choosing partners, entering and leaving small groups, initiating actions—all provide community members with significant choices that influence later work relationships.

5. High power for creating intense feelings such as warmth, anger, rejection, acceptance, loneliness, and exhilaration. It is important that the feelings arise as an emerging part of the action, and not as part of a set design that predisposes persons to give predictable responses or get predictable feelings.

6. High emergence power. Activities are best that start with loose structure and allow easy and unpredictable flow into other activities.

7. Focus upon spontaneity. Structured activities are suggested only at the beginning and occasionally during early stages of community life. The emergence of spontaneous or community-planned activities is explicitly encouraged from the beginning.

It is best to have a convener who has high transparence and availability, who shows his feelings and perceptions and total self easily and quickly, who is highly authentic, and who is flexible enough to flow with whatever happens in the community. The convener joins the community as early as he possibly can, takes no *special* responsibility for community events (other than as one member of the community), and encourages and accepts anything that happens (in the very early stages), and then reacts personally to all other events that occur at later stages. He is as personal, open, allowing, and interdependent as it is possible for him to be.

Especially early in the experience members make clear and insistent demands for freedom and self-determination. These needs have high priority and must be met before other activities can emerge. Members protect their life space, want to have freedom of choice, and want to "do their own thing." It is as if members are saying to the other people that they want to be sure they are free and will be given freedom before they will enter into intimacy and interdependence.

Given freedom and much psychological and physical space, the community *emerges and flows*. Things happen. Decisions come not so much from anything resembling formal decision making as from deep non-verbal sensing and the emergence of quasi-consensual activities that are continually tried out, changed in process, and ended when they become unsatisfying. Occasional brief meetings of the total group to voice feelings of the moment become helpful and sometimes lead to awareness of unmet community needs and to an emerging sense of totally new direction. This ability to flow and sense others' needs is particularly important back on the job when organizational and job decisions come to be made more easily, with less misunderstanding and unnecessary formality.

The community grows as *trust develops* and as fears are reduced. Trusts and fears are inherited from organizational life. All members of the community have many feelings of mixed fear and trust for other members present, dependent upon previous interaction. Past hurts and feelings are usually expressed and as quickly as possible brought into the present. Past misperceptions or miscommunications are verbalized, checked out, and reduced. Each member is of course free to initiate the interactions that he feels will lead to productive interchange and *for which he can feel responsible*. It is important that no individual feels pushed into waters that *he feels* are too deep for him. It is our experience that communities develop a high degree of sensitivity for their own interaction. We do not see the community experience as sensitivity training or as therapy and do not see skilled trainers or professional as necessary to a highly successful and powerful experience. Just as on the job, members take full responsibility for dealing with matters that seem to them to be job related and relevant to their lives in the organization. Members have a keen sensitivity about this—far better than an outside therapist or trainer who is not familiar with the life space of the participants involved. Whether or not a professional could make a "better" judgment, the participant must learn to handle what he can handle and take full responsibility for handling it.

In one sense the most important single development in the community is the growing sense that members come to *feel responsible for themselves* and their own experiences. It is our observation, both in the community and in the organizational life, that the most effective organizational member is one who makes his needs known, initiates actions that seem to him to be problem-centered and need-meeting, asserts himself in getting organizational activities started, and jobs done, and takes full responsibility for the organization and for his life in it. He thus tends less to project blame on the boss, the organization, other members, or the exigencies of organizational life. He is more assertive, less dependent, cuts through organizational tape, finds ways of getting done what needs to be done, takes necessary risks, makes occasional mistakes, and is less aware of organizational barriers than of organizational opportunities. Perhaps the single most rewarding outcome of the community experiences is that many people come to find such assertive behavior rewarding, far more possible in the organization than they had previously realized, and even approved by superiors who were previously felt to be disapproving of such assertive behavior.

Another significant development in the community experience is the *greater availability of spontaneous warmth* and affection. In the low-trust atmosphere of many organizations the expression of warmth is seen as strategic, as currying favor, as manipulative, or as rewarding or punishing rather than as a spontaneous response to inner feeling. As members interact in greater spontaneity and authenticity, feelings are expressed more freely and exchanged in an atmosphere of greater trust. Nonverbal and impulsive behaviors are often seen as more valid than the use of words, particularly conventional and stereotypic speech. People learn to give clearer and less contaminated messages. Questions become less frequent and are replaced by the direct messages underlying them.

The community experience usually starts with a direct focus upon relationships among members present. As the climate of trust and interdependence increases the community begins to deal with the basic problems of the organization as they are seen by the participants. The group tackles operational problems, and issues related to finance, personnel, marketing, research and any other relevant and high priority concerns. The community may make recommendations to management, plan for other meetings and community events, and take other action steps.

In general, our research and interviews indicate that behavior, during and following the community experience, becomes more personal and less role-related (Gibb, 1968a), more open and less covertly strategic (Gibb, 1969a; Gibb, J. R. & Gibb, L. M., 1971), more allowing and less persuasive (Gibb, 1961b, 1964b), and more interdependent and team-oriented (Gibb, 1969b, 1971a;

Gibb, J. R. and Gibb, L. M., 1967). These behaviors are probably related to increasing organizational productivity, creativity
(Gibb, 1971c), and vitality, but we have no direct measures of
these end variables at this stage of our research.

As stated earlier, the TORI community experience is most effective as an integral part of a long-range organizational development effort applying TORI theory. It is followed by related efforts to apply learnings in the community to actions on the job,
in the office, or in meetings. No single "intervention" is likely
to be very effective as a one-time shot, unrelated to the ongoing
life of the organization.

IN THE ORGANIZATION

Following are brief descriptions of two cases which show some
of the advantages, as well as some of the difficulties, in creating
a successful and powerful TORI community experience.

As part of a long range OD effort in a large utility organization, the total upper management group of 54 men who managed
a single division were taken off-site for a period of four days.

Several planning sessions over a period of two months pre-
ceeded the community event. Present at the planning meetings
were three line managers, two personnel and training managers,
and one outside consultant. The committee decided to determine
in advance the five or six top-priority operating problems as seen
by the total group of 54. After group interviews, questionnaires,
and team meetings, a list of five top items was made. High agreement in the group of 54 was obtained on the ordering of the items.

A total of four days were allotted to the event, with the open
possibility of later meetings. The outside consultant was given the
task of being convener of the workshop. Many of the people had
heard of the TORI community experience and there was a wide
variety of expectations in the group. Expectations ranged from
high enthusiasm to high skepticism. The decision was reached on
the basis of a high degree of confidence, from continuing experience, in the outside consultant, his abilities and his judgment.
An excellent facility was found, with plenty of indoor and outdoor
space. Material was mimeographed as background for the five
operating problems.

The group met and spent most of the first day in community-

building experiences, toward which there were highly positive reactions, even among the original skeptics. A variety of grouping
were suggested by the consultant-convener and by members of
the management group. People met in pairs, random groups of
5 or 6, and in five operating teams. The original committee plan
called for starting on the second day with the highest priority
operating problem. The total community decided, after much
fairly open and often heated discussion, to deal first with some
organizational issues that were arising within the work teams, and
in interface relationships among the teams.

With the verbalized sanction of the total community, including
the top executive and the planning committee, the planned agenda
(purposefully loose to begin with) was discarded in favor of hap-
penings and activities planned on the spot. Though this lack of
structure caused some frustration and discontent, it also precipitated several confrontations among key individuals in front of
the total community, something that had never happened in the
organization before. Some of the painful relationships had been
latent and unverbalized for a long period of time.

New norms of openness and confrontation were in the process
of development. Post-experience interviews indicated that the
confrontations initiated at the community experience were highly
functional, particularly for one key group head. The level of
openness was maintained at a higher degree than prior to the
community experience, but not as high as that during the experience itself.

The total community met often and continued to create new
interface groups as the conference developed. During the third
and fourth day the community dealt in depth with the first three
high-priority operating problems, and finally decided to postpone
discussions of the fourth and fifth priority items until later meetings. General discussion at the community meetings and post-
meeting questionnaires and interviews indicated high satisfaction
with the major actions taken at the off-site meetings.

Positive aspects of the experience included: total community
involvement among the group of 54 who met as a highly interactive and open community for the first time; the confronting of
some latent interpersonal conflicts in the group; the experience
with an emergent and flowing decision-making structure that was
seen as positive; a greater tendency following the conference to

take individual initiative; and the development of a newly-created set of norms around being more personal, open, and allowing on the job.

More difficult aspects of the experience included: the difficulty of making large group decisions on the job; the contrast between the spontaneous and unconstraining atmosphere in the community experience with the more formal and more constraining atmosphere on the job; the difficulty in measuring the effects of such an experience upon the hard variables of productivity and cost reduction; and the perceived importance by many of emergency-management procedures and philosophy in day to day operations.

All 54 of the managers rated the experience in the top two categories on a 7-point scale with regard to effectiveness. Overall reactions were highly positive. Many suggestions for improvement of design and flow were given. The organization has not as yet decided to repeat the experience during the year following it, but has engaged in a number of activities that flowed from the conference.

Another case example is a long range program of organizational development with a total faculty of a small university. TORI community experiences have occurred each fall for a period of four years. The faculty has about doubled in that period from 125 to 246. Different faculty groups over the period have acted as representatives of the faculty in designing the OD program and in planning the TORI experiences. The president of the university has been consistently positive about the OD program from the beginning. The faculty members have many diverse views, which, in general, have grown more positive over the years.

The four yearly TORI community experiences have increased in length from two days to about four and one-half days, with the general approval of the faculty, although the increased time has cut down on their valued free time. Activities have been increasingly more fluid, consensual, open, confronting, and less structured in advance. Decision making in the total group has become considerably more effective, less painful, and more satisfying. Decisions recommended at the community meetings have led to a complete reorganization of the structure of the administration and faculty organization, greater flexibility in curriculum, more faculty freedoms, a feeling of greater intimacy among the faculty members in spite of the large increase in size, more open expression of conflict, informalizing of the channels of communication and action, flattening of the organizational structure, and somewhat improved student-faculty relationships.

Although the TORI community experience has been used with dramatic success in freshman orientation programs and in large demonstrations with groups of 2,000 students, and although this is known by the faculty, there is as yet little interest in suggesting a TORI experience for the entire student body. The faculty is seen by the students as more close knit, but as less student-oriented. Individual faculty members see themselves as more free, more able to "do their own thing," less coerced into the comfortable paternalistic relationships with students that prevailed in the past. Individual teachers often build highly participative classrooms, and highly intimate relationships with individual students and groups of students. Many teachers choose to conduct more formal classrooms and not to engage in extracurricular activities with students.

While turnover and new additions create problems for a large community, there is in the case of this faculty a large enough continuing body of members to reenforce the gains made in the community learning sessions. The system is increasingly aware of itself as a system. There is an increasing awareness of the diversity of educational philosophy, administrative theory, and structure needs within the community. The diversity provides a continuing challenge, but also is a barrier to any one major group of faculty establishing a university-wide experimental curriculum and community that has a common thrust. It is our impression that much energy is wasted in dealing with the feelings surrounding the diversity.

The increase in communication, the improvement in problem solving, the general awareness of community, and the increased ability to plan are seen by the faculty as real gains and as at least partly due to the TORI community experiences. The yearly experiences continue to be different and more experimental each time. Unfortunately we do not have measures in a control-group institutional setting. We do not have enough experience with the method to warrant major research as yet. We continue to gather data that are useful to the system in planning, and useful in improvement of the method, but not as useful as yet in comparing various methods of intervention as we would like.

ADVANTAGES OF THE DESIGN

We see the TORI community experience as a design (1) for building a strong community in an organizational setting, and (2) for giving human-relations training and personal-growth experiences to homogeneous and heterogeneous groups. The advantages of the design as a community-building experience are several:

1. Problems of communication are reduced by having all members of the relevant community together for major and intense experiences. System-wide communication problems are handled as they occur.

2. The system *qua* system has a chance to acquire system-relevant learnings: decision-making skills, planning skills, work assignment, work structuring, etc. The system can learn whatever it needs to learn to do what it wishes to accomplish. Many problems of organization and living are unique to the organization, or are *perceived as unique,* and require custom tailoring by the people who are living in the system.

3. There is a minimal problem of transfer to the "back home" situation, because everyone in the back home situation is present in the learning community. This is in contrast to many decisions which break the community into small groups for more effective learning.

4. The experience is particularly good in making available the warmth and positive feelings in the system. People learn to express positive feelings, rather than hoard them. The positive valence of the organization is greatly increased. Feelings of isolation and alienation are reduced.

5. A functional feedback system can be created that involves all of the members of the organization. Diagnosis, feedback and problem solving can occur immediately rather than through the more cumbersome and long periods required for these processes in the formal segmented processes in most large organizations.

As a format for human relations and managerial training, the design has advantages:

1. It places immediate responsibility for learning upon the person himself rather than upon the community, a therapist, or a training leader. Each person seeks solutions to his own problems at the rate that he feels that he can learn.

2. Possibly for the foregoing reason, the experience is far less likely to incur destructive effects than other more intrusive designs currently in use. The destructive effects of training are probably greatly exaggerated, but there is some evidence that negative effects are increased by intrusiveness of trainer behavior.

3. Behavior is more public than in most other methods in use. A greatly augmented range of feedback is possible.

4. There is a wide range of persons, feedback, group size, attitudes and learning settings in which the learner can try out new behavior. The community provides a setting where people try things out *right now* in a physical way. It is the doing of something under one's own steam that brings enduring learning. One can confront someone in anger, choose a new partner, walk away from a group, be open with a stranger or a warm friend, get in a fight for one's rights—see the effects, take responsibility for the action, and try again.

5. There is a dramatic effect of trying out behavior in front of a large community. When persons on their own initiative get over the threshold of opening up in a large group, significant things happen.

6. There is a great similarity between the learning milieu and the back home environment. People learn right now how to do it back home (Gibb, 1971d). The transfer problem is negligible.

7. There is an economy of professional training resources. One competent professional can convene a learning community of 200 or more persons. Research indicates results comparable to those obtained in groups of 10 to 12 (La Boon, 1971; Pressman, 1970).

DISADVANTAGES OF THE DESIGN

As an organizational development process, the possible disadvantages include the following:

1. The design runs counter to many expectations in most formal organizations. The prospect of opening up organizational issues in front of a large number of people with whom one is working or living is for many a frightening thought. People fear large groups, and distrust large-group experiences. The prior experiences many people have in large group are largely negative.

2. The design and the assumptions underlying the development of the design run counter to many assumptions made by manage-

ment. The design is appropriate to participative styles such as McGregor's Theory Y or Likert's System Four management style. The design is most appropriate to organizations that stress functional communications, team planning, interpersonal warmth, and emergent structure.

3. The design must be embedded in a long-range OD program to be of sufficient effectiveness to warrant use. It is not suited to one-shot or crash programs.

4. The activities are new and have low face validity. When described to others, the activities seem minimally relevant to goals of productivity, creativity, and organizational vitality. Only the more sophisticated or creative managers will risk the intervention.

5. The community experience requires, at least for the first time in the organization, a leader with a high degree of professional skill in convening the TORI community, in using nonverbal activities, and in large-group decision making.

The disadvantages listed above are not as relevant to the TORI community experience when used as a growth experience as they are to the design used as an OD intervention. When it is used as a human-relations or management training experience, the following disadvantages seem relevant:

1. Many participants assume that highly competent professional therapists or trainers are necessary if participants are to learn to grow or to be effective. The TORI design requires an assumption that one can take responsibility for his own learning, and can marshall the resources necessary for such co-learning in a large community.

2. The physical requirements are difficult to meet. It is difficult to get large open space that is suitable for the experience.

VALUE ASSUMPTIONS

The values implicit in building the TORI theory are embedded in the structure of the theory itself.

The four values basic to the theory are difficult to separate out from the structure of the theory. It is probably true that the system stands alone without value statements or assumptions, but the values and the assumptions are so interlocked in the people who have formulated the theory and in the people who use it extensively, that it is not easy to try to divorce theory from values.

We place a deep value upon (1) being personal, people-centered, intimate, and close; (2) being authentic, open, transparent, honest, available, and direct; (3) being allowing, non-intrusive, non-manipulative, and non-coercive; and upon (4) being interdependent, collaborative, sharing, interactive, and not dependent or elitist.

It is probably impossible to be *too* personal, open, allowing, or interdependent—at least in the sense that we are using the terms. These behaviors cannot be too "extreme." If they are consonant with the deep-lying forces in the center of the person, if they are spontaneous and intrinsic, and if they are not too contaminated with organismic ambivalence, then movement in the direction of these values is "good," and results in highly positive outcomes: mental health, creative interpersonal relationships, and deep inner happiness.

It is possible to apply the theory to a wide range of organizational activities without dealing with the value system. The relationships within the system are empirically valid and consistent with hard research (e.g. fear leads to closed behavior; high fear leads to low creativity; high trust leads to intimacy; etc.). The development of TORI theory is a long range research program, part of which is directed toward understanding the relationships between values and conceptual models.

REFERENCES

Gibb, J. R. Defense level and influence potential in small groups. In L. Petrullo, & B. M. Bass (Eds.), *Leadership and interpersonal behavior,* New York: Holt, Rinehart & Winston, 1961a.

Gibb, J. R. Defensive communication. *The Journal of Communication,* 1961b, 11 (3), 141-148.

Gibb, J. R. Climate for trust formation. In L. P. Bradford, J. R. Gibb, & K. D. Benne (Eds.), *T group theory and laboratory method,* New York: Wiley, 1964a.

Gibb, J. R. Communication and productivity. *Personnel Administration,* 1964b, 27, 8-13.

Gibb, J. R. Fear and facade: defensive management. In R. E. Farson (Ed.), *Science and human affairs,* Palo Alto: Science and Behavior Books, Inc., 1965.

Gibb, J. R. The counselor as a role-free person. In C. A. Parker (Ed.), *Counseling theories and counselor education,* New York: Houghton Mifflin, 1968a.

Gibb, J. R. Group experiences and human possibilities. In H. A. Otto (Ed.), *Human potentialities,* St. Louis: W. H. Green, 1968b.

Gibb, J. R. Management tunes in. *Weyerhaeuser World,* 1969a, 1, 3.

Gibb, J. R. Building a teamwork climate. *Weyerhaeuser Management Viewpoint,* 1969b, 1, 10-12.

Gibb, J. R. Search for with-ness: A new look at interdependence. In W. G. Dyer (Ed.), *New dimensions in group training*, New York: Van Nostrand, 1971a, in press.
Gibb, J. R. Some psychological aspects of faith and trust. In J. A. Waterstradt (Ed.), *Festschrift for P. A. Christensen*, Salt Lake City: University of Utah Press, 1971b, in press.
Gibb, J. R. Managing for creativity in the organization. In C. W. Taylor (Ed.), *Climate for creativity*. New York: Pergamon Publishing Co., 1971c, in press.
Gibb, J. R. The small group experience: What does it mean? In L. N. Solomon, & B. Berzon (Eds.), *The encounter group: Issues and applications*, San Francisco: Jossey-Bass, 1971d, in press.
Gibb, J. R., & Gibb, L. M. Humanistic elements in group growth. In J. F. T. Bugental (Ed.). *Challenges of humanistic psychology*, New York: McGraw-Hill, 1967.
Gibb, J. R., & Gibb, L. M. Emergence therapy: The TORI process in an emergent group. In G. M. Gazda (Ed.), *Innovations to group psychotherapy*, Springfield, Ill.: Thomas, 1968a.
Gibb, J. R., & Gibb, L. M. Leaderless groups: Growth-centered values and potentials. In H. A. Otto, & J. Mann (Eds.), *Ways of growth: Approaches to expanding awareness*, New York: Grossman, 1968b.
Gibb, J. R., & Gibb, L. M. Role freedom in a TORI group. In A. Burton (Ed.), *Encounter: The theory and practice of encounter groups*, San Francisco: Jossey-Bass, 1969.
Gibb, J. R., & Gibb, L. M. The process of group actualization. In J. Akin, A. Goldberg,. G. Myers, & J. Stewart (Eds.), *Language behavior: Readings in communication*, The Hague, The Netherlands: Mouton & Co., 1971.
La Boon, S. TORI: A theory of community growth. Unpublished Master's thesis, United States International University, 1971.
Pressman, M. L. A study of an intensive TORI weekend group experience and its effects on interpersonal skills. Unpublished Master's thesis, University of Utah, 1970.

Organization and Family Viewed as Open and Interacting Systems in Grid Development

ROBERT R. BLAKE and
JANE SRYGLEY MOUTON

ROBERT R. BLAKE and
JANE SRYGLEY MOUTON

Grid Organization Development has been written about for a number of years. You probably know the character of its approach, at least in broad outline (Blake & Mouton, 1964, 1968, 1969). By comparison Grid Family Development is new. Therefore we would like to begin by describing to you what it entails. We will then be in a position to examine some interconnecting and synergistic possibilities between these two open and interacting systems: organization and family.

THE CHARACTER OF GRID FAMILY DEVELOPMENT

As with Grid Organization Development, the goal of Grid Family Development is to aid participants to learn theory alternatives. This aids people to be better able to comprehend their everyday experience as well as to plan and to implement desired changes. The technology makes extensive use of learning instruments (Blake & Mouton, 1962, 1971, 1972; Mouton & Blake, 1961). For a sample of what learning is experienced through use of this kind of an approach, we would like to ask you to complete two representative instruments.

First, read through items *1* through *3* below, with their alternative answers, so as to get a general idea of what's in them. Then, think about your own marriage. When you have picked the phrase that is most typical of your situation, place a 1 beside it. Place a 2 by the one you see as next most typical. Then place a 5 by the one which is most untypical.

1. When you get into *conflict* with your mate, what do you try to do?

Copyright © 1971 by Robert R. Blake and Jane S. Mouton. All rights reserved.

___Stamp it out.

___Smooth it over.

___Ignore it.

___Compromise the difference.

___Face up and solve it.

2. How would you rate your mate's approach to *teamwork?*

___Controlling.

___Gently encouraging.

___Cooperating like a turned-off robot.

___Maintaining an even keel.

___Zestfully getting with it.

3. When it comes to *intimacy,* I

___have definite ideas about when-where-how, and am displeased if things don't go according to my wishes.

___seek security and approval through intimate relations and feel apologetic when appreciation is not abundant.

___rarely feel involved or aroused by my mate.

___have a friendly, companionable approach and like our intimacy the way it is on a regular basis.

___express love for my mate as thoughtfully and imaginatively as I know how, in ways that bring richness to our relationship (Scientific Methods, Inc., 1971b).

So much for your rankings.

Now let's examine an instrument which illustrates a different data gathering method.

Here is a situation that might happen within any marriage. You are asked to write down what your mate's reaction would be. Then anticipate how your mate would probably respond to your reactions and write that down too.

Boss Frustration. You have just arrived home from work. You approach your mate, saying, "That job of mine is hopeless. The top dogs don't care what happens or how anyone below them feels and thinks. My boss was a real tyrant today, and it was the last straw. I'm fed up. I'm not going back to that place ever again. I'm looking for a new job starting tomorrow, even if it means less money."

A. What Would Your Mate Say   B. How Would You Respond
   or How Would She/He Re-   to Your Mate's Reaction?
   act?

_____   _____

_____   _____

_____   _____

We can now move on to examine the principal theories of
human relationships which are discernible on the Marriage Grid.
In this presentation we will restrict ourselves to the married-couple
part of the family rather than trying to analyze relationships between parents and children at the same time. The reason is this:
The quality and character of relationships between a couple is
prior to and highly influential on the character of their child rearing endeavors. This latter is a significant part of Grid Family Development but, one thing at a time.

THE MARRIAGE GRID

The *Marriage* Grid (Mouton & Blake, 1971) can help you and
your mate keep your relationship on track during your everyday-
and-everynight activities. It can also help you figure out situations
that might derail you.

As with other Grids, the Marriage Grid depicts two main areas
of concern; the ones here being the horizontal scale of *concern
for what happens* and the vertical scale of *concern for your mate*.

Concern for What Happens

Concern for what happens varies from individual to individual,
depending on the assumptions people are currently holding. In any
marriage each mate's own degree of concern for What Happens
may be somewhat different in degree from the other's. High concern means that you want to attain goals and get things done;
not just vegetate. Low concern means the opposite—to you, what
actually happens is within the providence of fate. There are various degrees of concern in between, often clustering about halfway.

Concern for Your Mate

The handily neutral term "mate" is used so that a relationship
can be examined without the connotational encumbrances of words

like "husband" and "wife," "breadwinner" and "spouse," and so
on. High concern for your mate means that the other person's
satisfaction is in the forefront of your attention. Low mate concern equates with disregard for the other person's feelings. Between low concern—symbolized by the number *1*—and *9*, high
concern there are the gradations running from *2* through *8*, with
5 at the midway point.

The Marriage Grid

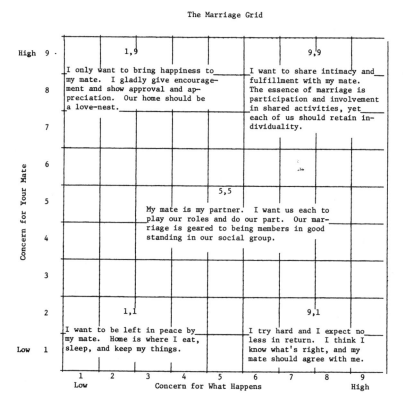

(Reprinted by permission from Mouton, Jane Srygley, & Blake, Robert R.
The Marriage Grid. McGraw-Hill, 1971, page 5.)

Figure 1 shows the Marriage Grid diagram. On it are represented 81 different combinations of *concern for what happens* and
concern for your mate. Five very distinctive combinations are defined on the diagram. There is no law of nature or of mate selec-

tion which says that both of you are bound to occupy the same position on the Grid. And even if you currently do, this might be no cause for congratulation, unless you're satisfied with *where* you are and can see no possible further progress. Here's a brief description of the five major Grid orientations.

9,1

The combination of concerns in the lower right corner of the Grid is 9,1. This means *high* concern for *what happens* coupled with *low* personal concern for your *mate*. What does this signify in terms of your thinking and feeling, your attitudes and behavior toward your mate? Predictably, that high "what happens" concern is primary. It's uncolored by sensitivity to your mate's feelings, far less by any cherishing of them.

Here are some clues to help you detect whether you are on or near the 9,1 position. One conviction that burns throughout your waking hours is that you're right—yes, absolutely right—by virtue of being *you*. Your keen discernment enables you to see in a flash what needs to be done. Since life is short, there's an urgency to things, and no time for argument. Your mate's views, if any, aren't worth considering. How could they be better than the ones *you* have? Someone's got to manage the marriage, and you've no doubts about whom that will be. In fact, you've no doubts, period.

Here's how it sounds in practice. Marcia is trying to get a message through to Sam as he marches along toward the airport departure lounge.

Marcia: Look, for the last time I'm telling you, war souvenir or not, you shouldn't be taking it onto the plane!
Sam: Calm down; you worry too much. I've paid for the tickets so I'm taking what I damn well want. That grenade's harmless, I removed the explosive when I was still in the Pacific. Besides, they only check out suspicious-looking characters and hippie punks.
Marcia: No, no, *everyone*—there's an electronic gadget and . . .
Sam: Hah! Trust you to get the story wrong—that's only installed at *international* airports. Come on, they're calling the flight.

Sam might be surprised later on at what happens, but for the moment there's no turning him around from his self-appointed course. If he's nabbed, no one else—be it Marcia, the airport cops or the Supreme Court—is likely to convince him that he's done anything wrong.

1,9

The style shown in the upper left corner of Figure 1 is one where there is *low* concern for *what happens,* together with *high* concern for your *mate.* Your major attention and interest focuses on your mate as a unique and lovable person. Sensitive consideration of the current state of your mate's feelings, with a desire to maintain these at a constant euphoric level, overshadows everything else. The field of perception and foresight, where practical matters and needs might be noticed, is blanked out of your attention.

An aspect of the 1,9 style is in constantly "giving oneself" to the other person. But it's no sacrifice. A 1,9-oriented person finds delight in being absorbed with the other mate's individuality as though it were his own.

Frank has learned to be a good listener. He is hearing Isabel as she expounds her program of civic activity and his new role in it.

Isabel: . . . of course, they already knew my husband was a well established lawyer, and I believe that was a factor in my getting elected to the Committee.

Frank: Oh, I'm sure it was *you* who impressed them, not me, honey.

Isabel: Thanks, but you're too modest. Anyway, these people we're trying to help have *so* many problems with their landlords, the police, the municipality and whatever; they need counseling, they need professional advice, they've no money—it's a godsend having you to call upon.

Frank: In what ways can I help them, Belle?

Isabel: In so *many* ways, it's hard to describe. The big thing is having you available, so that anytime I meet up with someone who has these difficult problems, I can just tell them to call you on the phone or go round to the office . . .

Frank: I'm only too happy to be able to help you and them, Belle, but I'm afraid it will have to be on my own time mainly. Y'know, we have a rather heavy caseload at present, and there's this system of recording our daily activities for billing purposes. And the other partners mightn't be very pleased to see these, er, unfortunate people wandering in to interview me . . .

Isabel: Now Frank, you're not starting to wiggle out of your commitment, are you? You *do* sincerely want to help, don't you.

Frank: Why, of course, darling. I was only saying . . .

Isabel: Good, well, that's settled, and I'll do my best not to embarrass you in front of the other partners. I *had* thought, that they'd admire you all the more for your public-spiritedness and social conscience. And as for not being a good discreet wife . . .

Frank: Don't get me wrong, please, I only meant . . .

So he's fallen into line, and the law office looks like being drafted into Isabel's voluntary social mission, even though it needs non-paying clients like it needs bookworms eating the library. This conversation, by the way, illustrates the point that awkward mismatches can occur between life at work and life at home. We'll return to that later. But here it can be said that poor Frank is in a tug-of-war he can't win, but can't afford to lose. If he pleases his wife, which he wants to do, he bugs his colleagues.

1,1

Low-low—these are the degrees of concern found in the lower left corner of the Grid. If you're a person in this position, *what happens* matters little. Furthermore, your *mate* is someone who's not worth bothering about.

Do people get married while in this state of mind, or does something suddenly happen to them, or does it gradually develop? All three are possible. There are those who marry each other grudgingly, expecting little from the years ahead. They drift together. Others, whose expectations are badly transgressed by what the other mate does, but who feel "obligated," might plunge into this Grid corner after losing hope or after a battle which has left a poisoned aftermath, but from which retreat is impractical. Yet it may be that the largest number of married 1,1s are those who have not noticed how their relationship is sinking downward into dullness over the years.

Here's an example of this kind of peaceful nonexistence. One night a row of books somehow started tumbling off the shelf one by one, and Alice, muttering irritably, went to pick them up. She hardly noticed what the titles were—Cliff and she didn't go in much for reading—so it was more the different size and shape of one of them, as she picked it up, that prompted her to look at it.

Alice: Hey, Cliff, here's the old honeymoon album.

Cliff: Let's have a look. My, we look happy in that one, don't we?

Alice: I remember where that was taken, it was just near the Wishing Well.

Cliff: What did we wish for, Alice?—I'm hanged if I can remember, can you? Alice? Great Scott, what are you crying for?

Alice: Suddenly . . . it all came back to me, how much we wished for. And look how little we've got!

Cliff: I don't understand you, Alice, are you feeling all right? "How little we've got?" Why, the mortgage is paid off, our investments are getting quite sizeable, and I can retire with a good pension in a few years' time . . .

Alice: I mean our lives and how we've wasting them. What do we do, sit around like this evening after evening til you retire, and then sit around some more until they cart us off to the funeral parlor?

Cliff: Well, I don't see . . . We have our interests and we pass the time . . .

Alice: That's not what we were wishing for! Look at us there, we were celebrating the future we thought we could have as lovers and friends. We've drawn apart, Cliff, terribly. Who would celebrate a future of "passing the time"? What can we do about this?

Cliff: Bear up, old girl, I know how it is with women who're having the change of life . . .

Obviously Cliff hasn't had the same awakening of insight into the contemporary poverty of their relationship that has stricken Alice. And with Cliff not cooperating, Alice can't see how to turn their marriage around.

5,5

What puts this style smack in the middle of the Grid is *half-and-half* concern on each axis. "Moderation in all things" is the keynote; anything more intense than that seems "way out." So it comes about that a "reasonable" degree of concern for What Happens is conceived of as balancing with and stabilizing a moderate personal concern for the other mate. Within the 5,5 orientation there is a sense of caution. The person restrains himself from "going too far," or "looking silly," or being "gung ho." It is as though he feels that if he put emphasis on performance in practical activities—the *what happens* axis of the Grid—he would be exerting an adverse influence on the *mate concern* marriage relationship dynamics; and vice versa. This is a quite prevalent belief and is closely associated with another core 5,5 notion. If you don't immediately know what's "right," how do you find out? *Other* people, whom you respect and admire, set the patterns and trends. You make their attitudes, thinking and behavior, part of your own, and this keeps you in step in the community, at the dinner table, and even in bed.

The "social models" that 5,5-oriented persons select for their guidance in married life are chosen mainly for respectability-and-status attributes. You copy them in the belief that what "they" have will become part of your own life style as well. Usually you focus upon what seem to be the average of current tendencies among your friends, for it might seem too risky to single out some distinctive individual for imitation. "Doing as others do" is a very easy way of avoiding decision problems about what, in a contemporary sense, is not too little, not too much, but just enough. Group behavior, as you know it, is the midpoint between all extremes, and thus "safer" as a model than might be the behavior of one person, however principled. Besides, from these social groups you can pick up the current line on what normal husbands and normal wives do, and so have a blueprint for arranging your own individual lives as mates. As for matters which are too technical or intimate to be brought up and discussed within your circle of friends, you probably rely on the advice of authoritative gurus you encounter in the popular media.

Russ is talking to Celia about their son, Johnny.

Russ: Hal and Bert and the other fellows want me to get young Johnny started in the Little League this Saturday when the season begins. I don't like them kidding me about our delicate little Lord Fauntleroy. I want Johnny to get interested in football, just like any other kid.

In this way, Russ has revealed the kind of 5,5 motivations to which he responds. He's trying to sweep his wife into agreement by using social pressure arguments rather than by giving direct consideration to Johnny and what would be helpful to his development.

9,9

The 9,9 viewpoint is summarized in the upper right corner of the Grid. This is where *concern for what happens* and *concern for your mate* are both high. They blend together and result in thinking, feelings and actions of the following kinds.

As a 9,9-oriented mate, you live by the premise that close attention to your mate's thoughts and feelings is essential for getting things done in a way that can be rewarding and gratifying to you both. Your assumptions lead you to conclude that no practical matter in which your mate has a vested interest should be ignored. You believe in going "all the way" on both dimensions of the Grid, with both concerns fusing with one another at a high level. This basic 9,9 aim can indeed be realized in everyday married life. Both concerns can be high *and* mutually supportive. They can be synergistic in the sense that their welding into a oneness of attitude promotes zest, achievement, and loving intimacy.

Carolyn and Alex are discussing what to do next weekend.

Carolyn: You know, we've never been into the National Forest; that's about a hundred miles east of here.

Alex: That's right. Where's the map? . . . What do you feel like doing—camping, walking the trails from the alpine part to the valleys, or just driving around to get to know the area?

Carolyn: They're all fun to do—maybe we could sample them all.

Alex: Let's see. If we started way up here, we could go down this trail and reach the Big Trees tourist camp by evening. Then we could spend the next day following the riverside path to Egret Lagoon. But that means the car's still parked up there at the Divide. Back to the drawing board!

Carolyn: There's a township here, just two miles from the Lagoon. We could leave the car there, and hire someone to drive us up this road to the Divide. I'll try telephoning the service station at Oxbow, to find out about transport.

Carolyn and Alex get a lot of pickup from each other's ideas as these are freely expressed and improved upon. Soon a highly original and mutually enjoyable program for their weekend is being selected from the possibilities they've explored. You may sense, too, how their considerateness for each other—*mate* concern— merges significantly into, and stimulates creative thinking about the practicalities—*what happens*. In this example it pertains to where and by what route they plan to go, and what are interesting things to do and see along the way. Yet their planning is by no means rigid, and we might expect that the spontaneity and intimacy so evident in this discussion will show up in many new activities, in the spirit of the moment, as they hike along the trails. On a larger scale, this self-renewing freshness, with perceptiveness to opportunities, can invigorate and enrich a lifetime for those who adopt 9,9 assumptions and follow through on their implications.

Here and There on the Grid

As you see in the diagram, there are nine different degrees of concern shown on the *what happens* axis and another nine that represent successively higher degrees of *concern for your mate*. So, as we mentioned earlier, each of the 81 positions on the Grid represents a particular combination of concerns for *what happens* and for *one's mate*; a combination that is different in some respects from all the other 80 possibilities. Nonetheless, the basic assumptions that underlie those positions adjacent to any one of the five distinctive Grid styles already described vary from these latter ones only by a degree or two either way. For example, 8,2 and 7,3 have close resemblances to 9,1 although their degrees of concern are "one degree up, another degree down" in relation to it. The same goes for 2,8 and 3,7 as compared with 1,9, and so on. Really, then, there is no need to be over-precise when trying to pinpoint your own or another person's position on the Grid. Probably it has more resemblances to one of the five main Grid styles than it has differences.

However, there are two exceptions to be made to this general rule. The first of these is that there are people who combine two or even more recognizably different Grid styles in a somewhat consistent way, as a general approach. For instance, the description, "mailed fist in a velvet glove," conveys the sense of a basically 9,1 style whose user knowingly applies a veneer of 1,9 personal warmth and responsiveness so as to apparently soften harsher aspects of a 9,1 attitude—at least, until the going gets rough. This blend of styles is recognizable in numerous actions by one of the mates. Our term for it is *paternalism* or *maternalism,* depending on the sex of the "heavy parent" type of mate. This approach has had a long history in child rearing and animal training—the latter giving rise to the phrase, "carrot and stick." In it there is the inconsistency of opposites, which can be mind-blowing in its long-term effects on your mate.

Other people are ready to occupy any position on the Grid which they feel is warranted so as to further their own individual interests. Hopscotching around the Grid in an attempt to adapt one's behavior to so-called "situational requirements" is what we term *Statistical 5,5.* More subtle manipulative approaches, in which one or a number of different Grid styles are employed as a calculated "front" behind which the person's actual intentions are concealed, are termed *facades.*

A further exception to the generalization that each person's typical approach resembles one of the five principal Grid positions, is the tendency of most people to have one characteristic Grid style which they habitually use when things are going well, plus one or more *backup* styles which come into play when the person is in difficulties which he or she despairs of resolving through the agency of a customary ("dominant") Grid style.

Jessie: Darling, could you come here a minute and help me unlace these granny boots? I'm so tired.
Nev: Hang on a moment, I'm in the bathroom.

* * *

Jessie: Now see what you made me do! I've broken a fingernail on this cussed knot I've been trying to untie! It's all your fault. Come here this minute!

There was no pre-planning in this sudden switch of Grid styles.

It was quite spontaneous and unpremeditated in the sense that Jessie didn't seem to have the maternalist orientation of "I'll coo to Nev first, but if he doesn't come, I'll roar!" Rather, her switch into 9,1 occurred as a consequence of resultless wrestling with the knot, climaxed by bursting her impeccably manicured fingernail. The guilty scapegoat then seemed to be Nev, with his tardiness in the bathroom. Whether he could help that, or whether her blow-up is going to help their relationship, are questions we needn't go into.

If you think of several people you know—including yourself—you can probably turn up many personally experienced examples of shifting from dominant Grid styles to backups. Perhaps you can identify your own typical tendencies in this respect. Dominant-backup shifts can go every which way across the Grid. There are people who have a 9,1 backup ever available behind a more usual 1,1 apathy, and there are those who, feeling defeat, switch from 9,1 into 1,1. 9,9-to-9,1 is not uncommon, and neither are other skids across the Grid.

Nonetheless, some people seem able to maintain the same Grid style, whichever it is, nearly all the time. A frequently-heard comment on this kind of consistency is, "he's just built that way. It's his personality," etc. But this kind of impression doesn't square with the just-as-common observation of people switching from one style to another. So what's at the bottom of it all?

This can be explained in terms of *assumptions:* axioms which are basic to your current interpretation of the world around you, of people and what "makes them tick," and so on. Though you might not presently be in the habit of doing so, it is easy to put assumptions into words and examine how they are related to Grid styles—your own included. "I have to be sweet and submissive, or no-one will love me," is a 1,9 assumption. "I alone know what's right," is a 9,1 assumption. "What's the use, to hell with it," has the flavor of 1,1; "Half a loaf is better than no bread," has a 5,5 ring; and "Onward and upward in unison" is a 9,9 theme.

Now, each of these different assumptions, not to mention others like them, is an *option* for guiding behavior. Each is alternative to every other one. None of them is bred in the bone, though, when habitual and unquestioned, any one of them can seem like the only platform upon which to base one's thinking and action. While being comparable, no one of them, in itself, is provable or measurable; in essence, it is a fundamental belief, and its soundness can only be demonstrated by acting upon it and comparing the consequences with those that would have ensued from action founded on a different assumption—for instance, one that underlay another Grid style. Analysis and comparison of this kind is at the heart of Grid development. Using the comparative approach, and with the help of experiments, people can identify and evaluate the present assumptions underlying their Grid styles, and, if they wish, work to change them in the direction of an alternative style that is seen as better. As for dominant-backup switching, this can be reviewed too. Maybe you will find one style suitable for handling peaceable, or conflict-laden, and even crisis situations, whether at work or within the family.

Getting it all Together

Even if you commute long distances in physical space between home and workplace, these two areas have common boundaries, and indeed, may have some common ground. Maybe your life is so busy and complex these days that the solution you've adopted— as a basis for not getting all mixed up—is to keep work life and home life in separate compartments. Perhaps you feel that it is desirable, as well as possible, to use one particular Grid style at home and another at work. If you're versatile, life can become even more subdivided. For instance, you and your mate may relate to each other with habitual Grid styles (whether the same or not), yet deal with your children in terms of still other Grid styles. It could even be that one child gets the adoring 1,9 treatment while another is being licked into shape according to 9,1 doctrine. Or a child could be experiencing two diametrically different Grid styles beamed at him by his father and mother respectively.

If there are complexities such as these in your whole-life relationships, now could be a good time to run a Grid style inventory on each and all of them, with the purpose of discovering whether across-the-board consistency within a selected "best" Grid orientation can transform your own life and cast favorable rays of influence on other people you live with or meet from day to day.

A key question is, "What particular assumptions would be the ones from which I would feel ready to extend my thoughts and feelings, with reasonable assurance that this personal style would work for me, throughout the many relationships areas of my life?"

HOW THEORY GIVES INSIGHT INTO BEHAVIOR

So this is what the Marriage Grid is all about. In ways analogous to the Managerial and other Grids, it puts emphasis on theory, conceptual understanding, and self-knowledge as a basis for illuminating your most personal experiences. Foresight, and consequently, one's future actions, can be improved by using it. Even more important, it provides a framework for seeing how to change.

Many authors have gotten a lot of tragic or humorous mileage out of the difficulties married people confront in getting clarity on the present states and tendencies of their own behavior and relationships. A common element can be found in the unique skills of Henrik Ibsen (1965), Arthur Miller (1958), Edward Albee (1963), Samuel Taylor (1950), Robert Anderson (1967), Paddy Chayefsky (1957), Tennessee Williams (1958), Frank Gilroy (1962), and Neil Simon (1969); not to mention others. These playwrights are justly famous because they illuminate the personal quandaries that people experience in relation to one another. A significant play or novel "gets to you" because you recognize the distilled reality of the relationship problems it illustrates. Often you are gripped by what you notice as a kind of mutual blindness of two characters as they grope for unity yet lurch past each other into further separateness. If they come together eventually, at the point of resolution of the play or novel, it's as though they've stumbled into mutual understanding by some crisis or happy accident. But as the curtain falls on *A Doll's House, Death of a Salesman,* or *Who's Afraid of Virginia Woolf?,* you will probably recognize that two married people have lost one another more completely than was the case when the curtain rose. The realism that has been sustained throughout these dramas is the realism of poignant human experience.

From our viewpoint in behavioral science, theory is important in altering human events. Some will disagree. Their thesis is that analytical theory has not done much to change behavior. In a way they are half right. Psychologists and sociologists seem to have found little that has changed as a result of their efforts to build theory and explain conduct. Though it might be highly *necessary,* theory by itself is not a *sufficient* basis for changing behavior. Something more is needed: a deep personalized understanding of how a theory illuminates your personal feelings, your daily experiences, and ongoing events. The next essential step after theory is examined experience, and after that, the testing of alternatives.

We can now return to the two instruments introduced earlier and make use of them as illustrating a basis for deepening your knowledge of how Grid theory can aid married couples to strengthen their life together (Scientific Methods, Inc., 1971a). Pressures arising within the operational system of work are potentially a major tension within the marriage system, and so, constitute a dilemma. The same is true of marriage-generated pressures which have effects on the job.

Here are instructions for a team discussion of the Boss Frustration dilemma (see page 128). If you are at home, you and your mate can be the team.

The purpose of the discussion is twofold. One is to determine what each person's Grid style is, as revealed in the reaction to this organization-and-family situation. The other is to determine what would be the "best way" for a mate to react to this situation, in terms of furthering the long-term strength of the marriage.

A suggested way to proceed is as follows. Start with one person who reads aloud his description of how his mate would react to the situation (i.e., what he has written under A, page 129). While he does so, the other team members make notes of what they think the mate's Grid style is, as evident from the description of her likely reaction to the dilemma. Then discussion begins, with the objective of reaching agreement on a team basis, as to the personal Grid style reaction revealed in the written description of this first person. (The question of whether the description is objectively accurate is not considered at this stage.)

Next, another person reads her or his answers aloud, and the same procedure of team discussion and diagnosis of the Grid styles involved takes place. The same procedure is to be completed for each member of the team. For each answer discussed, team agreement should indicate:

"The Grid style evident in my mate's described reaction was _____."

Once the personal reactions are diagnosed, then team agreement is sought in order to answer the following question, which relates to the B answer written on page 129: What would be the "best way" for a person to respond to strengthen rather than weaken the marriage? The answer to this question should be concrete, that is, what should the mate *say*—not in terms of a particular Grid style, but as the response would be expressed in words. Then you can evaluate and assign a Grid style to it.

Team agreement regarding the best way to respond to my mate's reaction: _____

_____

_____

You have now had the opportunity of evaluating your own answer in two different ways. One is from the standpoint of the Grid theory that *others* thought was revealed. The other is from the standpoint of how *you* would have responded in the situation, in contrast with how other members of your team would.

If the need exists, you and your mate could now examine whatever reservations either of you have regarding the accuracy of the "What Would Your Mate Say or How Would She/He React?" *A* answers. Does each of you recognize her-or-himself in the description which the other has written? If not, run a check by referring to the Appendix and picking out one or more sample answers from those listed there; answers which you feel you would typically give. Or, if you prefer, write your own. As a next step, try these out on your mate, and ask whether he or she finds them credible and characteristic of yourself in the here-and-now. Discuss any points of difference until agreement is reached as to how each of you typically would react. Then, if there are alternatives which either of you now consider might be better, discuss these too; and after finding consensus, try to set up an action plan for getting to the kind of relationship you both want.

At this point, the other instrument, whose three items indicate the five principal Grid approaches to *conflict, teamwork,* and *intimacy* can be re-studied. Note and discuss your self-descriptions. In each item, the sequence of Grid alternatives is: 9,1; 1,9; 1,1; 5,5; 9,9.

By now, you have become acquainted with *The Marriage Grid* and samples of instruments that are used by couples in learning how to strengthen their own relationships. This probably gives you a sense of what Grid Family Development is all about and yet, of course, it is much more complex in practice than has been demonstrated in these brief exercises. As mentioned earlier, a whole area of Grid Family Development involves parents and children. Of course it had to be omitted, though it is similar in approach and character to what has already been demonstrated.

To summarize, here are the objectives that Grid Family Development is intended to aid people to achieve.

1. Providing theory to bring insight to bear on personal experience and events.
2. Making learning and development a deliberate objective of couples and families, making these part of their continuing growth experience.
3. Introducing standards of excellence which open up new vistas of marriage enrichment.
4. Aiding couples and families to identify gaps between "what is" and "what is desired," thus providing a basis for marriage by objectives.
5. Inserting new material and providing new experiences that couples might not ordinarily discuss or have the opportunity to use in a growth-giving manner.

The sixth objective brings us back to the title of the paper. It is

6. To enable a person to be a "whole person" by contributing to the strengthening of his marriage in ways congruent with the manner in which he is pursuing growth and development in dealing with problems and people in his job.

GRID ORGANIZATION DEVELOPMENT AND GRID FAMILY DEVELOPMENT

The family is not only the nuclear unit of society, it also is the prototype of other organizations and institutions of society such as government, business, and school. The above seems true from the perspective of history, there being a family theme whenever adults have been able to survive. The nuclear significance of the family becomes apparent, too, from a comparative analysis of societies. Cultural anthropologists, for example, have noticed *variations* such as between the ancient Athenian and Spartan family patterns, the kibbutz, polygamy, etc., but the theme itself remains constant. It is accurate from the standpoint of systematic and conceptual analysis as Freud clearly recognized when he used the family model in studying military organizations and the Catholic church (Freud, 1960).

Family and organization: these are the two dominating social systems affecting the quality of our lives today. We live in one for fifteen or twenty years and then we live in two by taking a job, not to mention starting a new family.

Some people can keep the two pervasive systems closed and separate from each other. But most of us realize these are open systems, and that we can only be "whole" persons when our experience in one of them is both sound and congruent with our experience in the other. Otherwise, we are torn apart, or split asunder with divided loyalties. In the course of a day, for example, person A may argue with a subordinate, snarl at a salesman, harp at his wife, or bully his son. During the same day, person B may reach agreement with a subordinate, thank a salesman for being helpful, enjoy warmth and intimacy in his marriage, and discuss career hopes with his son. In either case, his personal effectiveness as a human being contributes significantly to the quality of his relationship outcomes.

Some of us seem to be effective in one relationship, but failures in another. Consider, for instance, person C who in one day argues with a subordinate, snarls at a salesman, but then, in a quick shift, is able to enjoy warmth and intimacy in his marriage and can discuss career hopes with his son in a constructive way. He is a somewhat unlikely possibility, though C's do exist. More generally, though, if relationships in one institution are bad, they spill over into the other. Every dog knows enough to stay away from someone who has had a bad day at the office. Equally, subordinates learn early to beware of a boss who gets up on the wrong side of the bed. There is another possibility too. At its extreme, person D throws himself into one of the systems and withdraws equally totally from the other. As a result he may be a great manager, but at home he is flesh without flash.

In our personal view, Grid Organization Development and some other approaches have aided men and women in business, industry, and government to develop as managers and working colleagues, thus enabling them to have, in certain significant respects, greater maturity and greater effectiveness in their jobs than women usually develop at home. Women in the traditional "wife and mother" model have not had the same opportunities of exposure to new ideas, new concepts, and new methods of learning. Thus, at this stage in time, it is possible that corporate life is contributing more to personal development than family life does. Yet, we all know that family life is the ultimate personal experience.

Integrated systems of development for organization and home, using the same concepts, the same learning methodologies, and which have been designed and engineered to be useful to people on a do-it-yourself basis, are now available to those who realize that their homes have the same developmental potentials as they have learned to appreciate within their work organizations (Scientific Methods, Inc., 1971c).

APPENDIX

Boss Frustration dilemma
A. What Would Your Mate Say or
   How Would She/He React?
   9,1:   "Stop whining, and shut up."
          "That's you all over—you haven't the guts to stand up to him."
          "Less money?!—you'll go back there in the morning and start earning *more* money."
          "What are you overcompensating for *this* time, little paper tiger?—you make me sick."
          "Biggest mistake I ever made was to marry a LOSER!"
          "Shut up."
          "You *aren't* going to quit."
          "I don't want to hear any more."
   1,9:   "You poor dear . . ."
          "How bad you must feel."
          "I'll get you a tranquilizer right away."
          "Of course you won't go back—they're *killing* you there!"
          "Let's go out somewhere, so you can forget *all* about it!"
          "You're so attractive when you get mad."
          "Let's talk about something more pleasant."
   1,1:   "Something bugging you, huh?"
          "Why bother?—all jobs are like that."
          "Play it cool, and things'll work out."
          "Looks like we're going from bad to worse all the time."
          "Is that all you wanted to say?"
          "I'm too busy to talk right now."
          Silence
   5,5:   "Everyone has days like that sometimes."
          "You'll feel better tomorrow."
          "Ask for a transfer—then you'll keep your seniority."
          "I'll talk to Mrs. Upper at our women's club—her husband can help you a lot."
          "Don't do that; we couldn't keep up appearances if you took another job for less money."
          "Why not talk to the personnel people about that?"
          "How many other people feel this way?"
   9,9:   "Tell me more about it."
          "What's happened to get you so upset?"
          "Before deciding what to do, let's find out whether we're hitting the real issues."

"That's an unusual way for your boss to act—do you have any idea of what got him uptight?"

"It might be worthwhile to look for a new job, but you'd be putting yourself under a handicap if you began by joining the unemployed."

"You're saying a lot. Let's take them one at a time."

P/M: "I'll come in with you tomorrow and straighten him out."

You oughtn't to be working at all. Stay home, and I'll do the bread-winning for us both."

"Now calm down, and don't start anything like that—I doubt whether you could go the distance."

"It's not for you to make a decision like that."

"Your boss was probably right—I've seen you goofing off recently too."

"If you'll calm down and stop acting this way, I'll think up something tonight that will make you feel better."

REFERENCES

Albee, E., Who's afraid of Virginia Woolf? New York: Pocket Books, Inc., 1963.

Anderson, R. You know I can't hear you when the water's running. New York: Dramatists Play Service, Inc., 1967.

Blake, Robert R., & Mouton, Jane Srygley. The instrumented training laboratory. In Wechsler, & E. Schein (Eds.), Issues of human relations training, Washington: National Training Laboratories, National Education Association, 1962.

Blake, Robert R., & Mouton, Jane Srygley. The managerial grid: Key orientations for achieving production through people, Houston: Gulf, 1964.

Blake, Robert R., & Mouton, Jane Srygley. Corporate excellence through grid organization development. Houston: Gulf, 1968.

Blake, Robert R., & Mouton, Jane Srygley. Building a dynamic corporation through grid organization development. Reading, Mass.: Addison-Wesley, 1969.

Blake, Robert R., & Mouton, Jane Srygley. Instruments to create involvement. Sales Meetings Magazine, 1971, 20(7), 62-68.

Blake, Robert R., & Mouton, Jane Srygley. What is instrumented learning? Training and Development Journal, January 1972.

Chayefsky, P. Middle of the night. New York: Samuel French, Inc., 1957.

Freud, S. Group psychology and the analysis of the ego. New York: Bantam Books, 1960.

Gilroy, F. D. The subject was roses. New York: Samuel French, Inc., 1962.

Ibsen, H. A doll's house, translated by Peter Watts. Baltimore: Penguin Books, Inc., 1965.

Miller, A. Death of a salesman. New York: Compass Books, The Viking Press, Inc., 1958.

Mouton, Jane Srygley, & Blake, Robert R. University training in human relations skills. Group Psychotherapy, 1961, 14, (3 & 4).

Mouton, Jane Srygley, & Blake, Robert R. The marriage grid. New York: McGraw-Hill, 1971.

Scientific Methods, Inc. An exercise on dilemmas of marriage. Austin, Texas, 1971a.

Scientific Methods, Inc. An exercise on ideal intimacy. Austin, Texas, 1971b.

Scientific Methods, Inc. The marriage grid: A catalogue of exercises. Austin, Texas, 1971c.

Simon, N. Plaza suite. New York: Samuel French, Inc., 1969.

Taylor, S. The happy time. New York: Dramatists Play Service, Inc., 1950.

Williams, T. Cat on a hot tin roof. New York: Dramatists Play Service, Inc., 1958.

SECTION II

Structural Interventions

A structural intervention in an organization is generally seen as a change in some tangible and usually, technical element of the organization, e.g., rearranging the layout of an accounting department, or some change in the organization chart. Such structural changes could easily be part of an OD effort (Burke & Hornstein, 1972). The kinds of structural interventions reported in this section, however, are different. The first one is a temporary structural change and the last two are permanent ones.

The temporary task force as an organizational intervention has been around for some time but, as Luke points out in his chapter, it has not often been used as an integral part of an OD process. Luke describes how the temporary task force was applied in an organization and then suggests a model for similar task force operations along with specific guidelines for implementing the model.

OD has been defined as a process of cultural change that attempts to *institutionalize* social technologies which regulate subsequent cultural and technological change (Hornstein, Bunker, Burke, Gindes, and Lewicki, 1971). This institutionalization process has three parts: Entry, normative support, and structural support. This latter part, structural support, means to alter the organization structure by placing internal OD personnel in the system who help to regulate subsequent cultural and technological change or, in other words, to regulate the process of OD. In their article, Schmuck and Runkel describe how they accomplished the "institutionalization process" in a public school system. A particularly helpful part of their chapter is a list of major tactics that they recommend to OD practitioners. It is clear that the recommendations are applicable to any organization, not just schools.

What if you had the power to (a) design the organization of a new manufacturing plant to your specifications and (b) select all of the people to man the operation so that you could be insured of the right "fit" of individuals to organizational design? This is probably *the* dream of most OD practitioners. Don King didn't have all of the control I've dreamed, but he did have a fascinating opportunity to influence such a process. In his article he describes a situation where a new food processing plant was to be built, designed, and staffed so that a System 4 (Likert, 1967) organization could be realized. King's opportunity, then, consisted of a chance to influence the organizational structure by placing people in the plant who were "compatible" with a team approach to management.

As every experienced OD practitioner knows, some people respond to and implement participative management processes more readily than others. For example, Jerry Harvey and I have demonstrated that certain personality types, i.e., people who score below average on Rokeach's Dogmatism Scale, are more attracted to laboratory training programs than other types—average or higher scorers (Harvey and Burke, in draft). If amenable people could be selected ahead of time and then given the authority to run a System 4 organization, the chances of actually achieving an open, participative organization should be greater than trying to change a management system that is already in place. King explains the unique design he and his management colleagues used to make their selections and the results.

REFERENCES

Burke, W. W., & Hornstein, H. A. (Eds.), *The social technology of organization development.* Washington, D. C.: NTL Learning Resources Corporation, 1972.
Hornstein, H. A., Bunker, B. A., Burke, W. W., Gindes, M., and Lewicki, R. J. *Social intervention: A behavioral science approach.* New York: The Free Press, 1971.
Likert, R. *The human organization.* New York: McGraw-Hill, 1967.

Temporary Task Forces:
A Humanistic Problem
Solving Structure*

ROBERT A. LUKE, JR.**

Problem solving is the business of organizations, and an organization's style of problem solving is the business of organization development. This article proposes, as one structural intervention, the use of temporary task forces as a means for problem solving that is both productive—moves the organization toward its formal objectives—and is expressive of humanistic values.

Organization development, like sensitivity training, is a term descriptive of nothing and everything. Organization development is not yet a profession. Standards for membership, training procedures for the practitioner and measurable performance standards for practitioners have yet to be fully developed. There are many available statements of what Organization Development is, is not, could be and should be (Bennis, 1969; Burke, 1971; Guest, 1962; Lippitt, 1969; Argyris, 1964; Blake et al., 1964; Greiner, 1967; Lawrence, 1958; Likert, 1967; Schein and Bennis, 1965) among others. In the author's opinion, organization development is the art of developing a process of management, organization administration—what have you—that expresses certain values. Among these processes are goal setting, rational planning, accountability for behavior, locating decision making authority at the source of information, appreciating and legitimizing human needs of individuals, personal growth and development, competence-based influence, self-direction, open and free flows of communication. These processes reflect certain values. For a listing of some of these values, see Burke (1971).

* The author would like to express his appreciation to Vernon R. Averch for his support and assistance.
** Reprinted by permission of the publisher from *Personnel*, May-June, 1970. Copyright 1970 by the American Management Association, Inc.

The model of an effective temporary task force, as described in this article, is not necessarily a new technology for organizational problem solving. The reader will recognize many familiar concepts and procedures. The model attempts to describe a problem solving vehicle which incorporates many familiar OD concepts into a viable structure designed for flexible and creative problem solving. There are six major components of the model each of which represent a departure from traditional modes of problem solving. One of these is expressly that of interpersonal maintenance, but the reader should bear in mind that a temporary task force is primarily a structural intervention, i.e., its effective use is dependent on a particular set of normative standards which, when taken together, support the expression of humanistic values on the job. The temporary task force is not intended primarily as an intervention to change individual's attitudes and relationships independently of an organization's normative structure, though this may well occur as a by-product. The major components, and their traditional counterparts, are described below. The article describes the model and reports on an actual temporary task force in relation to the model. Finally, some thoughts are offered on one strategy for implementing the temporary task force within an organization.

TEMPORARY TASK FORCE COMPONENTS

1. Competence as the criteria for member selection. To make the most effective use of a task force, it is suggested that competence and ability in the relevant areas be the criteria for member selection regardless of an individual's position in the organization. This concept may encounter resistance in those organizations where position and authority are the major criteria for choosing among people.

2. A commitment to long-range planning. To be creative and innovative, a task force needs support from the organization for intensive planning and experimentation in a manner similar to that provided for basic, as opposed to applied, research among scientists. It may be difficult to obtain this support in organizations who seek an immediate return on investment (read member time).

3. Interpersonal openness. To allow for the maximum in idea development, it is important that norms supporting openness and trust among members of the task force be developed. Tactful dis-

agreement and solicitous agreement often prevent a group from getting to the real issues. This may be a particularly difficult norm to develop in view of many organization's preference for interpersonal closedness, i.e., "let's keep personalities out of this."

4. A support giving executive. In these instances when a task force is convened by a major executive, his relationship to the task force can substantially enhance the group's creative potential and productivity to the degree that he actively supports and encourages independent thinking and personal risk taking. A tendency to over-control the task force can stifle a great deal of energy, commitment and creativity on the part of the members.

5. Task relevant interfacing. To avoid the potential implementation problems associated with ivory tower "blue skying," it is suggested the task force make a conscious effort to involve those who will be affected by the group's work in that work. Usually, cooperation from others in the organization will be needed to implement the task force's proposals and their early involvement can be a great asset. Tendencies toward empire building and territoriality needs of the organization's sub-units are possible sources of resistance to task relevant interfacing.

6. Open confrontation with resistance to change. The typical product of a task force represents a change and, for a variety of well known reasons, change engenders resistance. It is suggested this resistance be dealt with openly and directly and be regarded as a source of potential help rather than a source of blockage. When such resistance is avoided the result is usually either an attempt to railroad the proposal through or simply let it die. Either outcome wastes the work of the task force.

A TEMPORARY TASK FORCE MODEL

When there arises an organizational need to explore and develop new ideas, normal operational patterns are often not adequate to the task. An increasingly popular way to develop new ideas that will enable the organization to function more effectively has been to create a temporary task force within the organization—and this entails a wholly different kind of delegation. (An excellent theoretical discussion of temporary task forces is provided by Warren Bennis and Philip Slater in their book *The Temporary Society* [1968].)

Simply defined, a temporary task force is a group of employees selected from several formal organizational units and brought together to solve a specific problem, with the expectation that the group will dissolve when it finishes its work. The temporary task force design provides more flexibility in solving problems than is typically afforded by the traditional bureaucratic structure; it allows those in the company who have specialized skills and resources to form a problem-solving team, apply their special abilities to the task at hand, and propose thoughtful suggestions for action.

However, traditional models of organizational structure prevent the effective functioning of a temporary task force. Organizational norms governing employee rewards, status differentials, styles of management, and utilization of innovations need to be altered to support, rather than fight, the efforts of a temporary task force. The following eight sub-sections will be devoted to an examination of the nature of these changes, to some of the possible consequences for the organization, and to some suggested guidelines for the effective use of temporary task forces.

COMPETENCY OR SENIORITY?

It is assumed that members of the temporary task force are chosen because they possess a special skill or ability relevant to the problem under study. Their selection gives members favorable, and visible, expression of confidence from the executive, so status problems may arise. For example, if the staff person is chosen over his superior, the implicit message is that the former has more of the desired skills for this assignment than does his boss. While selection on a competency basis may be functionally most appropriate, it may create a storehouse of ill feelings on the part of those not chosen but with more organizational power than the task force members.

If a staff member is selected over his line manager, the latter may think that the company has decided to phase him out and replace him with the staff member, and he may then actively block the efforts of the task force, make life miserable for his staff member, or, reading the handwriting on the wall, make plans either to leave the company or to substantially reduce his contribution to it. If replacement of the manager is not behind a staff member's appointment to a task force and he has been selected only because of a specialized competence, the issues of status as well as the rationale for selection need to be made completely clear to both men.

Another frequent approach to selection is the blue ribbon panel concept—that is, appointment of those who have distinguished themselves in other areas and who have some degree of seniority within the company. This avoids the interpersonal issues associated with selection solely for competence, but there is no guarantee that the most revelant skills and resources will be represented on the task force.

Many companies use a promotion and reward system not unlike that of Congress, which rewards individuals for loyalty and length of service. Yet temporary task forces often have to chart unexplored terrain, where precedence and experience may not be appropriate and may, in fact, inhibit fresh, creative perspectives. Thus, it can be seen that the evaluation and status consequences of the seemingly simple act of selection make it by no means simple.

LONG RANGE PLANNING

Once the task force has been composed, the amount of time members have to devote to it needs to be considered. Is it to be a full-time commitment, with members' regular responsibilities postponed or delegated to someone else, or is it to be still another demand on an already overburdened person to be fitted in around his other responsibilities?

Ideally, perhaps, task force membership should be a full-time responsibility, free of other pressures, but this might seem to others in the organization as favored treatment, and their resentment could lead to uncooperative attitudes. On the other hand, to have members responsible for their regular duties in addition to their task force assignment obviously drains off energy from the work of the task force.

The issue of time available to the task force needs to be thought out in advance and considered within the context of the task force's major purpose—creating a new idea or product that calls for creative and intensive work, or a project that realistically can be accomplished simultaneously with other responsibilities. Since the expectation of a quick return on investment (read member time) is characteristic of many organizations, task force members could find themselves being expected and expecting themselves, to develop a new idea on the run. While it is certainly possible to do so, it will almost inevitably be more hit-or-miss than systematic planning and experimentation.

INTERPERSONAL MAINTENANCE

Most task forces are composed of persons who do not work closely with one another and, in many cases, may not even have met each other before. If they are to make maximum use of their collective resources, there is a clear need for the task force members to spend some time developing relationships with one another so that a climate of openness, support, and respect can be constructed before they tackle their assigned problem. The amount of energy that can be spent in carving out one's influence on the group, defending ideas and courses of action, and competing with colleagues is well-known.

The human relations aspects of a temporary task force are critically important. New ideas can be arrived at only in an atmosphere that legitimatizes high-risk approaches and suggestions for what may seem like radical departures from tradition. There must also be fluid and authentic communication, building on others' ideas, and motivations to continue working with this team to produce a final product. This kind of supportive climate does not develop accidentally or by executive whim or fiat; it has to be planned for.

Two steps may be needed—planning a start-up training activity and designing a continuing process in which the task force periodically considers its interpersonal maintenance needs.

PLANNING FOR START-UP

In addition to the usual task-oriented briefing that a task force gets from the executive, attention needs to be given to helping members get to know and trust one another. The company might engage the services of a qualified behavioral scientist for the explicit purpose of helping the members become a team by developing their skills in diagnosing elements of effective group operations, giving and receiving task-related feedback, and developing a climate supportive of personal risk taking. Such an experience would not only enable members to get to know each other more

rapidly, but would also serve as a foundation for continuing interpersonal maintenance work.

CONTINUING MAINTENANCE NEEDS

It might be useful for the task force to take time out periodically
for "stop action" sessions, to discuss how it's doing in terms of
leadership, communication, decision making and support. Fuzzy
communication, dissatisfaction with how decisions are being made,
lack of mutual encouragement, and inadequate leadership are
characteristic of far too many second-rate work groups. If these
issues can be discussed openly by task force members as they relate to the work of the group, the going should be considerably
smoother than if they are ignored.

ROLE OF THE EXECUTIVE

The support given to the efforts of the temporary task force by
the organization's key executives often determines the group's success or failure. The executive who meets with the task force for
a short time at the beginning and then is heard from no more implies that the problem is not a high-priority one or he would be
more actively involved. Merely calling a task force together and
leaving it to its own devices fails to motivate persons to work, except for a vaguely felt need to please the boss. All this does not
mean that the boss must become a member of the task force, but
it does indicate the necessity of his communicating, both formally
and informally, continued interest in task force activities.

The executive who forms a temporary task force has a stake in
the outcome of its efforts. His prestige and status in the company
can be directly affected by the product of the task force; if it is
successful, the executive can claim a share of the credit for being
innovative and imaginative, but if the efforts of the task force meet
with a great deal of resistance or produce nothing of substantial
benefit to the organization, the executive could receive a rather low
grade. Therefore, it is only realistic for the executive who is thinking about establishing a temporary task force to weigh the possible
personal consequences of his actions.

Since the temporary task force presents a challenge to established organizational norms, setting one up can represent a sig-

nificant risk for the executive. As a general rule; it can be expected that the higher the degree of personal risk, as he sees it, the greater will be the executive's tendency to control the work of the task force by making sure that no stone is left unturned. The executive's relationship to the temporary task force therefore involves a delicate balance between his tendency to actively control the task force—or be as inactive as possible—and the task force's need for organizational support that at the same times does not stifle bold and creative thinking.

TASK RELEVANT INTERFACING

As a postscript to these comments, it should be added that, while the executive's support and active interest are critical, a temporary task force has implications for many others in the company, from the initial stage of member selection to final implementation. The active support and collaboration of these people will be necessary if the task force's recommendations are to have any meaning, so they should be fully informed as to the purpose of the task force and involved in work of the task force when this is relevant. This cooperation might be engaged by periodic progress reports and requests for consultations and ideas. A major danger is completely isolating the efforts of the task force from the rest of the organization; its endorsement by the top man will not alone achieve the necessary cooperation.

COPING WITH RESISTANCE

The typical product of a temporary task force is a report recommending a new design for coordination and management or a new product idea. The mere fact that such a recommendation represents a change places substantial obstacles in the path of its implementation. Those most immediately concerned by the proposed change will probably be asked to alter their customary style of management, marketing, advertising, and so forth, and they may feel a degree of threat as a result.

New skills in which they have no training may be called for, the security built up over a long period of time is shaken, and the recognition that the task force's recommendation is an improvement over the current situation, which those affected may have had a large role in creating, may be seen as an implicit charge of in-adequacy. If the recommendations represent conclusions that both the task force members and others concerned have agreed upon, the transition from recommendation to action will be smoother than if there has been no prior involvement. The higher the level of threat, the less chance there is of active cooperation from those in the company who are central to implementing the recommendations.

Even if threat is not a major factor, sparking interest and commitment may present a problem. Inaction is a very effective means of blocking the implementation of any proposed change, so if the task force's recommendation is merely filed or returned for additional study, there is little hope of its being implemented. It follows that a good deal of thought should be given to involving in the task force's decision those who will be affected by it, in order to reduce the feelings of threat or disinterest that might nullify the task force efforts.

The value of involvement of task force members themselves in the implementation process is frequently overlooked, as once they have completed their report, the members disband and have little more to do with the project. But the recommendations of the report will have to be transmitted to a new group. Just as it is desirable to have continuity between task force members and organization members when the task force is at work, so it is desirable to maintain continuity between recommendations and action afterward by asking several or all of the task force members to become part of the implementation team.

In addition to the necessity for linkage between the task force and the implementation, it is suggested that the task force model be applied to the implementation process, i.e., those responsible for implementation be selected on a competency basis, realization that implementation of new programs takes time, planning for interpersonal maintenance and task relevant interfacing and openly confronting resistance as it is encountered.

A by-product of the success of a temporary task force may be an enduring change in organizational climate. The executive's major purpose in establishing a temporary task force lies in its superior problem-solving capabilities. As we have seen, the organizational climate in which the successful task force works is one that supports long-range planning and systematic problem solving, job-related human relations training, competency-based influence, innovative uses of the formal system, and perhaps most important, significant commitment to develop new ideas and see them through the implementation stage. The precedent established by the successful temporary task force can turn out to be the source not only of new ideas but of a more humanistic style of organizational problem solving style.

AN ACTUAL TEMPORARY TASK FORCE

So much for the model.[1] What follows is a description of the operation of a Temporary Task Force within a large, industrial organization. This particular Task Force experience was chosen because it rather clearly demonstrates the problems associated with this Organization Development technique within a rather traditional organization. The way in which the Task Force was initiated and implemented is similar to the way in which most major changes are initiated and implemented within this organization.

A large company was in the process of developing a new and comprehensive personnel payroll system. The need was to select a computer program which would meet the particular recording and retrieval needs of the company's information system. The task for selecting the right program was large and complex and the changes envisioned by the process would eventually affect 20,000 people.

A senior Vice-President convened a meeting of Vice Presidents and Corporate Directors from the revelant operation departments of the company. The executive charged the group to select a program and implement it. The executive defined those at the meeting as the Steering Committee for the Task Force. He further selected several staff members who would serve on the Working Task Force. Several other members were selected for the working task force by their immediate superior. The senior Vice-President convened a joint meeting of the Steering and Working Task Forces where he explained the need for the program, expressed his personal interest and commitment to it and asked the Working Task Force to commence work immediately.

1. The model was developed prior to the actual task force herein described and published separately (Averch & Luke, 1970). That article was itself used as an intervention to stimulate interest in a temporary task force.

Several important issues around the organization of both task forces were not taken up. Among these were the level of commitment to the project, the working relationship between both task forces, the amount of time task force members were expected to devote to the project and leadership responsibilities among members of the Working Task Force.

MEMBER SELECTION

The senior Vice President selected members of the Steering Task Force and some of those on the Working Task Force. Other members of the Working Task Force were selected by their V.P. In selecting the Steering Task Force members, he was concerned with having the top man from all affected departments represented. The criteria used for those he assigned to the Working Task Force are less clear. Presumably, he chose individuals in whom he felt the most confidence but whether a competency or seniority criteria was used is not known. Of central importance is the fact that the senior Vice President was the central person in selecting members for both task forces.

INTERPERSONAL MAINTENANCE

At its first meeting, the Working Task Force found itself (a) charged with a large and critically important task, (b) composed of people who had little influence over their assignment to the group, (c) lacking a formal leader, (d) expected to work on the task force in addition to their regular duties and (c) unclear about their reporting responsibilities to the Steering Task Force. Fortunately, the project itself was seen by members as in the best interest of their respective departments and this provided a large measure of motivation.

The group met twice without choosing a task force leader and was able to make considerable progress on its own maintenance. Early instances of inter-departmental conflicts were worked through, individuals were able to learn what they needed to know about the work of other departments and thereby identify the relevant resources of each task force member. The Director of Organization Development and a member of his staff joined the group as process consultants to identify and help the group resolve

interpersonal strains and to measure the group's progress in relation to its objectives. This consultant function was maintained
throughout the life of the Working Task Force.

At the third meeting, the Working Task Force selected one of
its own members as chairman. The individual chosen was acknowledged to have both the necessary technical and managerial
skills and was selected by his colleagues—a rare, and in this case
effective, process of selecting a leader. The chairman did an ad-
mirable job of coordinating work assignments, providing direction
and establishing a creative climate for work.

One continuing uncertainty experienced by the Working Task
Force was its authority to make decisions. The function of the
Steering Task Force and its operating relationship to the Working
Task Force was never spelled out. The Steering Task Force met
only twice as a group, though individual members had infrequent
and informal contact with members on the Working Task Force.
Minutes of the Working Task Force's meetings were routinely
distributed to Steering Task Force members and the senior Vice
President. The Working Task Force assumed that no response
equalled approval, and fortunately, the assumption proved correct.
The two Steering Task Force meetings were initiated by the Working Task Force at critical points during the project when explicit
support was needed.

TIME

Having to carry out their regular duties in addition to serving
on the task force caused members to have to work extremely long
hours. It was expected that the task force members themselves
would make a considerable sacrifice in time for the accomplishment of a high priority need of the company without having any
say about it. If the project really was of critical importance, why
could not others in the company take up the slack and thereby
allow the selected task force members to devote full time to the
project? There are continuing instances of a person's regular duties
being occasionally filled by others such as vacations and attendance at outside meetings and conferences. This issue of time rather
clearly demonstrates the assumption that task force work can be
superimposed on the normal routine of the company. While this
assumption proved workable in this instance, it happened only be-

cause task force members were willing to do double duty. One might wonder why the task force members received no support, in terms of extra time, from the company. Time is money, would go the traditional response, but time also reflects a sense of priority and importance. Had the program not been seen as important to the individuals, the necessity to do double duty could communicate to people that the program was of relatively low priority. It is also interesting to note that task force members were responsible to two executives—the senior Vice-President and their own V.P.—rather than the usual one, during the course of their work. This phenomenon raises the question of the V.P.'s commitment to the project for each department V.P. could have given the gift of extra time to his staff member on the task force. The fact that none did suggests the possibility that department V.P.'s supported the project only as long as it did not interfere with normal operations which suggests not all V.P.'s shared in the senior V.P.'s enthusiasm. Fortunately, the question of commitment did not prevent the Working Task Force from accomplishing its purpose but was a central problem during the implementation phase.

IMPLEMENTATION

The Working Task Force selected a program within the allotted time. It had been an intense, creative and productive experience as viewed by all members of the Working Task Force. Their esprit de corps and sense of accomplishment was high. The decision was made to implement the program on a small pilot basis first and then implement it company wide. It was during the implementation phase that the most serious problems arose.

The first need was for a full time project director to manage the implementation. There seemed to be general agreement among many members of the Working Task Force that the best suited person for this role would be the chairman of the Working Task Force. Unfortunately, other projects demanding his time were seen to be of higher importance. For the same reason, none of the other members felt they could lead the implementation phase. A decision was made to hire a project director from the outside who had both managerial and technical capabilities. The individual hired was not able to do an effective job and was shortly relieved. Those who hired him attribute his ineffectiveness to his lack of technical abilities and the fact that he did not formulate a plan for implementation. This being the case, the process of his selection and induction into the company becomes a point of concern. Perhaps a more intensive recruitment and selection process would have helped to guarantee the person's technical competence. In addition, the individual was expected to enter a new situation in a major role which is a difficult task under the best of circumstances. Such a person has to learn for himself what others on the Task Force already know, e.g., the informal patterns of influence and communication, the history of the Working Task Force and the personalities of people involved. The individual's failure to formulate a plan may be partly due to his lack of managerial skill but it may also reflect inadequate training and support from those who hired him and an indirect expression of the relatively low priority which was assigned by his superior to this particular project.

Also complicating the implementation was its timing. The implementation process was to begin at the same time that the payroll department was preparing year end employe tax forms which had to take priority over the implementation of the program. There was also a growing disagreement between members of both task forces over whether the existing system needed to be changed before the new one could be implemented. The senior V.P. felt the old system could be corrected while the new one was being implemented.

Hence, the implementation phase was stymied because of a lack of project management, varying degrees of commitment to its implementation and a disagreement over basic implementation strategy.

The situation came to a head as the result of an elevator conversation between the senior V.P. and a member of the Working Task Force who expressed his feelings of frustration over the lack of progress. This was the first indication the senior V.P. had of the severity of the situation. The senior V.P. responded by calling a meeting of the Steering Task Force and the Working Task Force within the hour which meant not all concerned could attend. The senior V.P. appointed two members of the Working Task Force to head up the implementation effort. One of the two was relieved of her regular job by the senior V.P. while the other was not.

At the time of this writing, the implementation moved slowly. The project competed with many others for scarce time on the

company's computers and no major executive of the company is
actively engaged in the program's implementation.

ROLE OF THE EXECUTIVE

The senior Vice President initiated the task force, decided on
the basic structure—a Steering and Working Task Force—selected
most of the members for both groups but then was not involved in
the on-going work of the Working Task Force. His involvement
came only at trouble spots. During the implementation phase he
was again active in appointing implementation directors and following up on deadlines. It had been mentioned that the executive
who initiatees a task force needs to assume a delicate stance of
control and support. In this case, the control functions outweighed
the support functions. His active involvement in deciding the structure and personnel of the project gave impetus to the effort but he
did not directly address, nor ask the opinion of the others, on
questions of commitment, which he may have assumed, the operating relationship between the Steering and Working Task Forces
or the question of his being continually involved in the task
force's progress.

In retrospect, it appears that he relied primarily on the traditional authority of his position to make major structural and personnel decisions which he then expected others to implement. The
result seemed to be an initial leadership vacuum, varying levels
of commitment and a lack of planning regarding the operation of
both task forces and the implementation phase. Perhaps most
significantly, the question of others' commitment to the project was
never discussed openly. It was just assumed that others in the company would do whatever was necessary to implement his decisions.

IMPLICATIONS

Perhaps the most striking feature of this particular temporary
task force was the process by which it was initiated, controlled and
the way in which work was done. The company relied almost
exclusively on the chain of command and the formal authority of
positions to activate and legitimize the task force. The senior
V.P. essentially ordered the relevant department V.P.'s and their

staff members to accomplish the project through an organization and personnel of the senior V.P.'s own choosing. Neither those on the task force nor those affected by the work of task force were involved in major decisions.

This suggests a need for organizations to consider more seriously the process by which a temporary task force is initiated and works. Of particular importance is the issue of developing the commitment of those involved. In this case, the assumption seemed to be that commitment would flow naturally from the fact that he senior V.P. deemed the project of high importance. Yet, such was not the case and one reason for the lack of commitment could well have been the lack of involvement by others in major decisions. For instance, why a group of V.P.'s as a Steering Task Force? Their steering function was minimally performed and probably not needed. Members of the Working Task Force was experts in their respective fields and the process consultation was able to help the group develop its own internal maintenance. Another factor which may have detracted from commitment was the V.P.'s lack of influence over the deployment of their own staff members. This could explain why task force members were expected to do double duty. The affected V.P.'s still had their department to run and the issue of changing a department's priorities to accommodate the task force was never raised. A clear conflict in priorities between implementation and normal business arose in two of the departments during the implementation phase. Again, the expectation was that implementation could proceed in addition to the normal business of the departments. To date, this has not proven to be a realistic expectation as both implementation of the task force's and peoples' regular duties have suffered.

If we review the experience of this task force in light of the proposed model for task force operations, we see some important deviations.

1. Member Selection: It would appear that the criteria of seniority was used in the selection of individuals to the Steering Task Force while the majority of Working Task Force members were chosen on the basis of the senior V.P.'s judgment of their competence. The experience demonstrated that the formal authority of the Steering Task Force members was not needed during the life of the Working Task Force. The senior V.P. evidently did know the competencies of those selected for the Working Task Force.

Yet, the process of member selection placed additional and unnecessary demands on members of the Working Task Force—
double duty and uncertainty about its relationship to the Steering
Task Force.

2. Priority and Member Time: The Working Task Force knew
the project was of high priority but the requirement that all do
double duty meant that individuals, rather than the company,
would make the necessary accommodations. To have been at least
partially relieved of regular duties would have been a welcome sign
of company support for the members.

3. Interpersonal Maintenance: The internal maintenance of the
Working Task Force was planned for and greatly facilitated the
work of the group. This experience, however, points up the need
for interpersonal maintenance work to be done between the executive who initiates a task force and those who carry it out. The relationship between the senior V.P. and both task forces was based
on the relative authority of positions. This resulted in relatively
low levels of commitment on the part of members on the Steering
Task Force and considerably slowed the implementation phase.

4. Role of the Executive: This experience would suggest that
the executive who initiates a task force needs to be more actively
concerned with questions of developing commitment, planning
with others the developmental and implementation phases and
maintaining contact with the task force. Reliance on the chain of
command, particularly during the implementation phase, did not
prove sufficient.

5. Interfacing: The problem solving of the Working Task
Force was creative rather than reactive. However, this task force
experience points up the needs for creative problem solving around
implementing a task force structure in an organization. The style
of the senior V.P., for instance, was largely reactive; no structural
changes or changes in departmental priorities were made to accommodate the task forces, and the managerial needs of the project
were not planned for.

6. Implementation: The lack of commitment to and a plan for
effective implementation was particularly noticeable as was the lack
of continuity of people from the task force effort to implementation. Members of the Working Task Force did creative work and
were satisfied with the effort. The difficulties with implementing
the program deflated the feelings of success and accomplishment

among those on the Working Task Force. Several members have indicated a lack of interest in serving on future task forces.

IMPLICATIONS FOR THE OD CONSULTANT

If it is assumed that the temporary task force model represents a vehicle for problem solving in a manner expressive of humanistic values, the case example demonstrates some of the consequences of trying to "shoehorn" such a vehicle into an organization which basically does not support such values. If we further assume that a humanistic value foundation is necessary as a growth culture for this and other OD technologies, the question for the OD consultant is how to develop such a culture? This is basically a strategy question. A frequent answer has been to confront the client with the array of OD technology-consultation services, attitude surveys with feedback, an assortment of workshops which have developed an endlessly creative flair regarding purpose, design and participants. The basic objective is usually to change attitudes and behaviors. Too often the client is left unconvinced, skeptical or downright hostile. Win-lose confrontations can develop between client and consultant around issues of hardness-softness, people *or* production. One reason for this unfortunate polarization is that consultants too frequently do not feel the client's basic need which is to realize the objectives of the organization be it making telephones or educating children. In addition, OD has yet to deal adequately with power and politics. Current behavior patterns and attitudes are influenced by what people feel will be rewarded. Those who distribute the rewards are the power figures. Hence, it seems realistic that it will ultimately be the power figures, and not the consultant, who will change the values, and therefore the attitudes and behavior of people. Lacking the power to staff the organization with "his men," one model of the consultant's role is to educate the power figures. Education has to occur within the context of the organization's objectives.

To return to the task force example, the senior Vice President initiated the project primarily because he felt the need for such a program was critical. He was willing to try the task force as a new form for work because he was interested in innovative work structures, the description of the model made sense to him and he had a relationship with and confidence in his OD Director. His style of initiating the structure and personnel for the task force was reminiscent of the traditional style of management. The important point is that he was willing to try out the model because he could see a direct link between this OD technology and his needs for productivity.

In this particular organization, OD consultants are seeking ways to educate key executives to try out, and hopefully finally become committed to, an alternative style of work with which to meet objectives. The continuing challenge for the consultants is to see the organization through the client's eyes, in addition to their own, and apply and invent OD technology that convincingly nurtures a growth culture. This approach to OD does mean the consultant has to buy into the objectives of the organization—ie., making a profit by distributing goods and services. A personal choice point for the consultant is raised. Does he or does he not feel good about buying into the client's objectives? It is a question worth answering explicitly.

REFERENCES

Argyris, C. *Integrating the individual and the organization*. New York: Wiley, 1964.
Averch, V., & Luke. R. The temporary task force: Challenge to organizational structure. *Personnel,* May/June, 1970.
Bennis, W. *Organization development*. New York: Addison-Wesley, 1969.
Bennis, W., & Slater, P. *The temporary society*. New York, Harper & Row, 1968.
Blake, R. et al. Breakthrough in organization development. *Harvard Business Review*, Nov.-Dec., 1964, pp. 133-155.
Burke, W. W. A comparison of management development and organization development. *Journal of Applied Behavioral Science,* 7, 1971.
Greiner, L. E. Patterns of organizational change. *Harvard Business Review,* May/June, 1967, Vol. 45, No. 3.
Guest, R. *Organizational changes*. Homewood, Ill., Irwin-Dorsey, 1962.
Lawrence, P. R. *The changing of organizational behavior patterns*. Cambridge, Mass., Harvard University Press, 1958.
Likert, R. *The human organization*. New York: McGraw-Hill, 1967.
Lippitt, G. *Organizational renewal*. New York: Appleton-Century-Crofts, 1969.
Schein, E., & Bennis, W. *Personal and organizational change through group methods*. New York Wiley, 1965.

Integrating Organizational Specialists into School Districts

RICHARD A. SCHMUCK and
PHILIP J. RUNKEL*

No school district, no matter how well adapted to its current community, can remain adaptive by preserving a particular structure and process. As the community changes, the functions of the school must change, and schools presently are being urged to change in thoroughgoing, even radical ways. As we see it, organization development for schools should strive primarily to develop an institutionalized capability for adaptive change. In fact, we think that training in organization development should become a regularized activity within school districts. It is the rare educational organization that contains systematic methods for scrutinizing its own functioning and redirecting its efforts toward new, more adaptive goals and procedures.

It is one thing to state that training in organization development should be built into every school district and something else to specify a practical means by which this can be brought about. Should every school district maintain a member of the OD Network on a retainer fee? Should the district call in some firm of management consultants during periods of crisis or when things get too much out of kilter? Should school districts hire their own, *permanent* OD consultants? From these and other suggestions for ways of making organization development available to school districts, we have chosen one referred to as the *subsystem of organizational specialists,* and we believe it holds great promise. In this paper, we describe the role of the organizational specialist, two actual groups of these specialists now at work, the values that guide us, some theory about the functioning of these specialists in OD

* Richard A. Schmuck is Professor of Educational Psychology and Philip J. Runkel is Professor of Psychology, both at the University of Oregon. Both are also members of the Center for the Advanced Study of Educational Administration (CASEA) where they have collaborated on research and development on OD for schools during the past five years. CASEA is a national research and development center established under the Cooperative Research Program of the U.S. Office of Education.

and a few practical steps for establishing a team of organizational specialists that we have learned from our theory and from our field trials.

ROLE OF THE ORGANIZATIONAL SPECIALIST

The strategy we propose by which organization development can become available to a school district on a continuous basis is that of establishing an agency for organizational training inside the district. But has not this scheme already been tried and found to have serious faults in many applications? Is it necessary when so many organizational consultants are looking for work? We believe our scheme is not one that has already been tried. We believe it is necessary because consultants from outside the district cannot provide the kind of continuous availability that school districts need. And we believe that establishing and maintaining teams of organizational specialists in school districts will provide plenty of work for professional OD consultants. Moreover, we believe our particular scheme endows the team of specialists with much of the advantage the outsider gains from not being entangled in the past and future of the organization. At the same time, our scheme has the advantage of the insider who has already made entry, who has a constantly ready fund of diagnostic information, and who is on salary and on the job.

Key features of the team of specialists

We now describe features of the team of organizational specialists that can give it its special effectiveness for a school district.

Team and subsystem. The first essential feature of organizational specialists is that they are organized into a team and subsystem. They must have confidence in the abilities of one another, and they must trust one another to carry forward the goals of the group. This mutual confidence and trust should be sufficiently thorough that specialists can form subteams quickly when a request for consultation is received. The entire team must also become a subsystem of the district; that is, it should be viewed as a group carrying out legitimate and important activities. It must be identifiable as a group, have a supporting budget, and be known by others in the district to have a budget. In a district of about 600 staff, we have found that a subsystem of specialists can operate well if it is financially supported on an annual basis by one-half the coordinator's salary, one-tenth to one-fifth of most other specialists' salaries, and a few thousand dollars per year for releasing occasional hours of the personnel with whom the specialists are working.

Part-time assignment. The second important feature of the subsystem of specialists is their part-time assignment to the role. This feature brings them the advantages of being both insider and outsider. The fact that the specialist, during most of the week, is a teacher, counselor, principal or assistant superintendent like anybody else means that he is already "one of the boys." Unlike the ouside stranger, there is little need to worry that the specialist may use the district for his own purposes and never be seen again. The part-time specialist, too, will not be likely to carry out his duties as organizational specialist at the expense of teachers or principals, because he is himself a teacher or principal. And while the part-time specialist gains these advantages of the insider, he can also acquire a vital advantage of the outsider. He can enjoy detached status because of the fact that most districts are large enough that a member of one school is in fact an outsider to a member of another school. We find that members of one school will accord trust and confidence to an organizational specialist employed as a teacher in another school in much the same way that they will give trust and confidence to a consultant on fee.

The part-time assignment of specialists gives the whole scheme certain advantages beyond those of the insider and outsider. One is the fact that each specialist becomes a channel of communication between his own segment of the district and the team of specialists as a whole. Another is that each specialist becomes a source of support and expertness when others of his specialist-colleagues are working with the segment of the district of which he is a regular part.

Own renewal. The third feature is that of self-renewal within the specialists' subsystem itself. The specialist should establish training and selection procedures by which to replenish their own ranks. They should employ procedures to maintain strength in their own group dynamics. And they should maintain liaison with outside agencies and consultants from whom they can learn more about organizational development and upon whom they can call for special help.

Readiness. The fourth feature is that organizational specialists do not administer, direct, supervise, or install. They wait for the school or department to demonstrate readiness to make use of aid before they offer their wares. Even when called on, the specialists sometimes make doubly sure of the client's readiness by working out tentative stages of mutual commitment to the project.

Process, not content. Finally, organizational specialists should not give advice about the content problems. They do not pose as experts in curriculum, finance, teaching methods, or whatever. Instead, they offer a greater range of group and organizational processes than school people ordinarily use as help to members of the district in working on their own important problems. The specialist offers methods, of working toward answers; he does not offer the answers themselves. As long as the specialist restricts himself to offering process and method, his client need never feel that his own expertness is being taken out of his hands.

Activities of the specialists

It is through work with the organizational and interpersonal processes in the district that the specialists become most visible. The specialists train others in communication skills, innovative group processes, and problem-solving procedures. They provide a source of fresh ideas on new ways of working together and serve as a channel through which other people's innovative ideas about organizational procedures—both from within and without the district—can be brought to points where they can be converted into reality. Seven kinds of activity that frequently recur in the work of the specialists are listed below. Along with each, we mention some skills the specialists seeks to transmit and some sorts of actions through which school people sometimes make use of their new skills.

1. Organizational specialists try to develop clear communication up, down, and laterally. Toward this end, they teach communicative skills such as paraphrasing and perception checking. It sometimes happens, as a result, that a school faculty asks for a workshop in which all its members can improve the communicative methods they use with one another.

2. Specialists seek to increase the understanding people have of the ways different parts of the district affect one another. A useful skill is that of using systematic information-gathering techniques such as questionnaires, interviews, and direct observations.

Members of the district often arrange sessions at which the information is given back to school faculties, central-office departments, parent groups, and others.

3. Specialists help spread skills in writing educational objectives and specifying operational definitions as an aid to understanding the educational goals held by persons in various parts of the district. Toward this same end, groups from different parts of a district sometimes meet to compare the observable and behavior outcomes toward which they are striving.

4. Specialists try to improve the skill of groups in systematic problem solving. Many different kinds of groups can invite specialists to help them make their problem solving and decision making more systematic and susceptible to monitoring; examples are teaching teams, departmental bodies, meetings of department heads, and committees of all sorts.

5. Specialists encourage schools and districts to develop new ways of assessing progress toward educational goals. They often refer school people to experts in collecting evaluative data, in systems analysis, and in other technical aids.

6. Specialists try to bring into use the relevant knowledge, skill, and energy of all persons involved in a task. Toward this end, they teach communicative skills that can increase participation in small group discussion. They offer consultation on effective procedures for running meetings. They also arrange confrontations between groups to reduce misapprehensions and increase the amount of correct and realistic information each group has about the other with which it must work. Groups in schools and districts can profit from diagnosing the influence processes in which they are embedded, comparing their diagnoses with diagnoses made by other groups, and developing plans for opening new paths for influence.

7. Specialists are always alert for innovative practices that can serve the goals of school and district. To locate structures and processes where innovation is needed, specialists watch for expressions of frustration and for creative practices even when they cause anxiety. Specialists teach others, too, to help make both frustration and creativity more visible to all. One frequent technique is to bring together the people with frustrations and those with creative ideas, in preparation for later problem-solving activity.

THE KENT PROJECT

Now that we have described the chief features of a team of organizational specialists and their typical activities, we shall describe briefly two projects in which teams of specialists have been established in school districts. The first is referred as the Kent Project.

As part of a 2½ year intervention, we as consultants from the Center for the Advanced Study of Educational Administration (CASEA), established a team of organizational specialists in the school district at Kent, Washington. As consultants from outside, we launched the organizational development project but later turned over the task of continued training to organizational specialists within the Kent district.

Our first contact with Kent came through a counselor who had obtained approval to visit us from members of the superintendent's cabinet. Early contact with the superintendent's office was cautious on both sides, since the district had recently spent a large sum of money for a management-consultant firm to study and recommend a reorganization of the district's organizational structure. This reorganization had been mostly accomplished, but among the consequences were a high degree of suspicion on the part of many teachers and a good deal of misunderstanding by all of the new structure.

The superintendent and his cabinet granted initial approval to the project during a meeting in September, 1967, and a steering committee was formed, containing representatives from all levels of the district's professional staff and one from the public sector. This committee was liaison between CASEA and the Kent district and was intended to have advisory responsibilities for the OD project.

In all, the period of entering the district lasted seven months. During this period we met with the building principals and representatives to the local educational association. We tried to gain approval from every level of the professional hierarchy so that the project would be "owned" by the entire district and not simply by the management. Because each building was being represented by a principal and at least one representative to the education association's board, and because we had sought approval at meetings of principals and of the education association's board, we hope'd that each building staff would also be agreeable to the project. As it turned out, this often was not the case, and the process of entering negotiating, and committing subsystems to engage in OD training had to be repeated through the tenure of the project.

We carried out training events in several important parts of the district during the year before the team of specialists was started. Although most of the personnel of the district were aware of the training at least vaguely, 30 percent or perhaps more were never directly involved because of limited time and resources of the CASEA staff. These training events were designed to increase the communication and group problem-solving skills of teams of personnel filling influential line and staff positions in the district, both in schools and in the central office. Our plan was to demonstrate the benefits of OD training to personnel in a variety of such key positions. A skeletal summary of these events is presented here; details can be found in Langmeyer, Schmuck, and Runkel (1971).

Stage 1: Training for Personnel with Line Functions

In April, 1968, we invited certain personnel performing line functions in the district to the first training event. Trainees included the superintendent and his cabinet, the elementary and secondary principals, and teachers who were leaders within the Kent Education Association. At least one teacher from every building attended the meeting, along with the officers of the association.

The event lasted four days, but only the superintendent's cabinet was present all of the time. On the first day, before others arrived, the superintendent and his cabinet discussed ways in which communication was breaking down among them, the lack of clarity in their role definitions, the ambiguous norms that existed in the cabinet, and, finally, their strengths as a group.

On the second day, the principals joined the cabinet in a specially designed intergroup confrontation that brought into the open organizational problems seen by each group as involving the other. Next, on the evening of that same day, teachers arrived to join the principals and cabinet, and for four hours these influential line personnel generated a list of organizational problems in the Kent district. The principals went back to their buildings the next day, leaving time for teachers and cabinet to interact in a modified intergroup confrontation. On the fourth and final day, the cabinet met alone to summarize the week and to schedule some dates for their own problem solving.

This initial training event served partly the purpose of direct training and partly the function of a demonstration in OD. Most of the participants were convinced of the usefulness of laboratory training for organization development, and many of them helped to bring us friendly receptions later in their own parts of the districts.

Stage 2: Training for Principals in Human Relations

All principals were strongly urged to participate in a basic human relation laboratory that was offered in June of 1968 by the National Training Laboratories of the Northwest, and all did. In general, the training brought about increased skill in interpersonal relations and increased awareness of the effects of one's own responses on others (Thomas, 1970). We have no evidence, however, that this training facilitated our own work of organization development in the district. On the contrary, we believe it hindered our work to some degree by leading the principals to believe that OD training and the work of the organizational specialists would be similar to the T-group experiences they had had.

Stage 3: Training for Personnel with Staff Functions

Personnel in staff roles in the divisions of Student Personnel Services and Curriculum Development attended a three-day conference in September 1968; they were joined for one-half day by the principals. Just as when the line personnel received training, these groups participated in a period of intergroup confrontation that unearthed a number of problems for systematic work. Each group began to work through a sequence of problem solving and made concrete plans to continue these efforts "back home." This event left the participants with mixed feelings.

Stage 4: Training for the Business Department

In November, 1968, the business personnel who had not yet been involved in the training were given two days of training in communication skills, group exercises, and problem solving. The training was similar in spirit and design to the events with the line and staff personnel, except that no confrontations with other role groups took place. The results seemed helpful but not remarkable.

Stage 5: Training for Selected School Staffs

From September 1968 to April 1969, we worked with five school staffs. These training sessions were aimed at introducing a large number of teachers to the benefits of OD and at reaching subsystems within the district other than the administrative personnel. The chief effect of these training events was to increase the awareness of a number of personnel of the meaning and procedures of OD. Certain of these schools later requested more work in OD from the organizational specialists; others did not. Perhaps the most significant result of these interventions was that many of the volunteers to be trained as future specialists came from the buildings in which some training took place.

Recruiting the Kent specialists

In the spring of 1969, information was circulated throughout the district that a workshop would be held in June 1969 for Kent personnel who wished to become organizational specialists. The mimeographed circular stated that the specialist would become knowledgeable and skillful in group processes. He would serve on committees to give feedback or as a trainer for special groups within the district. We hoped that personnel from all hierarchical levels would volunteer to become organizational specialists.

The first steps in establishing the role of organizational specialist in the district had already been taken when the school board approved the original contract, but it was imperative that the role be supported with released time, a part-time coordinator, and the official blessings of the district. There were several tense moments when the teachers were negotiating for a new contract and early reports seemed to indicate that adequate money might not be available—but commitments to the project were high and the matter was resolved with ten days allotted to each specialist for OD work during the school year. Further, a part-time coordinator was appointed.

Applications were solicited from all professional members of the school district. Twenty-three district personnel were selected from those who applied. They represented a very wide cross section of the district: teachers, counselors, principals from elementary and secondardy schools, curriculum and student personnel specialists, and assistant superintendents.

Training the Kent specialists

The Kent specialists began their training with a two-week workshop during June, 1969. The goals of the first week's sessions were to introduce them to many of the techniques, exercises, procedures, and skills that we had found useful in OD; to provide each of them with an opportunity to explore the impact of his behavior on a group; to establish them as a cohesive, vital, functioning unit; and to give them practice in leading some training activities. The participants spent the first three days in small groups going through many exercises and activities, with participants rotating in the role of co-trainer for these activities. In the last two days of the first week, the participants were asked to design activities for themselves that would help strengthen their team—activities focused either on the group or on participants' skills.

For the second week of the workshop, the twenty-three specialists divided themselves into six teams, each containing at least one CASEA trainer. The total group of specialists established potential target groups within the school district and each team selected one potential target with which to work. Among the target activities were workshops for several schools to be held prior to the opening of school or during the year, a continuation of work started with the cabinet at a senior high school, work articulating relations between principals and counselors, and work with a community advisory group. The rest of the week was spent establishing goals for training with the targets, gathering diagnostic data about the targets, analyzing the data to establish forces operating in the target groups, and designing the training events. We worked closely with these subgroups, anticipating the follow-up help we would give to the specialists during the academic year.

We worked with the Kent specialists during the first two-thirds of the 1969-70 academic year, withdrawing in March 1970. Thus, the training events that were engineered by the Kent specialists were observed and criticized by the outside consultants. This collaboration was part of a deliberate plan to support the development of training skills within the specialist team. Approximately ten different training events occurred with our assistance. Most of these events were successful in raising interest in the district in improving communication, group processes, and organizational problem-solving.

Coordinator of the Kent specialists

A key role in helping the specialists to function effectively was carried out by the coordinator. Many of his duties were very similar to those of curriculum coordinators; he handled budget arrangements, stored relevant training materials in his office, kept careful records of the project, served as a convener of the specialists' steering committee, and worked closely with colleges in the State of Washington to arrange for training courses to receive college credit.

Other of his duties were unique in the district. Because the organizational specialists cut across all important jobs in the district and because they served the entire system, the coordinator reported directly to the superintendent. All projects were discussed with the superintendent before they were launched. Unlike persons in line positions, however, neither the coordinator nor any of the other organizational specialists directed any work of people in the schools. And unlike persons in staff positions, their advisory and facilitative functions were not restricted to administrators. Everyone in the district had direct access to the organizational specialists; no one was required to have the approval of a superior before opening conversations with them.

The coordinator served as an active link between the specialists and the rest of the district. When the coordinator received a request for specialists' services, he and the person or group requesting the service typically listed the particular specialists who would be mutually acceptable. Only those listed would then be asked about their availability. In relaying requests to the specialists, the coordinator ordered the requests to rotate the work fairly evenly; the object was to avoid developing an elite corps who might become the only ones to take on difficult training tasks. As the project gained prestige and was recognized by other school districts as valuable, the coordinator processed all out-of-district requests for services. The coordinator was helped in his work by a steering committee formed within the body of 23 specialists. Membership in this committee rotates from semester to semester.

Work of the Kent specialists

During the first year of operation, the organizational specialists focused primarily on four target groups: an elementary school staff moving toward a multiunit structure, the superintendent and his cabinet, teachers interested in improving their communication skills, and a junior high staff. Limited work was carried out with a group of parents and with a senior high school. Of the four primary interventions, three appeared to be successfully executed.

The most successful training was carried out at the elementary school that was moving toward a multiunit organization. Several factors in this school were conducive to OD training. The school had few walls; the newness and freedom of the physical plant encouraged the staff to be creative about teaching strategies. The principal had been trained as an organizational specialist; he felt secure with the training process and encouraged the more retiring staff members to become involved. Another indicator of potential success was that some of the teachers aided the principal in selecting the particular specialists who were to work with the staff.

The first training with this school took place in August 1969 just before school began; it lasted for two days. The first day was spent in group exercises and in practicing communication skills. On the second day, the staff participated in group problem solving, making plans to short-circuit organizational problems that might arise during the academic year. The specialists met again with the faculty for three half-day sessions during September, October, and November. (These sessions were easily arranged because the staff was double shifting until Christmas.)

Assessment indicated that the teachers thought that the specialists had developed a well-organized training design, that the teachers were experiencing clear communication with the principal, and that they were working smoothly and effectively in their teams. Several teachers commented that they were gratified to see the specialists using the skills they were teaching.

A second successful intervention occurred when another team of specialists worked with the superintendent and his staff during cabinet meetings. Before any help from specialists was given, the superintendent and his staff generally agreed that communication at their cabinet meetings was poor. Participants seemed uncertain of their roles and hesitated to disagree at staff meetings with the superintendent even when debate might improve the group's decision making. Few decisions were made at the meetings; instead, cabinet members thought that decisions were being made on the outside in unknown ways. Other staff members in the district distrusted the lack of openness they perceived on the part of the cabinet. Much confusion and distrust persisted in the district.

In February 1970, the superintendent decided to open the cabinet meetings to broader participation. The group was renamed "staff" and the principals and teachers were invited to send representatives. In this new form, the meetings were open to participation by representatives of several district groups, the superintendent participated more as a group member and less as a laissez-faire leader, procedures were agreed upon by the total group, and time was devoted to discussing group processes at the meeting. In March, the superintendent and his staff agreed that one or two organizational specialists should attend staff meetings to serve as official observers of the communication processes.

As a result of feedback from the specialists at twelve weekly meetings, the following changes in group processes occurred:

1. The superintendent periodically stepped out of the role of "presenter." Presentations were made by a variety of participants.

2. The superintendent often relinquished the role of convener (chairman or moderator) to participate more freely in the discussions.

3. Agreements were made by the group on procedures to help the meetings run smoothly. The superintendent (who had been expected to prescribe such procedural rules) acted merely as another member while these agreements were being reached.

4. Time at the end of the meeting was used to discuss (debrief) the group processes that occurred during that meeting. The specialists gave feedback during this time on their observations.

As a result of these changes, less adverse criticism of the meetings was made by participants and less distrust seemed to be manifested by others in the district toward the superintendent.

A third successful intervention was a two-course sequence prepared for interested teachers in the district. In the first course, entitled "Techniques in Communication," the communication skills of paraphrasing, describing behavior, describing own feelings, and checking one's perception of others' feelings were taught. Also, the participants experienced several group exercises and learned how to carry out an organizational problem-solving sequence. The second course, entitled "Communications and Interpersonal Relations," was an advanced training experience in which the communication skills, exercises, and procedures were reviewed and related to group processes in the classroom. Those who successfully completed both courses and who were enthusiastic about them became candidates for posts on the team of organizational specialists.

Although no intervention created a great deal of strain or adverse criticism, one can fairly be called unsuccessful. The unproductive experience took place in a training event designed for a junior high school. One of the organizational specialists had reported that some staff members in one of the junior high schools were seen by other faculty as failing to take their share of responsibility for encouraging students to behave properly in the halls. The resulting tensions—so the specialist understood—had created several warring subgroups on the faculty; consequently, the faculty as a whole communicated and worked together very poorly. A team of specialists was assigned to the building and their conversations with the principal started during July, 1969.

In November, the specialists were taken aback to hear the teachers in the building state that the problem no longer existed. They discovered that during the summer the principal had taken steps to correct the lack of clarity about discipline in a way acceptable to most teachers. But the specialists did not learn of these steps until they had carried out several training sessions at the school. The specialists had intended the training to culminate in a problem-solving process to work on clarifying staff norms about disciplining students. The school staff was surprised that the consultants raised discipline as a problem soon after they had worked on it. The specialists were unsure about how to respond, imagining that some of the teachers were unrealistically defending the existing conditions of the school. The resulting confusions were followed by antagonistic remarks toward the specialists and a demand that they stop the training until further notice.

By March, 1970, we were giving no aid to the Kent specialists in selecting tasks, designing training, or carrying out the training. The specialists made the transition very smoothly. By the end of the summer of 1970 they had conducted OD training ranging from a half a day to a full week with seven elementary schools, the superintendent and his immediate staff, the program specialists within the Curriculum Division, a group of principals, some groups of parents, and a group of 80 students in a "multi-ethnic camp." Moreover, they had laid plans for the 1970-71 school year that included some continued or advanced work and some new work. For details of this second year of training see Wyant (1971).

THE EUGENE PROJECT

After the Kent experience, we decided to test whether an effective team of specialists could be integrated into a district without a prior period of district-wide OD training. With what we had learned in Kent about selection, training, and follow-up support of the specialists, we had a strong foundation for another try at creating a specialist-team. Moreover, we were growing toward a point of some maturity with our theory and technology of OD for schools (see Schmuck, Runkel, Saturen, Martell, & Derr, 1972).

The Eugene district offered an ideal setting for such an attempt. No district-wide OD had taken place; this meant that the district as a whole did not become accustomed to CASEA trainers before encountering their own organizational specialists. It also meant that the superintendent and his assistants were not given training before the organizational specialists. On the other side, many personnel were knowledgeable about our work, and many had also experienced demonstrations or college courses on communication skills and group problem solving. We already had been active in a part of the district, experimenting with OD in establishing the multiunit structure in four elementary schools. Discussions with Eugene personnel about creating a team of organizational specialists commenced in the fall of 1970.

Recruiting the Eugene specialists

Certain ideas and desires were paramount in our thinking because of the Kent project. First, we wanted a strong coordinator, highly respected by district personnel for his expertise, efficiency, and tactful interpersonal relations. We also wanted him to be knowledgeable, comfortable, and excited about OD training. We found our man in one of the coordinators of the multiunit project. Second, we wanted to reach clear agreements with the chief administrators in the central office about the nature of the project.

We accomplished this through several meetings during the winter of 1970-71, and by recruiting three of the four Area Directors (who serve substantially as deputies to the superintendent) to the specialist training program. Third, we wanted to publicize the project accurately, clearly, and widely; we also wanted the procedures for applying to conform to district policy and tradition. Fourth, we wanted to receive many more applications than could be accepted and we wanted to receive them from all professional jobs in the district. We did receive 75 applications and we could accept only 25 of them for training. As we had hoped, the trainees represented all professional jobs, including area directors, curriculum coordinators, counselors, principals, and teachers. Fifth, we decided to add a week to the summer training, making three weeks in all. Our period of co-training with the specialists during the school year was scheduled to run from August, 1971 to April, 1972. All totaled, we hoped to cut the time spent in Eugene to about one half the time we spent in Kent.

Training the Eugene specialists

The Eugene specialists started their preparation with two weeks of training in June, 1971. A third week of training took place in August, 1971, just prior to the start of the school year. Goals of the first week's sessions were similar to those pursued in Kent. The activities included practicing warm-up exercises, communication skills, and group and intergroup exercises and procedures. Heavier emphasis was placed on intergroup exercises and data feedback techniques than had been given in Kent. During the activities, trainees discussed their perceptions and feelings about the district, the resources they brought to the specialist team, their feelings about membership on the team, and their views of the goals of the team. We asked them to read theoretical expositions of such topics as clarifying communication, establishing goals, uncovering conflicts, and making decisions, and to discuss the topics amongst themselves.

During the second week, we focused largely on the stages of an OD intervention. We reviewed what we had learned in Kent about each stage and asked the trainees to carry out simulations of each stage. The stages were: entry and contract-building, diagnosing, designing, implementing major training events, assessing, follow-up training. We placed special emphasis on entry and diagnosis, because these represented problems for the Kent specialists. Also, we offered a great deal of conceptual input with our Handbook (Schmuck, Runkel, Saturen, Martell, & Derr, 1972).

Toward the end of the week the trainees established some agreements on how they would work as a team and developed a temporary plan to establish at least four different sorts of subteams within the specialist group during the fall of 1971. Our Kent experience helped us guide them in designating the teams. They were (1) a demonstration team to plan and carry out short meetings in the district to inform personnel about the goals, skills, and actions of the specialists, (2) an inservice course team to plan and carry out short courses for interested personnel on such topics as communication skills, problem solving, applications of OD to the classroom, etc., (3) a team to do OD training with schools and subsystems that had already received some previous training, e.g., the multiunit schools, and (4) a team to do OD training with subsystems that had not yet received training.

Between the June and August training, the coordinator made plans with several schools—some of which had undergone previous OD and some of which had not—to receive training in the fall from subteams of specialists. It was necessary that he make the arrangements by himself, because many of the specialists were on vacation and the target schools needed to make plans to receive the specialists. Also during this interim, the coordinator, along with a few specialists, laid plans for a slide-presentation to be used by the demonstration team.

During the one week of training in August, the specialists divided into subteams to plan for demonstrations, inservice courses and OD events. CASEA consultants joined each subteam as cotrainers. Each subteam tried out some of its plans on the other specialists to receive feedback before executing the plan in the real world of the district. At the time of this writing, the subteams are just getting into their work within the district.

VALUES

We wish now to pause in our discussion of the organizational specialists to state some of the values that guide us in these projects. Each of these projects has contained episodes that were sheer joy, when almost everyone seemed barely to be touching the ground. Some of the achievements of school faculties seem to us works of art—a sort of improvisation on a theme while modulating from one organizational key to another, with every member of the combo coming in on his own cue, without rehearsal. Yet, when we are asked to explain the *value* of these celebrations of human interaction, we often find ourselves saying that they lead to *other* things that are good—like more hours devoted to work instead of spells of suspicious anxiety, the use of more resources in building a more effective curriculum, or a more satisfying life for students. And then we are likely to ask ourselves why *those* things are good. A short-hand way of describing our most basic value position is to say that we value the *delight of joining and working with others to strive toward creating new, more adaptable human processes.*

Striving to create

Building a new phenomenon is deeply gratifying to us. It is a joy to produce a set of events that did not exist before, quite aside from what it does or what it leads tó. Joining with others in the joy of this creativity is even better. It is a good thing, not needing any other justification, to stand with fellow workers and gaze upon our handiwork. Comfort and pleasantness are not to be bought at all costs; creating events is sometimes hard and painful.

Joining with others

When there is disagreement about what to build or how to build it, one way to eliminate disagreement is to get rid of the people who disagree with oneself. This is like the conqueror who believes that he can win only if others lose. This is not the kind of achievement or creativity we value. We value the condition of joining with others to overcome obstacles. We enjoy, needing no justification for it, fitting our own well-articulated contribution into the contributions of the rest of the team. It is even better when it is very clear that everyone else is feeling the same kind of gratification.

Delighting in work

Work, we believe, is as human as play. Quite aside from what else work achieves—such as a knowledge of arithmetic, a plan for a basketball tournament, or the commitment of an employer to provide job experience for high school students—work can also achieve the satisfaction of individual human needs. While we grant that work must some times get done for the welfare of the group or society even though it is painful or even damaging to some of the individuals involved, we nevertheless value most the kind of work and the kind of organization that enable the most individuals to find most of their duties personally rewarding. In brief, work can be beautiful for many people much of the time, and that's the way we prefer it.

Implications

We also value behavior in organizations that will lead to these valued conditions. Since we value striving to create, we want organizations to state goals explicitly and pursue them flexibly and vigorously. We find that humans are very adaptable; almost everyone can contribute a valuable part to a goal that most others in a group want to pursue and almost everyone can find gratification in doing so. But people are not infinitely adaptable; in a group of twenty or thirty, there is often one who is overstressed by the changes OD brings. Sometimes the group cannot help this person to adapt without taking an exhorbitant amount of time from the organization's tasks. In such a case, the best course of action is to seek a place for the unconverted person in some other school or district. Always, the morphogenesis of the organization is a resolution of some sort of conflicts among individual needs and environmental demands.

Valuing striving toward explicit goals means that conflict and pain in the organization must be made known and treated as materials from which achievement is built. When an individual suffers for the sake of the group goal and he hides his suffering, others can remain unaware of his sacrifice and he can come to feel that others are profiting unduly at his expense. If his suffering is openly admitted, others can be grateful for the gift he has made to the group goal and can reward him with their appreciation. At later stages of the work, any necessary sacrifices can be equitably redistributed.

Since we value joining with others, we must seek to draw out the abilities, knowledge, and other resources of every individual so that all can be welcomed and valued. If one person contributes a disproportionately large share of resources, he can come to be valued because he can be exploited; others will come to feel that they cannot repay the one person's contributions, and they will develop rationales for accepting more than they give. The person with the extra resources will find himself "buying" pleasant relations between himself and others. We can freely join a group and be accepted only to the extent that all the others can freely join and be accepted. And this can occur only if everyone has something valuable to offer the group. In our experience, almost everyone does have something valuable to offer almost every group.

Similarly, we value ways of solving problems that maximize the gains of the maximum number of people and minimize the losses of a maximum number. And to do this, an organization must anticipate changes in the environment and initiate alterations before the demands from the environment produce strong stresses and polarize the members of the organization about responsive policy. If almost everyone is continuously or recurrently involved in adaptive problem-solving, then each person can be committed, at almost every moment, to action that moves him toward his own goals while at the same time moving the organization toward its goals. As long as this condition can continue, people will not need to choose up sides and try to win at the expense of the other side.

Just as valuing striving means that people must become aware of pain in the working group, whether their own pain or that of others, so valuing joining means that people must become aware of joy in the group, whether their own or others'. We cannot take joy in sharing the work of the group unless the others recognize the possibility, recognize our own state through their own empathy, and hold the moment for us while we express our gladness.

Since we value delighting in one's work, it is necessary that we know whether others are finding pleasure in their work. We cannot all enjoy every moment of our work. Sometimes one or another of us must undergo drudgery or even pain for the larger job to get done. If one person is not to get more than his share of unpleasantness, it is necessary for the pleasure and pain each person is finding in his work to be widely known in the group. Only by bringing feelings about the job into the open can an equitable sharing of pleasure and pain be assured.

THEORY

We draw strongly on two bodies of theory to guide our attempts at integrating organizational specialists into school districts. One is that of general systems theory, with its concept of the self-renewing or morphogenetic organization, making continuous, adaptive changes by maintaining a lively *variety pool* of resources and delicately monitoring its success in coping with its environment. For example, since one current tension revolves around inter-generational conflict, the self-renewing school of today will find ways to involve students in more decisions about the school's operation and what is to be taught in the classrooms. A self-renewing district maintains openness to its environment, responsiveness among its internal subsystems, and an open flow of its members' competencies so as to use its own resources as a district to cope with environmental changes.

Self-renewing organizations—whether they are teaching teams, schools, or entire districts—are adaptive in the long run; hence, they are not set in any single organizational structure or procedure. While there is typically some formal hierarchy, form follows function. People are organized into groups to solve specific problems; both the structure of the organization and the methods used in the groups change to suit the nature of the current problems.

In self-renewing organizations, decisions are made by the persons who have the information. Instead of looking to those who have the legitimate authority, emphasis is placed on the best possible decision. Decision-making requires adequate information; all too often, those in authority lack information or have it in a distorted form. In a self-renewing school, for example, a group of students and parents may decide on dress codes; teachers and students may decide on classroom procedures; teachers, principal, and superintendent may decide on whether to institute in-service leadership training for the principals.

A self-renewing organization has sensing processes and feedback mechanisms to tell when changes are needed. There is open communication within the school district and between the district and the community on the question of when the school needs to change. A self-renewing organization manages itself according to specified goals accepted by its members. It has systematic methods (e.g., problem-solving techniques) for dealing with obstacles to reaching these goals. The goals, naturally, are open to change as the environment of the district changes.

A self-renewing organization has a culture which permits the processes mentioned above to take place. There is open, direct, and clear communication. Conflict is viewed as inevitable and natural and is brought out into the open so that it can be used to bring about creative change instead of impeding the work to be accomplished. Creativity, even wild dreaming, are encouraged. New ideas and new persons and groups are seen as additional resources rather than as troublemakers and threats.

We view integrating a team of organizational specialists into a school district as a long step in endowing a district with the self-renewing capacity. In pursuit of the self-renewing school district, the job of organizational specialists is to increase the effectiveness of groups as task-oriented entities and to lead school personnel to function more effectively as components of working bodies carrying out their specific tasks. The key to a job well done lies in a school's capacity to solve its own problems by using the resources already present. These resources include information about different curricula, willingness to take risks, and creativity in teaching. Staff resources are not simply ideas residing in a filing cabinet. Rather, resources are truly available only when a work group calls upon members for fresh ways of doing things, when each member feels unafraid in offering his own ideas for use, and when the norms of the group enable a new idea to be moved into action with reasonable speed and commitment. It is the specialist's commitment to enhance these capabilities.

Work of the organizational specialist differs significantly from the sort of help offered by a traditional management consultant. Traditional consultants work on problems as they are defined by the administrators of the organization. After interviews and observations are made, reports are issued that recommend solutions to the original problems. Rarely does a traditional consultant stay with an organization long enough to help it carry the recommendations into practice. Organizational specialists, on the other hand, explore problems from the perspectives of all parts of the organization and include relevant parties within and without the organization in designing and implementing change. Frequent training sessions help the school personnel to carry out the changes they themselves designed.

The work of the organizational specialist also differs significantly from that of the sensitivity trainer. Although the specialist makes use of the organization as its own laboratory for experiential or inductive learning techniques, he uses these "laboratory groups" in very different ways from sensitivity or T-groups. The targets of the OD training are the membership as a whole and as subgroups. The specialist seeks to help modify norms and the definition of roles. He does not seek to change personalities, nor is the OD training aimed at facilitating personal growth.

The other chief body of theory upon which we draw is the branch of group dynamics that studies the helps and hindrances that individuals bring to the group task. The writings of McGregor (1967) sum up our position on these matters very well. See also Katz and Kahn (1966) and Schein and Bennis (1965) as other representative examples.

Schools are complex organizations stabilized by role expectations and interpersonal norms. Faculty members behave predictably largely because they adhere to shared expectations for what is appropriate in the school. Norms are compelling stabilizers because individuals monitor one another's behavior. It is the strength of this shared feeling that makes a school organization so resistant to modification but at the same time offers the specialist a leverage point for planned change. Norms provide the school organization with its structure and coherence. Members of a staff behave in patterened and predictable ways because their behaviors are guided by common expectations, attitudes, and understandings. Norms are especially serviceable and tenacious when individual staff members intrinsically value the normative behavior in the school or when they perceive such behavior as instrumental in reaching other valued goals. In any case, norms are strong stabilizers of organizational behavior.

Norms about relations between individuals produce role prescriptions. Role-taking is done as part of an interaction with other role-takers. If it is said that an organizational member is performing poorly in a given job, it means that the interaction between the job-holder and his role reciprocators is breaking down. In this sense, the point of a specialist's intervention for improving a subsystem is not a person but rather the interaction patterns linking role reciprocators.

A specialist's intervention must bring a subsystem new ways of carrying out interpersonal interaction; further, these new procedures should be entered into by the actual role reciprocators who make the subsystem run. Changes in organizational norms and roles are most efficiently brought into being and made stable by asking staff members to behave in new ways in their actual work-group setting while, at the same time, other role-takers observe these new behaviors. Norms will not be altered unless other relevant role-takers are allowed to see that their colleagues actually accept the new patterns of behavior in the setting of the school.

Many subsystems in school districts call for staff members to interact daily in mutual interdependence and reciprocity. These subsystems, especially when they are face-to-face and intimate, require more detailed norms than does the district at large. The norms of such subsystems center on methods for work, interpersonal values, and social-emotional customs. Each face-to-face work group rewards certain manners of speech, behaviors, gestures, etc., and not others; it also approves certain topics for discussion and not others.

In these groups, individual differences in personality become important, sometimes crucially so. Especially important are emotional predispositions and interpersonal competencies or skills. Alteration of some interpersonal patterns can be brought about by administrative directive, but patterns of interpersonal interactions that deeply involve the egos of the participants can usually be changed only through the same process by which they are maintained—through new one-to-one actions supported by other members of the subsystem and legitimized through the formation of new intra-group norms.

Because man's rational and emotional sides are inextricably mingled, organizational change can achieve stability only if it takes adequate account of the participants' emotional natures. Research, shows that men invest emotion in at least three domains: (1) *achievement,* also labeled curiosity, exploration, or activity; (2) *affiliation,* also delineated by some as the interpersonal dimension of love, indifference, and hostility; and (3 *influence or power,* also described as the dimension of dominance-submission. Most interpersonal relations and the motivations concomitant with them can be construed as having achievement, affiliation, and influence components. Emotional experiences can become problems when any one of these motivational states is frustrated.

Any job becomes attractive and draws upon the best abilities of its incumbent to the extent that it satisfies one or more of these three needs. Feelings in the area of achievement can be harnessed by the specialist when he helps staff members gain a clear conception of one another's goals. Affiliative feelings can be gratified by helping to build a cohesive unit in which staff members find friendliness and the reciprocal exchange of support and warmth. Feelings related to power can be satisfied by helping a subsystem to allow for influence at all levels. All these emotional states are potentially harnessed through taking a problem-solving orientation to organizational life in schools.

USING THE THEORY

Our theory points us toward working with subsystems, not with individuals or with opportunistic collections of individuals. We reject the strategy of making better organizations by improving the members as individuals. Instead, we seek to alter organizational functioning by changing the *interactions* among members. In training, furthermore, we deal during any one unit of training with the interactions within the subsystem: a group of individuals held together by norms and roles and interdependent in carrying out their tasks.

Furthermore, we do not spend much time studying individuals and directing our interventions to individuals. Instead, we help subsystems to design ways of working that will offer opportunities to satisfy the three needs we mentioned earlier. We then leave it to the initiative and ingenuity of individuals to take advantage of the opportunities to satisfy their uppermost needs. And they do so.

The tactics or sub-strategies we use in the overall design of a large intervention do not follow in simple logic from the theoretical assertions we made earlier in this paper. One reason (among others) is that the tactics also rest on the practical experience we have had with alternate sequences. We shall skip a good deal of explanation and describe briefly some major tactics we recommend to organizational specialists. Each tactic focuses effort upon a particular function in the organization. Improving these functions, we believe, is essential if the self-renewing capacity is to be achieved.

1. Organizational specialists should first judge the sorts of discrepancies that exist between the school's goals and its actual organizational performance. Some features to be diagnosed are: (a) the school's current level of tension in relation to achieving its goals, (b) the possible directions that the school might move in achieving its goals, (c) the goals that are or are not being achieved, (d) the problem-solving processes that the school uses to cope with discrepancies, and (e) the ways that the school now checks to see if it is achieving its goals.

2. Organizational specialists should assess the level of role clarity in the school. The important features are (a) sufficiently promulgated definition and support from the school district's administration (central office), (b) adequate level of confidence in the role-performance of others vis-a-vis oneself, and (c) sufficiently understood roles of others in distant parts of the school so that the entire organization can be perceived as an organization to which one sees that he belongs in a meaningful way.

3. Organizational specialists should pay attention to the flow of communication in the school organization. Almost inevitably, malfunctioning in a school will show itself in weakened and distorted communication at crucial links. In contrast, schools that undergo successful organizational training evince continuing formalized activities for improving communication. The specialists should diagnose a school's attempts to improve its communication by checking to see if new forms of communication remain reasonably stable, to see if more than just a few staff members get involved in the new mode of communication, and to see if there is agreement in the school that the new form is legitimate and that it helps the staff to accomplish its goals.

4. Organizational specialists should assess the extent to which the school has a repertoire of interpersonal techniques for collaboration in small task-groups. They should assess the success of staff members in performing communication skills such as paraphrasing, describing one another's behaviors objectively without imputing motives, and expressing their own feelings openly and constructively.

5. Organizational specialists should assess to what extent a variety pool is available for producing new and appropriate ways

of solving organizational problems. Neither people nor organizations take on a new way of behaving merely because someone conceives of the new mode. Formalized ways for adopting new patterns must be present; the variety pool, if it is to be effective, must represent a capability for organized action. It must be institutionalized and rewarding.

To locate the variety pool in schools, the specialists should look for recently altered interrelations of roles, the diverse ways of transmitting information present in the school, commitments of man-hours to temporary projects, the variety of choices and classroom innovations actually being tried out, and the like. Often new activities in schools take the form of committee work, curricular alterations, financial changes, alterations in schedules, procedural innovations at meetings, or finding new roles for students or new jobs for the faculty. An important evidence of an active variety pool in a school is the practice of new forms without prior approval of administrators, at least up to the point of disruption of existing routines. Further, in seeking possible new contributions to the variety pool, the specialists should look at the deviant behavior in the school and assess its potential for being converted to constructive use.

6. Organizational specialists should assess to what extent the school contains means for selecting some innovative activities to be maintained in the variety pool and means for rejecting others. The school should have a method for deciding whether any proposed innovation points sufficiently close to a goal to justify keeping the innovation in readiness for use. Significant individuals in the school should be able to verbalize goals in ways with which others would agree. Norms in the school should support continuous comparisons between expressed goals and the implications of current action, and committees should exist for deciding what is to be done about the lack of matching between expressed goals and proposed ways of doing things. The specialists should insist on clearer statements of goals, should help convene frequent conferences of a problem-solving type to seek ways of bringing current action into harmony with goals, and should suggest "trial runs" of new organizational forms for bringing about an understandable correspondence between the variety pool and proclaimed goals.

7. Organizational specialists should assess to what extent the school has a method for institutionalizing an innovation after it has

been judged suitable and worth keeping. OD training that helps a faculty to search its own members for useful resources will create a school in which the staff members invent their own methods of maintaining an accessible variety pool. A variety pool will probably be more accessible when the distribution of power in a faculty is more equalized. Conscious modes of maintaining innovations will be more likely to appear after training that gives practice in using feedback-loops and in seeking evidence of successful innovations.

8. Finally, the organizational specialists—as a team—should become a permanent and legitimate body in the school district. The team must be supported both intellectually and financially by the district's decision makers. It should be established as a formally differentiated subsystem with a coordinator who reports directly to the superintendent and its own budget. The team remains integrated and in touch with other parts of the district because of its heterogeneous membership. Composition of the ideal team would include members from all parts and role levels of the district.

A RECOMMENDED SEQUENCE FOR INTEGRATING SPECIALISTS INTO OTHER DISTRICTS

A team of organizational specialists in a school district is one way of developing the self-renewing character of the district. Especially when the specialists are drawn from different roles and hierarchical levels in a district, their work together can build useful techniques whereby intra-district communications are clarified and constructive attitudes are taken to problem-solving. The success of the specialists depends on their ability to open up communication and to improve problem-solving skills in ways that allow existing resources to be used. Certain preconditions for a successful cadre of organizational specialists can be sketched as a result of our experience in Kent and Eugene.

From the beginning of the project, all significant job sectors within a district should be involved in defining objectives and delineating problems. Second, a vertically organized group of persons of high influence should attend a short training event in which OD theory and techniques are demonstrated. The demonstration should explicitly reveal the differences between OD and sensitivity training (Schmuck, Runkel, & Langmeyer, 1971). Third, this high-influence group should form a steering committee for the project from one of its own subgroups. The steering committee should decide on a means of advertising and of selecting the recruits for the training. A coordinator of the steering committee should be identified as the coordinator for the specialists. He will report directly to the superintendent. The recruits that are sought by the coordinator and his steering committee should represent most of the significant professional roles in the district. Fourth, the specialists should experience intensive initial training during three weeks in which they learn how to perform as group-process facilitators. Fifth, the team forms into several subgroups for the first round of training attempts. The specialists try out skills under the guidance of outside consultants. The subgroups focus upon (1) a public-relations function to inform others in the district about OD through demonstrations, (2) an inservice course in communication skills, group exercises, and group problem-solving to educate individuals in the district about the building blocks of OD, and (3) OD interventions for schools which have already had some training and for those which have had none. Finally, the team develops its own best set of procedures for monitoring its own performance for improving the skills of its members, and for getting new members.

HELPS AND HINDRANCES IN ESTABLISHING TEAMS OF SPECIALISTS

Our experience in both Kent and Eugene indicates a number of things the outside consultants can do to help the organizational specialists get off to a good start. A number of features of the Kent and Eugene projects speeded and heightened the effectiveness of the teams of specialists in their work. Members of both districts were able to comprehend something of the probable role of the organizational specialist through participation in some of the training that had been conducted by the CASEA consultants. (Actually, almost everyone who applied for training as a specialist in Kent had experienced the work of CASEA first-hand. In Eugene, most of the recruits had experienced CASEA-like events through demonstrations, inservice workshops, and college courses.) These facts minimized false anticipations on the part of applicants and gave the summer training events something of a head start.

Because of participation in CASEA-led or CASEA-like events, many members of the two districts also had some familiarity with the kind of work the specialists would be doing. The superintendent in Kent, for example, knew what the specialists were talking about when they proposed to help with the processes during his staff meetings. The Area Directors in Eugene knew very clearly what the work of the specialists would be like. The principals of both districts had at least a beginning understanding of what they were contracting for when they asked for help from the specialists. This familiarity lessened the likelihood of crossed signals, misapplications, and disappointments. The familiarity with the specialists' sort of work on the part of others in the district also resulted in confidence and support from others. The two superintendents supported the work by allowing two very capable curriculum specialists, one in each district, to spend time as coordinators of the specialists. They also supported the specialists by releasing ten days a year to each for his work as a specialist.

The many jobs represented among the specialists made available to them a wide variety of resources. These resources included intimate knowledge of particular schools, liaison with the local education associations, and access to the superintendent and his cabinet (called clinic in Eugene).

In both districts, the specialists were soon recognized as available to any segment of their district. No doubt this occurred because the wide range of jobs among the specialists prevented them being looked on as an adjunct of any one school or division, and also because they sought out, for their early projects, work that would take them into various segments of the district.

In Kent, a norm was established early that maintained respect for diversity among the specialists. As early as the end of February, 1970, the steering committee of the organizational specialists had stated that a member of the district could participate in the work of the specialists in several ways: (1) as an occasional observer and reporter, (2) as an instructor of an inservice course, (3) as an active member of a team of specialists in a particular OD intervention but not as a regular member of the specialist group with duties to the specialists as a body (4) as a regular member of the specialist group, and (5) as a regular member with additional duty as a member of the steering committee. This tolerance of various roles within the specialists has enabled them to make optimum use of the talents and time of each person who works with them. Moreover, the gradation of responsibility among the roles provides a natural channel for developing new members of the body as a whole. Although at the time of this writing it is too soon to tell, it appears that Eugene, too, will adopt a norm of flexibility and diversity for its specialists.

Our theory of organizations leads us to believe that a key cause of the successful functioning of the specialists is their image, not merely as a list of individuals, but as a team or subsystem within the districts, with a group identity as clear as that of a school or central office division. This subsystem character was produced among the specialists by giving them tasks during training that increased their interdependence and their readiness to call upon one another for help with the expectation of receiving it. The subsystem character, in turn, made it easy for the specialists to allocate duties, establish and disband subteams, and call upon the resources of one another on short notice.

Our experiences in Kent also showed that our strategy for building the specialist team had some weaknesses and limitations. In the earlier part of the Kent project, sites for interventions were picked mostly by the specialists; the projects did not arise at the initiative of the people occupying the sites. In a few instances, the trainees felt as if the OD were being imposed upon them. One way specialists can give a school the opportunity to invite them in (and increase the likelihood of such an invitation) is to make opportunities for the faculty to discuss its own problems within itself, with the specialists serving as little more than conveners of the discussions until an opportunity arises to offer their other skills. Another way—the way currently being adopted in Eugene—is to offer brief (two hours to two days) demonstrations of "what OD is" and then to let the recipients choose whether they want OD training.

A second weakness of our approach in Kent was the perception on the part of many of the Kent staff that the specialists were part of the outside CASEA consultant group rather than an integral part of the district. We believe this perception was intensified among those personnel who never actually participated in any of the OD training as a result of certain fears many of them formed about what the CASEA consultants—and consequently the specialists—might ask them to do. The most prominent fear was that of self-disclosure and the release of strong emotion that many people associate with "sensitivity training." This misapprehension was strengthened in Kent by the principals' attendance at the Human Relation Laboratory in June, 1968. That event consisted mostly of experience in T-groups, with personal growth rather than OD as the goal. Some Kent principals communicated the belief to teachers that the training done by the CASEA consultants and Kent specialists would be similar to their T-group experience. The CASEA consultants should have devoted more time to demonstrating the nature of the projected OD training to interested teachers in the district. In Eugene, we are being careful to do this by urging a subgroup of specialists to develop strategies for demonstrating OD throughout the district.

Perhaps the most serious limitation to both the Kent and the Eugene cadres relates to the professional expectations and workloads of the specialists. Both districts are vigorously pursuing other change-oriented programs and many of the specialists are committed to some of these other programs. For some specialists, conflicts will develop in their own minds over which of the projects should receive highest priority. In Eugene, we have attempted to seek clear commitments from the specialists with the understanding that some extra time will be required to make the project successful.

Another limitation is that the specialists will sometimes encounter role conflicts; they will inevitably obtain diagnostic data about others than can be used for evaluative rather than facilitative purposes. Or they may wish to move back from certain confrontations if they think their own status in the district could be threatened. Currently, we are trying to mitigate limitations like these in our work with the Eugene district. A final limitation is the lack of a clearly worked out set of procedures for increasing the knowledge and skills of the specialists. In brief, the specialists will need their own mechanisms for self-renewal. Currently, we are developing a strategy for refurbishing local teams of specialists through regional linking organizations (Runkel, 1970).

To sum up briefly our current recommendations for developing a cadre of organizational specialists, the district should involve representatives of all ranks and types of jobs, demonstrate repeatedly the nature of OD in various segments of the district, and wait for subgroups in the district to ask for help. Administrators and influential teachers should be encouraged to indicate their support of the project in concrete ways; payment for training events, offer of secretarial services, and offer of space for meetings and storing supplies. Since most organizational specialists will be expending a great deal of extra time and energy in the project, the fragile relationship between the district and the project must be carefully nurtured.

If it exercises due regard for the nature of a subsystem in a human organization, a school district will find that the development of a cadre of specialists in organizational training can be a relatively inexpensive way of refurbishing ineffective group processes and of bringing about a greater capacity for self-renewal.

REFERENCES

Katz, D., & R. Kahn. *The social psychology of organizations.* New York: John Wiley, 1966.

Langmeyer, D., R. Schmuck, & P. Runkel. Technology for organizational training in schools. *Sociological Inquiry.* Vol. 41(2), Spring, 1971.

McGregor, D. *The professional manager.* New York: McGraw-Hill, 1967.

Runkel, P. Linking organizations to maintain organizational development and transmit innovation. Eugene, Oregon: Center for the Advanced Study of Educational Administration, 1970.

Schein, E., & W. Bennis. *Personal and organizational change through group methods.* New York: John Wiley, 1965.

Schmuck, R., P. Runkel, & D. Langmeyer. Theory to guide organizational training in schools. *Sociological Inquiry.* Vol. 41(2), Spring, 1971.

Schmuck, R., P. Runkel, S. Saturen, R. Martell, & B. Derr. *Handbook of organization development in schools.* Palo Alto, California: National Press Books, 1927.

Thomas, T. A. Changes in elementary school principals as a result of laboratory training. Technical Report No. 5, Eugene, Oregon: Center for the Advanced Study of Educational Administration, 1970.

Wyant, S. Organizational specialists in a school district: A follow-up study. Unpublished Master's Thesis, Eugene, Oregon: Center for the Advanced Study of Educational Administration, 1971.

Selecting Personnel For
a System 4 Organization [1]

DON KING

A common approach in instituting markedly more participative forms of organization is to introduce them into new units rather than to attempt major change in existing units of a complex organization. Among the organizations which have followed this approach are Procter and Gamble, General Foods, DuPont, Westinghouse, and Olin Conductor.

The introduction of forms of organization such as Likert's System 4 (Likert, 1967) or McGregor's Theory Y (McGregor, 1967) represents major change for most organizations. Therefore, working with new social systems within an organization has several obvious advantages. Many difficult problems in overcoming resistance to change are obviated. New norms, different from traditional norms in industry, can be developed. Rather than the problem of changing established roles and role expectations about how supervisers or employees "should" act, roles are established anew. The newness of the physical setting and technology is congruent with the institution of a new approach to organization and interpersonal relationships.

At the same time, such an approach makes the selection problem all the more critical. People, many or most of whom are unknown to company personnel making selection decisions, must be selected for very different kinds of organizational roles than they have previously experienced. This poses an interesting transactional problem. The selection decision makers must obtain an accurate indication of whether or not the candidate is likely to function well in a participative organization. At the same time, prospective employees need accurate information to assist them in deciding whether or not it is advisable for them to join such a new system. They are more likely to make valid decisions, and

1. I would like to thank Messrs. Lyman Ketchum, Ed Dulworth, Phil Simshauser, Don Lafond, and Bob Mech, of General Foods for inviting me to work with them on the project and for their critical review of and contributions to the material reported in this paper.

if selected, make quicker, more effective transitions in their behavior, if in the selection process they clearly experience (a) this
organization as truly "different" and (b) what the major differences are and how such differences will affect them.

The fact that a Systems 4 form of organization is not everyone's cup of tea is well documented. Red Jacket Manufacturing
Company of Davenport, Iowa was an early leader in the movement toward participation maangement in industry. A number
of years ago James E. Richards, President of the Company gave
these replies to questions about his organization, (Lawrence &
Seiler, 1965, p. 971-72):

Q. What about the selection of personnel?
A. This question is a very real problem. An organization that
   develops in this way becomes very closely knit, with a constructive capacity to deal with disharmony as well as harmony. So it's hard finding someone to walk into this atmosphere who's unused to the business of squaring off. It's
   hard to find the man who's developed a tolerance for direct
   contact. I'm inherently suspicious of projective testing and
   that kind of thing. For selection I don't know at the moment of tests that can tell me, in a way I can believe, how
   a man's going to be in action. . .
Q. Does anyone want him to go ahead and talk about it? I
   think he should. [performance of people in the system]
A. Well, all right. We've fired men. We've downgraded men.
   We've upgraded men. And we've transplanted men and re-
   shaped functions. We've pulled some real boners. But by
   and large, I think we've found some effective methods. . .

Vroom (1959) has demonstrated that need for independence
and authoritarianism moderate the response to opportunities for
participation. Tosi's (1970) results did not support Vroom's findings but did support the existence of an interaction between personality and the effect of opportunities to participate in decision
making. Recently one of my Ph.D. students, Peg Rucker (Rucker
& King 1971), in a laboratory study found that low ascendant,
externally oriented subjects preferred assertive and manipulative
supervisers to participative ones.

In a symposium in 1964 (King, 1964), I suggested that laboratory training concepts and techniques might usefully be applied

to problems of selection and placement, particularly for unusual or temporary assignments. The basic idea is to set up a series of interactive experiences which provide all parties involved with richer more realistic data about how prospective members would fit in rather than the data provided by more traditional selection procedures.

Typically, selection on the one hand and team building and other O.D. efforts on the other have remained separate and distinct activities in most organizations. This is unfortunate in several respects:

1. Employees may well receive very different sorts of treatment before and after their selection and hence form ambiguous expectations or expectations at variance with System 4 values.
2. As indicated above, traditional selection procedures and criteria may not be relevant or at least may be inadequate.
3. The organization may miss opportunities to begin organizational development at the very moment of birth of a new organizational unit.

A NEW PLANT

Recently I had the opportunity to assist in the selection process for a new General Foods plant located in Topeka, Kansas. The plant is committed to a Systems 4-Theory Y form of organization. The major tasks, such as producing a product, are assigned to teams. The division of more specific responsibilities is one of the tasks of the team. First line supervisers are called Team Leaders. Status differentials are at a minimum—one parking lot, one cafeteria, etc.—and rules have largely been made by committees whose membership is drawn from throughout the organization. One could extend the list of differences between this plant and traditional organizations but these may suffice. The four operating managers who formed the basic cadre for the plant asked me to work with them in developing appropriate selection procedures for Team Leaders. I was later peripherally involved in the selection process for nonsupervisory employees. The remainder of this chapter discusses the rationale which was followed, the selection procedures themselves, and how things worked out.

The principles which guided our work explicitly or implicitly include:

a) All selection decisions are made by the men who are to work with those selected.

b) Decisions should be based on how prospective employees function in collaborative and conflictual group situations, as well as how well they handle themselves in one-on-one situations.

c) All prospective employees deserve direct, immediate, and "non sugar coated" feedback from those making the selection decisions as to why they are or are not offered a job.

d) The selection process should mirror, as much as possible, the jobs for which these candidates were being considered— that is, status differentials between selectors and applicants should be minimized; the process should be personalized; the emphasis should be on the implications of the candidates' behavior for their own growth and development; and dialogue should be two way, selectors should be accessible and they should be as exposed as the applicants.

e) Paper-and-pencil test data are (1) to be used only as secondary information to validate the reactions of the managers making the selections or to indicate strengths that might not be readily ascertained in directly observable ways, (2) collected by outsiders (the author for supervisers, the Kansas State Employment Service for hourly paid employees) and (3) not to become part of a person's file.

f) Contact between current members of the system and prospective members should become more extensive and open as the selection process progressed.

SELECTION PROCESS FOR TEAM LEADERS

The selection was managed by a group of four operating managers and a consultant. The plant personnel were the Plant Manager, Operations Service Manager, Manufacturing Manager and Technical Manager. The selection process for Team Leaders is described next. A step-by-step approach was used where application blanks containing rather extensive, albeit traditional, information were first screened. Those applicants who looked as though they might be promising were then independently interviewed by at least two of the operating managers. The interview's purpose was twofold: to convey to the applicant the nature of the organization for which they were being considered and to gather information about the applicant. If there was consensus among the interviewer that the applicant should be given further consideration, he was invited for a weekend at the company's expense. The company also paid each applicant a modest sum for his time. Ten applicants were invited to spend a weekend at a motel in the city where the new plant was being built. The design of the weekend was the most unusual part of the selection process and is outlined in detail:

SATURDAY

12:00-1:00	Lunch
1:00-2:00	Plant Visit
2:00-3:30	Detailed briefing regarding the organizational system of the new plant followed by a description of the rest of the weekend.
3:30-4:30	Role-Play of an Organizational Problem: a role-playing problem involving conflict between processing and packaging supervisors. The problem was one which the applicants would face if selected. The four managers designed the role-play, played ancillary roles, and observed how applicants handled the problem. All attempts to refer the problem to higher authority or duck the problem in other ways were blocked. The senior managers sent clear signals that this was their (the applicants') problem, and they were expected to work it out. This was exactly what the senior managers expected when the plant opened.
4:30-5:00	Mechanical Comprehension Test Form CC: a difficult form of the test designed to assess knowledge of physical and mechanical relations and laws. The author administered and scored this and all tests.
5:00-5:40	Purdue Creativity Test: test is designed to measure the extent to which one can think in novel and innovative ways.
5:40-6:30	Cocktails
6:30-7:30	Dinner
7:30-9:30	Group Problem-Solving Task and Compensation Task: the applicants were divided into two groups of five and completed the NASA[2] exercise. After each group made its decision the group's decision was scored. The winning, i.e. more accurate, group was then told that the company would provide $13 for them to divide in the following fashion: $6 to the member who contributed most to the group's decision, with $4, $2, $1, and nothing for the other four members. This was again to reflect his relative contribution to his group's effort. The losing group was given $6 to distribute $3, $2, $1, with two

2. In this exercise 15 items are ranked, first individually and then by groups, in the order of their importance for survival in reaching a mother ship on the moon.

applicants receiving nothing. The groups were given a time
limit to reach their decisions as to how to divide the money.

SUNDAY

8:00-9:00	Breakfast
9:00-9:30	Personnel Classification Test: a short test of mental ability which provides separate verbal and quantitative scores.
9:30-10:00	Survey of Interpersonal Values: a forced-choice questionnaire which provides scores on the following dimensions: support, conformity, recognition, independence, benevolence, and leadership.
10:00-11:30	Shift Division Problem: applicants were divided into two groups of five and were asked to make tentative assignments for themselves to the first, second, or third shift. No more than two men in each group could be assigned to a shift. They were informed the tentative assignments would be one factor considered in making permanent assignments, if they were selected for employment.
11:30-1:00	Lunch
1:00-2:30	Bridge Building Exercise: the group was split and two sub-groups were given materials with which to build a bridge between two tables. Issues as to what type of design to employ, how to divide the work, etc. were to be decided by the groups.
2:30-3:30	Plant Role Discussion: as a total group the applicants came to tentative decisions regarding whether they would prefer working in the processing or in the packaging phase of the plant's activities. Again, the applicants were informed that their decisions would have potential relevance in actual future assignments.
	During most of this hour the senior managers and I met separately to share reactions, make final decisions about who would talk with each applicant, and agree upon any special information we would want to be certain to convey or obtain in the interviews which followed.
3:30-5:00	Individual Feedback of Reactions, Ovservations, and Test Scores: each applicant met for approximately 30 minutes with one of the operating managers to discuss the manager's reactions to him during the weekend and also met separately for about 10 minutes with the author to discuss his test scores.

Several features in the fiow of activities can be noted:

1. The activities moved from a focus on the applicant's functioning as an individual, to small group activities, and ended with the total applicant group working together.
2. Activities became more collaborative as the weekend progressed.
3. The last activity, Plant Roles Discussion, was self regulating and gave the managers who designed the weekend a final

opportunity to compare reactions to the applicants before their closing interviews with them.

After this weekend, offers of Team Leader positions were extended to six of the ten applicants. Five accepted and are now working in the plant. One was currently earning $3,000 more than he could be offered and reluctantly declined the offer. The reaction to the experience was uniformly highly positive. It is of interest to note that, of the four men not offered positions in the new plant, one was offered and accepted a position at another plant in the company and two later applied for nonsupervisory jobs in the new plant.

SELECTION PROCESS FOR NONSUPERVISERS

In line with the criteria previously discussed, the Team Leaders were then charged with working out a selection process for nonsupervisory employees. My involvement was limited to consulting with the Team Leaders for two days on the plan which they were devising.

Over 700 people applied for 63 production job openings. Initial interviews were conducted by Kansas State Employment Service personnel. If the applicant met several specific criteria, e.g. willingness to work rotating shifts, desire to learn multiple skills, and mechanical aptitude, he (or she) was interviewed by one of the Team Leaders in the offices of the State Employment Service.

Those who appeared to be good prospects were then asked to complete the General Aptitude Test Battery. This was also administered by the Kansas State Employment Service Testing Department. Since broad skills would be required of employees in the new plant, adequate performance across all nine aptitudes measured by the test battery was the criterion for further consideration.

Subsequent interviews were then conducted in the General Foods office. Background checks were conducted (after approval of applicants to do so), and applicants were given an extensive physical examination.

After these steps, approximately 95 applicants remained. They were invited to spend a Saturday at the plant site after which the final selections would be made.

Team Leaders decided that a balance of experience and talent was necessary to mold well rounded teams by shifts. Team Leaders agreed that the Team Leader who initially interviewed an applicant had first choice of selection.

A letter of invitation to the selection weekend was drafted and sent out individually by Team Leaders. The letter explained events, time, place, date, and requested confirmation of attendance. When confirmation of attendance was not given to Team Leaders, there was telephone follow-up on some applicants.

The Saturday session began by greeting applicants and giving each individual a name tag to wear during the day's activity. The groups assembled at one of the two construction trailers at the site of the new plant which was then nearing completion. The sessions opened by welcoming each group and explaining the four hours of activities. Following this, there was a plant tour of about 1½ hours.

After the plant tour, everyone met in one of the trailers for coffee and rolls. The next portion of the program was handled by one of the four senior managers. Applicants worked on the NASA exercise. This was the same problem used in the Team Leader selection. This part of the program took about 2 hours during which time the Team Leaders acted as observers. The NASA problem was first completed individually, then in two separate groups. The winning and losing groups divided prize money as designated by the exercise leader.

Following the NASA problem there was an open question-answer period. After spending some time informally, the session ended and each applicant was given a modest amount of money for his time and effort.

Sixty-two of the sixty-three people to whom job offers were made accepted the offer. This is remarkable considering almost all were currently employed, and the starting rate (which was the same for all new employees) was competitive, but not particularly high.

WAS THE SELECTION PROCESS EFFECTIVE?

The approaches described here are similar in some ways to those used in assessment centers (Byham 1970), however, there are important differences. Every effort was made to play down the evaluative component of the process. Two way interaction between those doing the selection and those being considered was maximized. In both assessment center activities and these selection procedures, the implications of individuals' performance for his own growth and development were stressed.

What was learned from the process that might not have been learned via other procedures? There are no hard data which can answer this question, but a couple of specific situations are interesting. At least two of the prospective Team Leaders who looked very good on paper and handled themselves well in one-on-one interviews did not function well in the group activities. Neither was made an offer. On the other hand one prospective Team Leader who had been characterized as bright, but bitter and sarcastic before the weekend, handled himself well and demonstrated strong interpersonal and technical competence.

The careful, step-by-step approach, and the fact that it was a different approach to selection, clearly signaled this was going to be a significantly different kind of operation, and that the advertising material which said the company was looking for employees to, "Work in a new modern . . . plant with an exciting new organization concept which will allow you to participate in all phases of plant operation," was not merely designed to get people to apply for jobs.

Also the survivors felt, with justification, that they were a carefully selected, high-power group. I am certain this helped establish positive early expectations regarding what one could expect from fellow employees and oneself.

Lastly, I continue to be impressed by the high level of commitment to one another and to the concept of organization in the plant which has been exhibited by all the employees. I feel that the selection process helped to get members of the organization off to a good start in this regard. The interest and excitement generated carried over to the work itself.

When this paper was written (October 1971), approximately nine months had passed since these employees were hired. During this time only two employees left the company, one of these for an excellent opportunity to become a partner in a new business venture. Absenteeism has averaged less than one percent. Productivity data indicate that, after initial difficulties due to delay in completion of the plant, productivity gains are exceeding those projected in a stringent nine month start up plan developed before the plant was operational. Figures for amount of spoilage are also excellent.

Several cautionary notes should be voiced, however, in assessing how the system has worked:

1. The plant is still quite new and there has not been adequate time to collect longitudinal data.
2. All the members of the organization are fully aware that they are a part of a social experiment. Thus some of the positive data may reflect a "Hawthorne effect" phenomenon which may wear off in time.
3. The data reported in this paper are as seen through my eyes or those of people in the plant. While effort was made to be aware of biases and to present a balanced, accurate picture, all the sources of data would obviously like the plant to succeed.

A final cautionary note is in order. One applicant filed a complaint charging discrimination with the Equal Opportunities Employment Commission (EEOC). The EEOC investigators ruled that there was no basis for the complaint. They cited the fact that the percentage of minority group employees was higher than the percentage of minority group citizens in the community as the primary reason for their finding. They did express concern about the division of money in the NASA exercise by applicants. You will recall that the applicants themselves decided on this division on the basis of relative contributions to their group's decision. The company was interested in the accuracy of self assessment and assessment of others, not who received the most money. The EEOC investigators concluded (correctly I think) that this process would inevitably be viewed by the applicants as a peer rating with possibilities or probabilities of racial, sexual or other biases involved. Plant officials have concluded that they will eliminate this phase of the selection process for production employees if and when they face similar selection tasks in the future.

REFERENCES

Byham, W. C. Assessment centers for spotting future managers, *Harvard Business Review*, July-August 1970, 150-162.

King, D. C. Theoretical and research implications of the laboratory approach for divisional interest groups in the APA. A Symposium, American Psychological Association, September 1964.

Lawrence, P., & Seiler, J. A. (editors). *Organizational behavior and administration,* Revised Edition. Homewood, Illinois: Irwin-Dorsey, 1965.

Likert, R. *The human organization.* New York: McGraw-Hill, 1967.

McGregor, D. *The professional manager.* New York: McGraw-Hill, 1967.

Richards, J. E. A president's experience with democratic management. In P. R. Lawrence, & J. A. Seiler, *Organizational behavior and administration.* New York: Irwin-Dorsey, 1965, 960-973.

Rucker, Margaret H., & King, D. C. Reactions to leadership style as a function of personality variables. Paper No. 312, Institute for Research in the Behavioral, Economic, and Management Sciences, Krannert Graduate School of Industrial Administration, Purdue University, 1971.

Tosi, H. A reexamination of personality as a determinant of the effects of participation. *Personnel Psychology.* 1970, *23,* 91-99.

Vroom, V. H. Some personality determinants of the effects of participation. *Journal of Abnormal and Social Psychology,* 1959, *59,* 322-327.

SECTION III

Interventions to Cope With
Manpower Reductions and Demotions

It is probably not difficult to recall the economic slump of the 1969-71 period in the United States. While this decline hit the aerospace industry particularly hard, practically every organization experienced fiscal difficulties. Frequently during these periods organizations make cutbacks in many areas, including the workforce. Cutbacks in the workforce may take the form of layoffs and/or demotions. Lehner and Golembiewski, Carrigan, Mead, Munzenrider, and Blumberg explain what they did as OD practitioners to help the persons involved and the organizations to cope with cutbacks. It should be pointed out that these interventions were implemented in organizations that were already involved in an OD effort. Thus, the interventions were planned and implemented as a function of a prior diagnosis and as part of an ongoing process. There was a receptive climate in these organizations for invention in the "people areas." This climate undoubtedly contributed to the success of these interventions. Stated differently, it is important to understand that these events were not conducted in isolation but, rather, within the framework of a continuing OD process.

In this chapter, Lehner explains more than one useful technique for helping persons to cope with job loss. These techniques are easy to understand and transferable. Lehner explains more than the techniques, however. Specifically, a particular strength of the article is his thoughtful and all too brief treatise on the "personal meaning of work."

Using specific elements from laboratory training methodology, Golembiewski and his colleagues designed and conducted small group discussion sessions to help those affected cope with a sudden demotion in organizational position. Consultation with new boss and subordinate relationships, as a result of the demotions was a major part of the follow-up to the small group discussions. Golembiewski *et al* have quantitatively documented their work and present persuasive evidence that their intervention made a difference.

From Job Loss to Career Innovation

GEORGE F. J. LEHNER

"It was a totally brutal experience," said an engineer who had just been laid off from the job he had held for nineteen years.

"We were treated like objects . . . given no severance pay, no matter how many years we had served. Some of us were dismissed a few days, or even hours, before being vested in the company's retirement plan. Some of us were notified one morning not to return the next—that this was our final day. One fellow spent the day sitting at his desk in a sort of stupor, struggling to keep tears from running down his cheeks. He had spent twenty years with the company."

These sample remarks reflect typical reactions of professional persons who have been subjected to involuntary dismissal. Statistics indicate that such individuals have lost their jobs during the last   months. The man-years of training represented by this number, based on an average of six years of combined undergraduate and graduate training, comes to a staggering figure of man-years presently going unused in our problem-ridden society.

Dismissal is usually direct, sudden, and irrevocable. The act is often performed with guilt feelings by the person responsible and experienced with anger and shock by the person dismissed. The absence of either skill or regret is too often evident. Too many managers simply regard the firing of an employee as an unpleasant duty to be accomplished as quickly as possible.

How can OD improve such a situation?

As a social technology for promoting organizational *effectiveness,* OD generally is thought of in terms that apply to relatively stable—or expanding—organizations. The opposite situation—when contraction is called for—is usually overlooked. Greater attention needs to be paid to the personal and organizational dynamics related to the process of contraction.

This paper is specifically oriented toward the problems facing persons trained in certain scientific and technical specialties (such as aeronautical, electrical, or mechanical engineering, mathematics, physics) who, having lost their jobs because of organizational contraction rather than through any fault of their own, must now cope with the realization that another job in their particular field may not become available. These former employees have been dismissed for reasons external to themselves, such as contract expiration, work cancellation, fund reallocation, economic recession, mergers, plant automation or re-location, or technological changes.

DEVELOPING MANAGERIAL CONCERN

How can a manager deal more constructively with these layoff victims?

He can begin by learning to understand—through increased awareness—what the loss of a job means to a professional man.

Before introducing some material that might help to fill this particular need—the need for increased awareness of the meaning(s) of job loss—we might indicate a process for increasing awareness in *any* area when specific information is not readily available or when personal sensitivity affords no immediate cues.

The process of increasing awareness involves such steps as 1) providing *time* to focus *attention* on the topic; 2) asking *questions*; 3) accumulating *facts* and *feelings*; 4) relating these facts and feelings to possible *courses of action*; 5) exploring possible *consequences* of such actions. After this has been done, we may select and implement the action desired, provided action is called for.

The elements of this process can be made part of an interaction between consultant(s) and manager(s) or between consultant(s) and affected groups. If layoffs are pending, it is desirable to arrange interactions which will involve consultant(s), manager(s), and those facing dismissal. The time needed would vary from one to three hours, depending upon the number of persons involved.

To return to a consideration of the manager's need for increased awareness of what job loss means to a professional man, the following information may be helpful.

It has been learned that for some highly trained persons the loss of a job is a "castrating experience," creating feelings of impotence and helplessness. For others it creates an "identity crisis," because identity for many people derives from the nature of the jobs they hold. Some find that job loss is "image shattering," creating a "failure complex" of guilt and worthlessness. Still others find it a process of regressing to childlike dependency, apathetic withdrawal, and effacement. The emotional shock waves that spread from these reactions create further dilemmas and concerns in each man's relationships with others—especially with members of his family.

There is, however, another side. Though they may be angry about *how* the layoff occurred, a small percentage of the victims react to the loss of their jobs with such remarks as:

"I felt relief."

"I felt it was a new opportunity to look at my career."

"I was elated because it gave me the guts to check out some things I'd always wanted to do."

"I felt relieved to get out of a dehumanizing job."

"I was glad to get away from a miserable tyrant of a boss."

For such men job loss is a liberation from occupational boredom (as divorce might be from marital boredom), from bureaucratic stifling, and from festering disillusionment with themselves. Some it compels to knock on new doors, to gamble on new paths and goals. Many are prepared and willing to take sizable reductions in salary in order to initiate new careers. ("I'll take half of what I was earning to get into something I like better, that's more worthwhile—like cleaning up pollution.") I would estimate, from my consulting experience in industry, that about ten percent of laid-off professionals react in such positive ways.

Reactions to job loss vary according to our perceptions of the meaning of *work*. Thus, understanding the personal meaning of work facilitates understanding the meaning of job loss.

Let us consider what work signifies—first to the individual and then to our society.

Work, for most of us, absorbs the major portion of our time—at least eight hours a day, and often more. Work fills our days. It fills our lives.

For the fortunate man, work is a source of pleasure . . . an absorbing, even consuming activity that makes him feel alive, vital, worthwhile. It gives structure and meaning to his time. It reinforces his actions as it nourishes his zest for living.

For another man, work may be a dulling process, compelling him to lead a life "of quiet desperation" and to hate himself for doing it. It can create emotional and physical illness. It can cause a man—even a professionally trained man—to count the weeks, months, and years as he waits for the liberation of retirement.

For still others, work may provide both pleasure *and* pain, as well as many other ambivalences related to the multiple characteristics of a variety of jobs. But whether it provides pleasure or pain, or a mixture of both, most of us prefer work to unemployment, for even the dullest job satisfies some of our essential needs.

When we honor a man, we honor him primarily for the work he has accomplished. We glorify his performance and the results his work has achieved—as with a Nobel prize. Our Western culture is a working culture, an achievement-oriented culture. If we do not work we have nothing to show for our time—whether in products, services, or satisfactions. If we do not work, we do not expect society to reward us.

Speaking to a U.S. Senate subcommittee engaged in a study of retirement, John Gardner commented, "How much of life's fullness disappears is one of the tragic surprises of retirement." This "tragic surprise" is even more vivid for those whose enforced idleness comes early and unexpectedly during a cutback.

Summarizing the significance of work to most individuals, we might say that it represents. . . .

Self-confirmation—as a valued contributor to society;

Self-assertion—as a producer, working alone or with others;

Self-aggression—as one who tries, and sometimes succeeds, to outdo others;

Self-love—as a prerequisite to loving others;

Self-fulfillment—as a source of pleasure and rewards from functioning to full capacity;

Self-therapy—as a tranquillizer for anxiety and stabilizer of inner turmoil.

Thus when a man shifts from the rank of "employed" to the rank of "unemployed," the addition of that simple prefix brings with it an emotional shift in self-image from "worthy" to "unworthy." Suddenly he feels like a bargain-basement cast-off. He resents the indignity which has been thrust upon him. And he finds his altered status untenable.

The meanings of work for society are reflected in the artifacts of our culture. Work—including creative effort—is the process that produces civilizations. It provides us with the accumulated achievements of past generations. It is the only process available to us for improving our imperfect society. The process of working together supplies our social, technical, and industrial needs and conveniences. It differentiates us from other animals and determines the physical and social conditions under which we live. So when work is taken from us—or denied us—our deepest fears are aroused.

OFFERING SPECIFIC ASSISTANCE

Beyond giving some hard thought to the meaning of job-loss and work, a manager should recognize that cutback victims *do* deserve attention and consideration. This awareness is the primary condition for mobilizing a manager's feelings and skills, so that when he lays off an employee he can be prepared to help the man explore other options for employment and income. It provides the basis for creating new ways of *perceiving* and, therefore, *dealing* with the problems of layoff victims.

With this backdrop, let's now look at specific things that can be done by management, especially top management, to help professionally trained cutback victims. Some of them may seem eminently practical, even obvious. Others you may find "way out." Taken together, they provide the outlines of an attack on a vexing problem.

Provide cutback victims with the longest possible advance notice. This is of utmost importance. The longer the time, the easier it is to adjust—emotionally and operationally—to the departure. A man finds it easier to look for a new job while still on the payroll. His panic feelings are attenuated, and he will present himself more favorably in critical interviews. The objection to longer advance notice—namely, that "the man will lie down on his job once he knows he's leaving"—has not been observed by many managers I've talked to.

Provide precise information on the local and national employment situations. This is useful input data for developing choices and making better decisions. If, for example, a laid-off mechanical engineer is informed by his manager that men in his specialty are a glut on the market in his locality, he will not waste time (a) finding this out for himself or (b) trying to sell his talents if he doesn't yet know it. It is management's responsibility to develop such information, which can be obtained from many sources—including government agencies at the state and federal level concerned with manpower policy and administration.

Offer group counseling to those who wish it. Getting small groups of cutback victims talking together under the guidance of a competent counselor has two main values: It helps them deal with the emotional shock of finding themselves unemployed (perhaps even unemployable in their specialty); and it helps them transform their anxiety, despair, and self-pity into hope and renewed enthusiasm.

I have found that management can develop the necessary counseling capability—in themselves or in other interested persons—in a one-day workshop with a competent specialist in this area. What is needed are candidate counselors who *care* about helping others and are motivated to acquire the necessary helping skills.

Make available services which facilitate the job-hunting process. In California, for example, Lockheed and TRW have set up Employee Information Centers. In addition to counseling, these centers provide such assistance as a practical guidebook on "Finding That Next Job;" lists of job openings in industry and government throughout the country; help in resume preparation and mailing; office space and telephone use; classified advertising and finance sections of Sunday newspapers from different parts of the country; and lists of relevant books and special reference volumes. The cost of these services is estimated at "a few hundred dollars—and worth a lot more." Hundreds of laid-off professionals have used them since they were established.

Develop intercompany talent-sharing opportunities. It should be possible for a physicist, for example, to work two days of the week with Company A, two days with Company B, and devote one day to some personal entrepreneurial activities. Through such an arrangement, the professional would be only *partially* laid off. The company cutting back would have first call on his services, perhaps in exchange for some real effort on its part to line up opportunities in Company B. It would require careful coordination among companies in the depressed region.

Another option available to the concerned manager is to offer to his layoff victims—or potential victims—the opportunity to explore employment and income-development possibilities through three types of workshops: 1) the Income Development Workshop; 2) the Job Search Workshop; and 3) the Career Optimization Workshop. Additional information about a fourth type of workshop which might be of interest to workers not faced with immediate job loss will also be offered.

Income Development Workshop

Purpose: To assist in the development of immediate income opportunities by encouraging professionals to explore how they might generate income by means not necessarily involving their technical specialties.

In a typical workshop, up to fifty participants gather in groups of five or six persons. In each group the discussion is guided by a trained counselor and deals with the following questions and topics:

1. What did I feel when I received my layoff notice? How did I deal with my feelings? Were my actions constructive or destructive? How am I dealing with my feelings now? These are the kinds of questions dealt with in group counselling, discussed earlier, and confronting them in a group session helps the individual cope with the emotional shock and anxiety induced by the cutback.

2. What have other professionals done to generate income outside of their regular jobs? Learning about the experiences of others in earning side income leads to the conviction on the part of those laid off that "If they can do it, I can do it."

3. What *can* I do to generate income? This usually leads to an inventory—drawn out of the individual, in part, by the other members of the group—of personal experiences, resources, and desires which might lead to immediate income generation.

4. What would I *like* to do? The intent here is to help each person to explore possible new goals and to discover how they might overlap the previously generated income possibilities. Some individual career planning is added to the workshop process in this regard.

5. Where can I get the experience I need to get started? Here, presentations are made to the group on such topics as: establishing a new business; Small Business Administration services; special business opportunities like franchising, real estate, and export-

import; personal finance; and converting ideas and patents into marketable products.

6. All right, here's what I think I'll do; what do you fellows think? Individually developed action plans are assessed by the group, and additional possibilities are suggested and explored.

Here is an example of an idea that emerged from this process:

During step 4 Jim commented, "I've got a boat I'd like to keep. I wish I could make a living with it."

The group "brainstormed" this idea and came up with *sixty* possibilities. Jim's favorite was a suggestion that he stock the boat with food items and sell refreshments to the thousands of other boat enthusiasts in the marina. As a result, he began exploring methods for turning his boat into a "Vittles Vessel" or "Burger Barge."

Reactions to Income Development Workshops have included such comments as:

"At first I was reluctant to attend because I feared I would be with a bunch of losers. Now I see us as winners."

"I arrived depressed. I'm leaving optimistic."

"I feel more confident that I can find something interesting to do."

"Each day was worth at least $100 to me."

"I never realized my company cared so much for its employees."

Job Search Workshop

Purpose: Ten to twelve persons, meeting together for one and one-half to two days, learn how to become more effective job seekers.

Activities Outline (A sample program which may be modified and adapted as circumstances require.)

Facing the search together: What needs doing? How can it be done?

Presenting oneself:

1) In writing—biographical summaries, case histories, letters, resumes

2) In person—interview procedures, role-playing, mutual coaching

Searching for job opportunities—preparing job prospect lists, use of executive search firms.

Special participant needs

Following through
Getting feedback

Career Optimization Workshop

Purpose: To enable small groups (up to twenty) of persons with technical training in rapidly changing areas: 1) to examine their present situations; 2) to anticipate future job possibilities; 3) to prepare to bridge the gap between what is and what might be.

Activities Outline

Identifying and discussing the present job for
  1) "Follow-on" or "Add-on" career opportunities
  2) New, alternative career possibilities
Surveying future career possibilities
Developing individual ideal-career fantasies
Integrating career fantasy and reality components
Listing options and preparing time-phased action plans
Implementing personal career optimization programs

The most significant result of such workshop activities is the encouragement of participants to take a more active role in shaping *future* careers while pursuing *current* careers.

This process of self-direction and self-management is new for many reasons. Relatively few of us actively design our futures. More often we simply let them happen. Why do we take so passive, reactive an attitude toward so critical a dimension of our lives? Speculatively we might say that by letting our future happen we somehow absolve ourselves of responsibility for what becomes of us. However—and this is a critical insight to note—such irresponsibility leaves each of us the victim of his own reluctance to plan.

To plan or not to plan?

Planning necessitates the making of choices.

Planning entails resolving dilemmas and ambivalences—difficult tasks for many of us.

Yet to refuse to make choices is to run the risk of having others make choices for us.

Then we become victims, not of our own choices, but of choices others have made. We become pawns of our failure rather than initiators of our success.

Workshop participants frequently indicate that they had felt it was taboo to discuss plans or career opportunities with bosses or peers. OD procedures can facilitate greater openness in a team, creating a climate and norms of communication which permit 1) dialogue about career opportunities and aspirations, and 2) exploration of opportunities for individual growth and career enhancement. In short, career development shifts from a hidden agenda to an open blueprint of explicit career planning.

To achieve this openness requires a recognition on the part of the manager that personal growth motivation may increase job effectiveness rather than threaten it. It provides an opportunity for the manager to demonstrate his concern for assisting people rather than merely manufacturing products.

What-If: Job-Confrontation Workshop

Purpose: To confront persons with the question: "What if I lost my job?" in order to test reactions in two areas: 1) at the feeling level; 2) at an action level where alternatives are generated. Experience has indicated that individual confrontation or groups of no more than three persons are preferable.

(Incidentally, people sometimes admit that they have occasionally, usually briefly, entertained this question but have not thought or talked about it in detail. Other data collected in career counselling with individuals suggests, however, that few persons really confront themselves with this question and that it might be helpful for a facilitator to provide external confrontation.)

Activities Outline

To focus mainly on such questions as the following:
If I lost my job. . . .
     What would I feel?
     How might I deal with my feelings?
     What actions might I take to find another job?
     What are my strengths and how might I build a career around them?
     Who might serve as resource persons for me?

OD INTERVENTION IMPLICATIONS

Workshops and other techniques for assisting career exploration, though focused on different aspects of job search and career development, all emphasize certain values and modes of functioning, such as the following:

The individual who "owns" the problem takes primary responsibility to "work" the problem.
The process for working the problem involves high dependence on
   —openness
   —trust
   —sharing
The process is mutually collaborative rather than individually competitive. The process involves the utilization of both fact-data and feeling-data in working the problems.
The process stresses shifting the mode of functioning from
   —passive to active
   —reactive to proactive

Furthermore, these different interventions, whatever their specific purpose or design, have similar expected payoffs, such as:

—to provide persons with help to reduce emotional turmoil and personal dysfunctioning resulting from lost work opportunities or threatened job loss.
—to provide search techniques for new opportunities.
—to provide new ways to preserve and possibly enhance individual productivity and work satisfactions with optimum self-realization social contributions.

The underlying "values" of these OD interventions might be stated as follows:

—that individual and team productivity and creativity are needed by all of us as part of our specialized training and social interdependence.
—that opportunities for productive functioning must be both individually and organizationally (socially) determined and implemented.
—that work rewards and satisfactions are an important personal value for many and that jeopardizing this value creates profound personal and social dis-ease.
—that critical work and career problems, including layoffs, are valid OD concerns.

Integrating Disrupted Work Relationships: An Action Design for A Critical Intervention

ROBERT T. GOLEMBIEWSKI, STOKES B. CARRIGAN, WALTER R. MEAD, ROBERT MUNZENRIDER and ARTHUR BLUMBERG

ABSTRACT

This study has two central themes, both of which are relevant to applications of the behavioral sciences in "real-life situations." First, considerable psychological trauma can be generated by events such as the demotions reported on here. Second, substantial evidence suggests that a learning design based on the laboratory approach can significantly moderate such trauma. Methodological problems inhibit assigning all observed effects to the learning design. But the presumptive evidence is strong that this action design is one way to apply in organizations the massive forces often observed in sensitivity training groups, one way to apply in vivo the values that commonly guide the development of the miniature societies that are T-groups.

This study details one example of a broad family of critical interventions at work. The focus is on the demotion of 13 field sales managers, many of whom were senior employees. The basic intent of the intervention was to help ease the inevitable stresses on the demotees. These stresses inhered in diverse personal adaptations required of demotees as they changed jobs, schedules, and routines, and as they modified levels of aspiration of perhaps self-concepts. Stresses also inhered in the need to develop viable work relations between the demotee and his new manager, who formerly had been a peer.

The intervention had both personal and organizational aspects. For the demoted men themselves, the intent was to ease what was probably a major and even painful emotional experience for all of the men, and one that was economically costly for most demotees. For the organization, the intent was to preserve its valued human resources. Although they were demoted, that is to say, the men's past efforts and their anticipated future contribution were perceived as significant enough to warrant risking a difficult transition.

The intent of the intervention also can be suggested by two crude equations (Jones, 1968, p. 77). Equation A sketches the grim consequences to be avoided. It proposes that the imaginings or speculations induced by the demotions, given the aloneness of the field situation and the helplessness

Equation A:

$$\left(\begin{array}{l}\text{imaginings}\\ \text{triggered}\\ \text{be demotion}\end{array} + \begin{array}{l}\text{relative}\\ \text{aloneness}\end{array} + \begin{array}{l}\text{relative}\\ \text{helplessness}\end{array}\right) = \begin{array}{l}\text{initial}\\ \text{increases}\\ \text{in}\end{array} \left\{\begin{array}{l}\text{anxiety}\\ \text{depression}\\ \text{hostility}\end{array}\right.$$

to do anything but resign, would generate immediate increases in anxiety, depression, and hostility. Such effects probably would not serve the individual, nor would they help in making necessary adjustments at work. In contrast, Equation B proposes to confront the imaginings induced by the demotions with the sharing of resources in a community setting that hopefully will increase a demotee's sense of mastery over the consequences of his demotion.

Equation B:

$$\left(\begin{array}{l}\text{imaginings}\\ \text{triggered}\\ \text{by demotion}\end{array} + \text{community} + \text{mastery}\right) = \begin{array}{l}\text{effective}\\ \text{coping, or}\\ \text{reductions}\\ \text{in initial}\end{array} \left\{\begin{array}{l}\text{anxiety}\\ \text{depression}\\ \text{hostility}\end{array}\right.$$

LABORATORY APPROACH AS *GENUS*

The action design for this critical intervention is based on the laboratory approach (Golembiewski & Blumberg, 1970). Perhaps the term "action design" is dramatic, but we wish to distinguish the design from sensitivity training in several major senses. To illustrate these differences only, the design in this case deals with a "very real" problem; the target-concerns are rooted firmly in specific organizational relationships, although the focus may extend beyond the worksite; and the thrust is toward a working resolution of major concerns that have long-run implications rather than toward dealing with reactions and feelings in a temporary group. Although they differ in important particulars, however, this action design and sensitivity training are viewed as *species* within the *genus* laboratory approach. The "laboratory approach" is, in brief (Schein & Bennis, 1965, p. 4):

"an educational strategy which is based primarily on the experiences generated in various social encounters *by the learners themselves,* and which aims to influence attitudes and develop competencies toward learning about human interactions. Essentially, therefore, laboratory training attempts to induce changes with regard to the learning process itself and to communicate a particular method of learning and inquiry. It has to do 'with learning how to learn'."

THE DEMOTED POPULATION

As part of a broader reduction-in-force, 13 regional managers from the marketing department of a major firm were given two choices, of accepting demotion to senior salesmen, or terminating. The demotees were a heterogeneous lot. Table 1 presents some descriptive data about the men and their eventual choices. Relatedly, although most of the demotees would suffer a major reduction in salary, reductions would range from less than $1000 to approximately four times that amount for the demotees with most seniority.

Several forces-in-tension influenced the decisions of the 13 men. In favor of choosing termination were such factors as the generous separation allowances available to those with seniority affected by reductions-in-force. To suggest the countervailing forces, the job market was tight, the company was considered a good employer, and market conditions required cutting as deeply as the 13 managers, all of whom were satisfactory performers.

All but two of the managers accepted the demotion and, as Table 2 shows, were given an early work assignment intended to facilitate their making the required adaptations as effectively and quickly as possible. The demotees knew that the "integrative experience" had been discussed with, and approved by, several managerial levels in the marketing department. In addition, almost all of the demotees and all of their superiors had long-standing relations of trust with four of the authors of this paper, who variously participated in the development and implementation of this action design.

BROAD PURPOSES

Five broad goals of the critical intervention may be distinguished. First, the action design was intended to build on the values of the laboratory approach. The company had invested in a major way in a program of Organization Development, in which

Table 1. Selected Data About Demotees

Demotee	Age	Years with Company	Years as Regional Sales Mgr.	Decision to Accept Demotion
1	36	12	1	No
2	35	10	5	No
3	40	7	6 mos.	Yes
4	39	9	7 mos.	Yes
5	51	23	16	Yes
6	33	5	10 mos.	Yes
7	43	12	5	Yes
8	44	17	7	Yes
9	43	12	5	Yes
10	35	11	8 mos.	Yes
11	55	24	17	Yes
12	35	10	2 yrs. 6 mos.	Yes
13	50	13	10	Yes

Table 2. The Timing of the Action Design

Day 1	Day 2	Day 6	Day 7	Day 45
13 managers informed of choices:	Decision required:	Three major activities:	Two major activities:	Demotees and superiors respond to MAACL:
—demotion to salesman	—11 managers accept demotion	—demotees and superiors respond to MAACL: pre-test	—demotees meet individually with their new superiors	test of persistence of changes
—termination			—demotees and superiors respond to MAACL: post-test	
If demotion accepted, an early work assignment would involve reporting to a midwestern city for an "integrative experience" along with their new superiors		—demotees spend balance of day in discussion —superiors have briefing meeting		

an offsite sensitivity training experience was a major early learning vehicle.[1] Eighteen of the 22 participants—the 11 demotees
and their immediate supervisors—had such a learning experience earlier. The other 4 men had their sensitivity training postponed only by the major reduction-in-force at issue here. Moreover, 19 of the men had been involved in various "team development" activities that attempted to extend the initial offsite training directly into organization activities.

The thrust of the initial sensitivity training experience is to help
organization members in two ways: to build a specific set of norms
or values into their workaday relations; and to aid in the development of attitudes and behavioral skills appropriate to those norms.
Table 3 sketches three sets of such norms, or values, and suggests
some of the appropriate behaviors. The norms are meant in the
sense of ideals-to-be-strived-for, as individuals become increasingly convinced that it is safe to do so, and as they learn by experience whether they can meet their own needs by following the
norms.

The challenge posed by the demotions was simply to apply the
norms of the laboratory approach in a specific case that was personally and organizationally meaningful. Significantly, the specific case is a complex matter. Demotions involve difficult and
subtle adjustments, in emotions, in work routines, and in relations. In the case of most of the present demotees, as was noted,
major salary cuts also could require economic adjustments for
many of the men.

Second, the purpose was to begin developing integrative linkages at the earliest possible time after the demotion announce-
ments. The focus of the derivative two-day design was on common
personal or interpersonal data. On the first day, these data included the reactions of the demotee, his concerns about attending
regional sales meetings as a peer rather than as superior of salesmen, etc. On the second day, the focus was on supervisory relations between the 11 pairs of men who had been peers, the demoted one of whom would sometimes have substantially more
seniority than his new superior.

Third, the intent was to provide a specific action arena in which

1. For the basic design, see Robert T. Golembiewski and Arthur Blumberg,
"Sensitivity Training in Cousin Groups: A Confrontation Design," *Training and
Development Journal*, Vol. 23 (August, 1969), pp. 18-23.

Table 3. Four Value-Loaded Dimensions Relevant In Laboratory Aprroach to Organization Change and Development

A	B	C
Meta-Values* of Lab Approach	Proximate Goals of Lab Approach	Organization Values Consistent with Lab Approach†
1. an attitude of inquiry reflecting (among others): a. a hypothetical spirit; and b. experimentalism 2. expanded consciousness and sense of choice 3. the value system of democracy, having as two core elements: a. a spirit of collaboration; and b. open resolution of conflict via a problem-solving orientation 4. an emphasis on mutual helping relationships as the best way to express man's interdependency with man	1. increased insight, self-knowledge 2. sharpened diagnostic skills at (ideally) all levels, that is, on the levels of the a. individual; b. group; c. organization; and d. society 3. awareness of, and skill-practice in creating, conditions of effective functioning at (ideally) all levels 4. testing self-concepts and skills in interpersonal situations 5. increased capacity to be open, to accept feelings of self and others, to risk interpersonally in rewarding ways	1. full and free communication 2. reliance on open consensus in managing conflict, as opposed to using coercion or compromise 3. influence based on competence rather that on personal whim or formal power 4. expression of emotional as well as task-oriented behavior 5. acceptance of conflict between the individual and his organization, to be coped with willingly. openly, and rationally

*Adapted from Edgar H. Schein and Warren G. Bennis, *Personal and Organizational Change Through Group Methods* (New York: Wiley, 1965), pp 30-35; and Leland P. Bradford, Jack R. Gibb, and Kenneth D. Benne, editors, *T-Group Theory and Laboratory Method* (New York: Wiley, 1964), pp. 10, 12.

† Philip E. Slater and Warren G. Bennis, "Democracy Is Inevitable," *Harvard Business Review*, Vol. 42 (1964), 51-55.

feelings could be expressed *and* worked through, if possible. The working symbolism was the cauterization of wound, not pleasant but preferable to the possible or probable alternatives. The anti-goals were obsessiveness, and the postponement of a required facing-up to new work demands that would probably loom larger with the passage of time.

Fourth, the goal was to provide diverse support to the demotees at a critical time. The support was to come from demoted peers, superiors, and the employing organization. The common theme was: "We want this to work for you as much as possible, and not against you." At the most elemental level, most managers perceived that the expense of the integrative experience itself was a signal measure of "the organization's" concern and support.

The vicious cycle-to-be-avoided can be sketched. Depression was an expected result of the demotions, for example, especially for the more senior men. Unless carefully managed, depression can work against the man. The consequences of believing "the organization is against me" can be both subtle and profound, especially for the field salesman. Incoming cues and messages might be misinterpreted, and outgoing projections of self might trigger unintended consequences. More broadly, Kiev (1969, p. 2) traces an unattractive catalog of the "manifestations of depressions," which include "diminished incentive, interest, morale, and ability to concentrate, feelings of alienation, inability to assume responsibility or to follow a routine, diminished ability of self-expression, self-assertiveness and decreased pride, irritation with interference, feelings of being unappreciated or worthlessness. . . . [The] psychophysiological concomitants of early depression . . . include insomnia, loss of appetite, excessive worrying, indigestion, and decline in energy."

Fifth, the integrative experience was intended to provide early readings about possible adaptive difficulties, readings for managers, the demotees, and the training staff. Efforts were made to legitimate early contacts from both supervisors and demotees if future help were necessary.

CHARACTERISTICS OF THE ACTION DESIGN

A simple learning design was developed to meet these multiple goals. The constant target was adaptation to the new status, which implied the development of new work relations. In terms of time, roughly 50 per cent was spent with the demotees working together, and 50 per cent with the demotees individually attempting to work through issues of concern with their new supervisors.

The first design component brought the demotees together for discussion of their concerns, problems, and needs. Approximately

4 hours were devoted to this exploration, with two resource persons available. The formal afternoon session was kept deliberately short, although it provided the model for several informal sessions in the evening. The announced design intent was to help prepare the demotees for the next day's sessions with their individual managers concerning work relations. This action-thrust sought to harness emotional energies to organization purposes rather than to diffuse them through ventilation.

The role of the resource persons in this initial phase to harness emotional energies rather than to diffuse them was a mixed one. In capsule, the resource persons sought to direct attention to "content" as well as to "process," whereas the trainer's role in sensitivity training emphasizes "process." The distinction is not an easy one to make briefly, but the notions refer to an emphasis on *what is done* and on the *way things are done,* respectively (Schein, 1969, pp. 13-75).

Specifically, the first design component began with personal reactions to the demotions and then trended toward an emphasis on the problems that demotees perceived as relevant in developing the required new work relations. In the later phases, the reactions of the men to the problems expected in their new roles were stressed, as were their concerns about facing these problems. Whenever possible, alternative ways of coping with problems were explored. The following list provides some flavor of the main themes dealt with, beginning with personal reactions and trending toward issues that were more work-related:

1. comparing experiences, especially about the diverse ways in which various relevant organization policies were applied to their individual cases;
2. encouraging expression of anxiety or hostility about the demotions themselves or about the associated processes or their style, timing, etc.;
3. surfacing and testing suspicion of management, as in the concern that another personnel purge was imminent;
4. isolating and, as possible, working through demotees' concerns about authority/dependence, as in the complaint that the demotees did not see themselves being treated as adults, or that they were men enough to take the demotions without the integrative experience;
5. dealing with a variety of topics—e.g., explaining the demo-

tions to clients or other salesmen—so as to develop norms that would reduce the probability of either avoiding the topics or awkwardly handling them in the field; and

6. identifying relevant others with whom interaction had been stressful, or with whom it might prove to be so, the emphasis being on strategies for handling such interaction.

Surely success varied from case to case, but the intention of the resource persons was constant. That intention, in sum, was to: facilitate expression of feelings and reactions; to help reveal the diversity of the demotees' experiences and coping strategies; and to work toward a successful adaptation to the demands of the new job. More specifically, the model for interventions was an insight-action model, with the emphasis clearly on the action. To illustrate, assume that Individual A was sending signals of fear and anger concerning some technical aspect of his new job. The resource persons sought to intervene at a process level as in a T-Group, with the goals of making A aware of those signals and of putting him in touch with the inducing emotions, if possible. The seven old-T-Group hands among the demotees were very active in this regard, also. The capstone intervention here tended to be associated with the readiness of Individual A to raise the concern and the associated feelings with his new manager, with whom he would meet the next day. The action-thrust is patent. Moreover, the technical content at issue also would be explored. Sometimes the resolution was easy, as in clarifying a misunderstanding or a misinterpretation. When the resolution was difficult, interventions by the resource persons tended to be questions with an action-thrust. What does Individual A prefer? What are the other alternative strategies? What role can or should his new manager play in the matter, especially in the meeting between the two that was scheduled for the next day?

More broadly, resource persons were not advocates of management actions; nor were they neuters without emotional response to the sometimes tragi-comic dynamics of the demotions. But they were committed to helping the demotees face their demotions as clearly and realistically as possible. Hence the resource persons considered it an open option that some demotees might decide to accept termination after the integrative experience. None of the men did so.

It is not possible to convey the diversity of the products of this first design component, but two themes provide a useful substantive summary. First, almost all demotees emphasized the positive meaning of the integrative experience, whatever its specific outcomes. The design implied to them their value to the organization, and also reflected a continuing effort to provide resources which would help them do the job. From this perspective, the design had substantial value as a sign that efforts to act on the norms sketched in Table 3 would be made even under conditions of substantial stress, which no doubt provide the best test of managerial intentions. This positive evaluation was variously shared by all the supervisors. One of the demotees took a different approach. He resented the integrative experience as "hand-holding" and "coddling."

Second, the first component of the learning design emphasized some common elements among the demotees, as well as some differentiating factors. The training staff saw both the commonality and differentiation as being reality-based, and their conscious strategy was to avoid at all costs a strained display of ardent but feigned homogeneity or good fellowship among the demotees.

The elements of commonality that emerged in discussion among the demotees were expected ones. They include: the impact of the demotion on the self; experiences with important referents such as wives, colleagues, or salesmen from other firms; and concerns about taking on the salesman's job, about "picking up the bag again" to cover a sales territory, about participating in sales meetings, and so on.

The differentiating elements were harder for the men to openly identify, but they were no less clearly reality-based. For example, the demotees included both long-service employees, as well as recent managerial appointees. Reasonably, on balance, the younger men could be expected to feel more optimism about being re-promoted. The future for the longer-service men was far less bright, realistically, and they generally if sometimes grudgingly asknowledged the point. Relatedly, some men professed shock at being confronted with the choice of demotion or termination. Others maintained they more or less expected some action, because of falling demand in the industry, or performance problems, or both. A few even expressed pleasure that the action was not so severe for them as it had been for many others affected by the major reduction-in-force.

The second component of the integrative experience took two approaches to extending demotee concerns into action, via the development of new working relations between the managers and their new subordinates. First, the managers met for some two hours to discuss the design for the next day and their role in it. The meeting's initial tone was a kind of gallows humor, which the training staff interpreted as understandable anxiety among the managers about their role. This initial tone quickly dissipated into the theme of making the transitions as easy as possible for all concerned. The basic thrust was to empathize with how the demotees were feeling, and to channel those feelings toward making the most successful adaptation possible.

Second, the demotees spent approximately 3 hours with their managers in one-to-one situations. The resource persons sat in on some of the dyads, as time permitted, and especially the dyads with senior demotees. The major concerns invloving these dyads were:

1. The building of early supervisory relations, as in mutual pledges to work harmoniously together, which was easy enough in some cases because some of the demotees were able to choose their new managers;
2. technical problems such as going over sales territories, etc.;
3. developing strategies by which the manager and man could be mutually helpful, as in discussing ways to moderate the formation of cliques that the demotions could encourage; and
4. isolating likely problems and cementing a contract to agree to meet any such problems mutually and early.

Some dyads concentrated on one of these concerns, while others gave attention to several themes.

MEASURING INSTRUMENT

The effects of the action design for helping integrate disrupted work relationships were judged by changes in the Multiple Affect Adjective Check List (MAACL) developed by Zuckerman and Lubin. MAACL is a brief instrument for tapping the psychological aspects of emotion, which conceives of affect not as a trait but as a state. That is, a time referent is specified for the respondent, who reacts as he feels "today" or "now" as opposed to how he feels "generally" or "occasionally." The researchers (Zuckerman & Lubin, 1965, p. 3) explain that MAACL

was designed to fill the need for a self-administered test which would provide valid measures of three of the clinically relevant negative affects: anxiety, depression, and hostility. No attempt was made to measure positive affects but some of the evidence indicates that the scales are bipolar, and that low scores on the full scales will indicate states of positive affect.

Its authors place MAACL "in a research phase and . . . not yet recommended for routine applied use," but accumulating evidence suggests its value (Zuckerman & Lubin, 1965, pp. 6-16). In an initial study, the validity of the test was suggested by changes in the Anxiety scale administered just prior to an examination showed significant increases from an established base, as expected. Similar changes in the Depression and Hostility scales were induced by administering a classroom examination a week earlier than announced. An extensive bibliography provides detailed reinforcement of these illustrations of validity (Zuckerman & Lubin, 1970).

The expectations in this case were direct. The demotees were expected to have high initial scores on Anxiety, Depression, and Hostility, which a successful intervention would reduce significantly in a post-treatment administration of MAACL. Lower initial scores were expected for the managers, and the post-treatment administration was not expected to reveal any major shifts in scores, except perhaps on anxiety. This expectation is based on the assumption that the managers, who had to develop new relations with their former peers, might be somewhat anxious initially about their role in the learning design. This anxiety was expected to fall as the design unfolded and especially as it proved useful.

A third follow-up administration of MAACL was administered by mail approximately a month after the planned intervention. The purpose was to develop data about the persistence of any before/after changes. A potent training intervention was expected to preserve over time any reductions in anxiety, depression, and hostility induced by the demotions, in the face of the relative isolation and threat of the field situation.

Respondents were given code numbers that permitted comparing the before/after responses of specific individuals.[2] One of the 22 subjects did not respond to the third administration. Hence the N in the several statistical tests reported on below varies.

SOME MAJOR RESULTS

Five themes emerging from the results deserve spotlighting. First, as expected, the demotees initially generated high scores on all three MAACL scales. That the demotions were traumatic can be demonstrated in several ways. For example, the demotees initially scored higher than the managers on all three MAACL scales, the differences being statistically significant far beyond the .005 level. To a similar point, Lubin and Zuckerman (1969, p. 488) tell us that a transformed "score of 70 is generally accepted as the point beyond which scores on a psychometric instrument are considered to be unusually high, as that point represents a score higher than that achieved by 98 per cent of the standardization sample." Only two of the 33 transformed scores for demotees on the three scales reach that level on the initial administration, but an additional 8 men have transformed scores of 60 or above on the pre-test. In sum, the demotees reacted strongly to the demotion, but their scores were not "unusually high."

Second, the data meet all expectations concerning changes attributable to the training intervention. Specifically, as Table 4 shows, demotees reported statistically-significant decreases on all three scales on the second administration of the MAACL, and these sharp and sudden reductions were at least maintained through the third administration. As Table 4 also shows, indeed, a comparison of the Anxiety scores on administrations 2 vs. 3 shows a statistically-significant reduction following the earlier and major reductions.

The major and sudden reductions in MAACL scores between the first two administrations imply the potency of the brief training intervention. The conclusion is reinforced by the lack of evidence that respondents become adapted to the MAACL items in responding to successive administration. What is not known

2. Note that on the third administration, researchers made an assignment decision in one questionable case. Statistically, it turns out, the assignment affects the results in trifling ways only.

Table 4. Overall Effects of Intervention on Three MAACL Administrations

	Mean Scale Scores, by Administrations			t = test values for paired administrations		
	1	2	3	1 vs. 2	1 vs. 3	2 vs. 3
Demotees						
Anxiety	9.8	7.5	6.5	2.59†	2.74†	2.14*
Depression	17.8	14.8	13.6	2.88‡	2.65†	1.09
Hostility	9.5	7.2	7.2	2.90‡	1.98†	0.15
Managers						
Anxiety	6.3	5.3	4.6	1.24*	1.83*	0.83
Depression	9.8	9.5	9.5	0.23	0.38	0
Hostility	5.1	5.3	5.7	— .30	— .87	— .62

    * indicates .05 level of statistical significance.
    † indicates .025 level of statistical significance.
    ‡ indicates .01 level of statistical significance.

is how long this initially-high level would have been maintained in the absence of the training intervention.

Third, the scores of the managers showed a significant change only for Anxiety. That reduction is most easily attributed to a successful intervention, a building-down from a realistic prior concern about what the integrative experience would demand of the supervisor. Interestingly, scores on the Hostility scale increased for the managers, although not significantly so. This may reflect a reasonable reaction against the action design, or against the training staff, whose focus was clearly more to help the demoted men than the managers. The moderate increase in Hostility scores suggests a neglect of supervisory needs, in sum, which subsequent design variations should recognize.

Fourth, a variety of analytical approaches establishes that the design had quite uniform effects for all demotees, regardless of their other differences. For example, correlation analysis revealed insignificant associations between changes on MAACL scores and four variables describing individual demoted managers: age; years with company; years as regional manager; and loss of salary involved in the demotion. The four individual variables were highly and positively inter-correlated. The inter-correlation matrix contains these 5 values: .7309, .7430, .8317, .8593, and .9545, all of which attain at least the .01 level of statistical significance. However, in only 1 case in 72 does one of these four variables correlate significantly with any of 18 measures of outcomes: the 9 absolute scores on Anxiety, Depression, and Hostility in each of the three administrations; and the 9 measures of relative change on the 3 MAACL scales which compare scores on the three administrations, taken by pairs. Consider "salary loss," for example. Not one of its 18 correlation coefficients with the various outcome variables attains the .05 level of statistical significance, $\pm.60$ by two-tailed test. In fact, only 3 of the 18 coefficients reach $\pm.40$, while 9 coefficients fall in the interval $\pm.199$ through $-.199$.

Such data support the dominance of treatment effects. No attempt was made to deal with partials in the correlation analysis, however, given the small N.

Fifth, the effects on individuals also establish the efficacy of the design. Three perspectives on the data provide evidence. First, consider a crude comparison of the first and second MAACL administrations. Of the 33 comparisons—11 demotees three MAACL scales—26 were reductions and 3 were no-changes in scores. No demotee had an increased score on more than one scale, in addition. Looked at from another point of view, second, the data show only a single demotee who has even one score significantly greater than the mean of any scale on the first administration, and whose scores were not significantly lower in later administrations. Using a more demanding convention, third, the demotees can be divided as:

1. 3 men all of whose scores on the third MAACL administration were "major decreases,' that is, they were at least one standard deviation less than the means on each of the three scales on the first administration;

2. 3 men who had major decreases on two MAACL scales and a more modest reduction on the third scale;

3. 1 man who had a major decrease on one MAACL scale and more modest reductions on the other scales;

4. 2 men who experienced no reduction of greater than a standard deviation on any scale; and

5. 1 man who had a "major increase" on the third administration of one standard deviation greater than the initial mean on one MAACL scale and who was at or near the initial means on all three scales; and

6. 1 man who had a major increase on one MAACL scale plus a major reduction on another, and who was substantially above the initial means.

Sixth, post-experience interviews with the demotees and several levels of their managers underscore the value of the design. Many of the details cannot be revealed since they might identify individuals. But the overall thrust of the interviews is clear. The integrative experience was considered valuable in smoothing what had been predicted to be a very stormy and costly transition. Significantly but not conclusively, all 11 demotees are still on the job some 6 months later, and 10 are considered to have made the transition "in great shape" a "more than adequately" on a 20-point scale running through "adequate," "somewhat inadequate," and "critically inadequate."

CONCLUSION

The application of a learning design based on the laboratory approach, then, seems to have induced the intended consequences. Conservatively, the intervention seems to have quickly reversed emotional states that can generate consequences troublesome for the individual and the organization. Specifically, scores on Anxiety, Depression, and Hostility scales were reduced significantly for a small population of demoted field supervisors, following the learning experience. These reductions were maintained or augmented in a third administration of the measuring instrument, spaced in time far enough after the intervention to test persistence.

Note also that it seems likely that the present learning design profited from earlier work in the host organization to develop norms, attitudes, and behaviors consistent with the laboratory approach. No concrete proof exists, but the training staff feels strongly that the observed effects derive in some substantial part from the earlier work in sensitivity training groups, as that training influenced individual behavior and as it helped develop appropriate attitudes and norms in the host organization. At least in the absence of very compelling (and presently unavailable) evidence, this design may not be applicable in organizations as a first-generation effort.

Methodological inelegancies prohibit uniquely attributing the effects to the learning design, but the presumptive evidence is strong. For example, the initial reductions cannot easily be attributed to the passage of time. The interval between the first and second MAACL administrations was a brief one, and the demotees had patently developed and sustained high scores on the three marker variables in the five or six days intervening between the demotion notices and the integrative experience. It is of course possible that the observed changes were artifacts of the design. But it does not seem likely that, for example, the announcement of the integrative experience alone triggered the high MAACL scores, which naturally dropped when that experience proved benign. Post-interviews with the demotees largely scotch this explanation, although some minor "anticipation effect" no doubt existed.

In other senses, however, more substantial reservations must hedge attributing the observed results to the learning design. For example, was the real magic in this case in the "process analysis" and the values of the laboratory approach? Or did some or all of the potency derive from the very act of bringing the men together, a kind of Hawthorne token that management really cared, and no matter about the specific learning design? Similarly, it is not known how long the initial levels of anxiety, depression, and hostility would have persisted if nature had been allowed to run its course.

Only a fool or a very wise man could definitely answer the latter questions. The issues are incredibly complex. This pilot study at least suggests one promising extension of the laboratory approach into large organizations and urges the comparative analysis of other designs that can safely be added to the kit of the change-agent.

REFERENCES

Golembiewski, Robert T., & Blumberg, Arthur, Editors. *Sensitivity training and the laboratory approach.* Itasca, Ill.: F. E. Peacock, 1970.

Jones, Richard M. *Fantasy and feeling in education.* New York: New York University Press, 1968.

Kiev, Ari. Crisis intervention in industry. Paper delivered at Annual Meeting, New York State Society of Industrial Medicine, Occupational Psychiatry Group, Dec. 10, 1969.

Lubin, Bernard, & Zuckerman, Marvin. Levels of emotional arousal in laboratory training. *Journal of Applied Behavioral Science,* Vol. 5, October, 1969.

Schein, Edgar H. *Process observation.* Reading, Mass.: Addison-Wesley, 1969.

Schein, Edgar H., & Bennis, Warren G. *Personal and organizational change through group methods.* New York: Wiley, 1965.

Zuckerman, Marvin, & Lubin, Bernard. *Manual for the multiple affect adjective check list.* San Diego, Calif.: Educational and Industrial Testing Service, 1965.

Zuckerman, Marvin, & Lubin, Bernard. *Bibliography for the multiple affect adjective check list.* San Diego, Calif.: Educational and Industrial Testing Service, 1970.

SECTION IV

Training Interventions

Training continues to be a prominent part of many OD efforts. The training programs described in these three articles have not, however, been typical in any OD effort to date. Oshry's power lab has been conducted as an intervention in an organization once, but it was not part of an OD process. These training programs, then, represent new designs.

As I stated in the introductory chapter of this book, power is probably the most neglected dynamic of organizational behavior today. In my opinion, most OD practitioners are woefully naive about power in organizations and inexperienced in dealing with the uses and misuses of power. The power lab described by Oshry doesn't promise to solve what I am advocating as a problem for OD practitioners, but it is one of the few steps I know that approaches the situation experientially and holds the promise of providing a significant learning experience for participants.

Dyer contends that very little effort has been devoted to investigating organizational conditions that foster creativity among employees. He also contends that the knowledge for *changing* an organization to provide these conditions is lacking. After describing what he thinks certain organizational conditions are that facilitate creativity, Dyer explains the design of a training laboratory which was an attempt to learn (a) the nature of the creative process, (b) how to identify and assess creative potential in individuals, (c) which conditions in an organization facilitate or block creativity, (d) how to manage the creative process, and (e) how an OD practitioner can influence a change process toward more creativity.

In the final chapter of this section, Ferguson describes a training design which helps individuals understand how they influence the psychological climate in an organization. Managers and consultants do not always see the direct cause and effect relationship between the kinds of attitudes they choose to mobilize and express and the psychological climate, with its inevitable results, that they thereby produce. The design is one that facilitates understanding that psychological or organizational climate can be influenced and to a significant extent controlled.

Power and the Power Lab

BARRY OSHRY

I. INTRODUCTION

"Power" is an emotionally loaded word. It conjures up images of riots, revolution, destruction, and the overthrow of established order. It also conjures up images of class struggles, and of open or covert warfare between the have's and have not's, between the Establishment (who supposedly have all the power) and the disenfranchised (who supposedly have none of it). To confound matters still further, the emotionalism surrounding power is often cloaked in supposed moralistic concerns—whether or not power itself is good or evil or " in the natural order of things," or whether or not man has the right or duty or obligation to fight for power when he has none, or whether or under what conditions violence is a legitimate weapon in the struggle for power.

Given the skittish state of our nation with regard to power upheavals—Black power, Woman power, Consumer power, Radical power, and so forth—it is reasonable that the "clients" of O.D. services should look with equal skittishness at interventions promising to elevate and deal with issues of power in social systems. In short, there are far more marketable products.

Our reasons for pursuing matters of power and the Power Lab, despite this apparent paucity of potential clients and applications, are as follows:

1. Power and power differences are realities of social systems. They are there and will continue to operate whether or not we are comfortable with them and whether or not we choose to deal with them.

2. It is our belief that increased knowledge with regard to power will make such phenomena more understandable, hence more manageable, eventually less anxiety-provoking, and ultimately even enjoyable.

3. It is our belief that power differences, specifically the effective management of power differences within social systems, is a source of considerable human energy. Conversely, it is our

feeling that those who, because of their own blind spots surrounding power, attempt to develop systems interventions
aimed at minimizing or reducing power differences, inadvert-
ently act in ways which reduce the creative energy of these
systems.

4. Finally, it is our belief that "feelings of powerlessness," regardless of whether one is in a position of power or among
the disenfranchised, are considerably more widespread than
"feelings of power," and that, in fact, it is *shared powerlessness*
within institutions and societies which contributes greatly to
the emotionalism surrounding this area. It is our belief that
people at the very top—people at the so-called seats of power
—share with the disenfranchised the psychological state of
feeling blocked in (a) identifying that which they want to have
happen and (b) making it happen. Powerlessness is not the
exclusive property of the disenfranchised.

Those at the top, who fear that others are "out to get them"
or want to take something away from them, are justified in such
fears since that may in fact be part or all of the motivation, and
that certainly may be one possible outcome. But, our purposes in
creating laboratory learning experiences around power are not:
(a) to encourage the "disenfranchised" to overthrow the "establishment" nor (b) to encourage the "establishment" to give away
(or share, which is the "O.D." way of putting it) power to the
disenfranchised when, in fact, they may not be feeling very powerful in the first place. Our goal is to create learning conditions regarding power which can result in a diminution of "feelings of
powerlessness" *throughout* a social system and an increase in
"feelings of power" *throughout* that system.

The Power Lab is intended as a first step in that direction.

II. HIGHLY SELECTED APHORISMS[1]

This section is inserted to stir the reader's "juices" regarding
some complex issues surrounding power and social systems before proceeding with a description of the Power Lab and related
design issues.

---

1. The writer apologizes for some confusion in his multiple uses of the word
"power." Sometimes it is used to refer to "positions of power" and sometimes it
refers to "feelings of power."

1. Power differences are a major source of human energy within social systems. But, energy in and of itself is neither good nor bad. Just as it may lead to growth and creativity, so may it lead to violence and destruction. The goal for systems growth and maintenance is not the elimination of power differences but the development of skills in the management of these power differences.

2. Crippling strikes, riots, massacres, and wars result from power confrontations. Improved living and working conditions, more equitable distribution of goods and services, and the overthrow of tyranny also result from power confrontations. The morality of power confrontations depends heavily on where you were before the confrontations and how it turns out for you.

3. Most people who have any kind of continuing relationship with others have the potential for some power in that relationship. They may or may not be aware of this power; they may or may not be comfortable in the exercise of this power; but that power is still there. Power is the *potential to withhold from another that which the other needs or wants, such withholding being in the service of realizing one's own goals.* Even the most powerless of us are frequently confronted with options for exercising our power. We can ask, "What's in it for me if I do what you want?" We can say, "I'll do it *if....*" We can say, "If you want it so badly, do it yourself!"

4. There is a difference between being "In" or "Out" of a social system, on the one hand, and being "Powerful" or "Powerless" on the other. O.D. Specialists, like most middle management people, tend to be "In" and "Powerless." You can be "In" a social system—i.e., have relatively free access to the goods, services, and privileges of that system—while at the same time being "Powerless"—i.e., having no control over how these goods, services and privileges are distributed throughout the system. Those who are in seats of power and are motivated to maintain the status quo thrive on the willingness of "Powerless Ins" to barter away power in order to remain "In."

5. The condition of being "In" produces its own perceptual framework. "Outs" see their conditions and the total social system differently from how it is seen by "Ins." Both groups

then, viewing the same conditions, see different "realities." This is particularly true around issues of power. Whereas "Ins" may be largely oblivious to the operations of power around them, "Outs" may be acutely aware of the finest nuances of power.

6. Militants and O.D. Specialists are both change agents. Since the former arise from the Outs and the latter from the Ins, each brings quite different diagnostic perceptions to his work, particularly around issues of power and what constitutes legitimate grounds for moving against power. To the militant, a "rip-off" is a "rip-off" and all rip-offs are equal fair game for confrontation. An O.D. Specialist is likely to be more discriminating in his perceptions and, consequently, more lenient in his judgements regarding the actions of power people.

7. Man is frightened by his own aggressive impulses. Just as he is aware of his own capabilities of and tendencies toward violence and destruction, so is he aware of and frightened by the same in others. Throughout Man's history, various religious, philosophical and psychological schemes have been developed promulgating Man as an essentially non-aggressive creature. Yet, whenever the conditions have been right, these same schemes have been modified to support the most brutal and violent forms of aggression. Wishing away Man's nature is not the same as altering it. It is suicidal to confuse the two.

8. The quickest and most economical path to team development is to confront those team members with an adversary having power to adversely affect their lives. The person-to-person glue resulting from such a condition is more quickly produced and more durable than that arising from helping team members identify and work through their work and interpersonal issues.

9. Love/trust models for systems growth and development are based on fantasy notions regarding the nature of Man. Love and trust are naturally emerging phenomena occurring among members of a sub-system when that sub-system is confronted with an adversary sub-system which threatens to oppress and overwhelm it. For two such systems to deal with one another on a love/trust basis seems idealistic, uneconomical, and self-destructive.

10. Maintaining the status quo is often justified as the basis of "tradition." If this use of tradition in any way implies assumptions about the basic nature of man or the basic nature of social systems, then this must be dismissed as short-sighted demagoguery. The United States of America is less than two-hundred years old; the industrial revolution itself only began in the mid-eighteenth century; super corporations and giant conglomerates are still more recent; multi-national corporations are a phenomenon of the past decade. By contrast, man as a social animal has been around for over a million years. Many civilizations—each with its own implicit or explicit theories regarding the nature of man and social systems— have risen and fallen during this period. Some of these have endured for *thousands* of years. Given the dire predictions emanating from many quarters regarding the future of our little experiment, and given the widespread discontent, the rampant lawlessness, the increasing number of societal "drop-outs," and the deterioration of cities once cited as the jewels of our way of life, appeals to tradition must be based on something other than rationality.

11. Sometimes "pure" research is the last hope. There are things we need to know about human systems—the conditions under which they can and cannot succeed—even though it may appear that, given the nature of our society and its social systems, we haven't the slightest chance of ever applying this knowledge.

III. THE POWER LAB

A. Experiential Conditions Created

The Power Lab is designed to provide participants with direct experiences in *power* or *powerlessness* in a social system and *inclusion* (being "in") or *exclusion* (being "out") in a social system. The design structure is such that participants experience these not so much as individuals but as members of different social sub-systems each with its own set of special conditions.

B. Beginning Structure of the Power Lab

Participants find themselves assigned to one of three social subsystems within a society.

1. *The Social Sub-Systems*

   Powerful Ins:[2] This group *has power* (that is, it controls all goods and services; it can make rules and change rules) and *is in* (that is, it has easy access to all goods and services).

   Powerless Ins: This group *is in* (that is, it has easy access to all goods and services) but has no power (that is, it cannot make or change the rules; it has no direct control over goods or services).

   Powerless Outs: This group has no power and is out (that is, it has no easy access to goods or services).

2. *Goods and Services*

   The goods and services which participants do or do not have control over and do and do not have easy access to include such things as:

   a. *Housing*—The location and quality of living arrangements at the lab; the amount and quality of services provided with these living arrangements (e.g., maid service, room service, whether or not one or more room keys are available, number of participants sharing a room).

   b. *Transportation*—e.g., possession of car keys; availability of cars, buses, bicycles; number of vehicles available.

   c. *Food*—Location and quality of dining accommodations; amount and quality of meals; timing of meals; quality of meal service.

   d. *Entertainment*—Amount and quality of entertainment; availability of recreational facilities.

   e. *Treasury*—Personal belongings (e.g., cash, credit cards, luggage, clothing, car keys).

   f. *Education*—Availability of staff or other educational resources; availability of books, films, tapes or other teaching material; accessibility to various seminars or other educational activities.

3. *Starting Processes*

   a. The Powerful Ins meet with the Lab Staff before the other participants.

---

2. Again, in this section, power refers to "positions of power" and not to "experiences of power."

b. The lab staff orients the Powerful Ins with regard to:
—the nature and purposes of a Power Lab (that is, a design to create a set of conditions in which people can learn about the social system phenomena of power and powerlessness and inclusion and exclusion).
—the specific function of the Powerful Ins (that is, to create a power base for themselves and to make provisions for maintaining and using this power).
—the nature of the specific goods and services available for control at this particular laboratory site (that is, who the local facilities people are, how to make arrangements with them, what variations exist with regard to housing, recreation, food, etc.).

c. The Powerful Ins, with staff consultation, work out the details of securing, maintaining, and using their power. They may deal with such issues as:
—What specific housing, transportation, tax, and other arrangements will exist for themselves, the Powerless Ins, and the Powerless Outs?
—What arrangements need to be made in order to ensure that the Powerful Ins can make these arrangements stick?
—What rules (or constitution, if you like) should be established to maintain law and order in this social system?
—What strategies are to be adopted for dealing with the Powerless Ins and the Powerless Outs?
—What specific plans need to be made to receive the rest of the lab population?

C. Possible Learning Outcomes of the Power Lab

1. *Systems Learning*

    a. Increased empathy for people occupying different class positions within organizations, institutions, communities, and societies. Increased awareness of and empathy with the very different "cultures" which grow out of conditions of "in-ness" or "out-ness," power or powerlessness.
    b. Increased sensitivity to power as a pervasive factor of organizations, institutions, and societies. Increased sensitivity to the power games played within social systems.

Increased understanding of ways of breaking these power games.

c. Broadening repertoires for creating change within systems —from positions of power or powerlessness, from In positions or from Out positions.

2. *Personal Growth*

Three conditions for emotional learning are:

a. That the individual be confronted with choices which are difficult for him,

b. That at these choice points he take actions which are personally threatening and which he tends to avoid under non-laboratory conditions, and

c. That when such non-normal action steps are taken, the consequences are positive for him.

These conditions occur at numerous times in the naturally emerging processes of the Power Lab.

Much of the personal growth which comes from participation in Power Labs stems from behavioral coping with action crises. Relatively little comes from the sharing of interpersonal feedback.

D. Design Issues

The following factors are critical to the design of an effective Power Lab:

1. *Site Selection*

Because the Power Lab involves all facets of the participant's life, twenty-four hours a day, the issue of selecting the appropriate site assumes even greater significance than it does in most other types of laboratories. The following facility characteristics are particularly critical:

a. The "space" of the lab needs to be both physically and psychologically distant from competing spaces. Ideal sites are ones which are physically isolated and are not being used by anyone else at the time. If discriminatory treatment regarding food services is a major lab issue, the power of that variable is greatly diminished by having easily accessible alternative sources of food.

b. The facilities management and staff need to be aware of

the special characteristics of this lab, committed to making it succeed, directly involved in the planning of details, and completely at the service of the Lab Staff and the Powerful Ins.

c. The accommodations, facilities, and services need to have sufficient variability as to allow for differential treatment of participants (e.g., variability in room quality and location. variability in menu, control of maid service and room service).

2. *Learning Contract*

In addition to the usual issues regarding the establishment of a learning contract between staff and participants, particular attention needs to be paid to the special contract between the Powerful Ins and the staff. It is critical that the Powerful Ins:

a. understand the rationale for this training design,

b. are committed to accepting their role in the society and, therefore, to the processes of securing, maintaining, and using their power, and

c. understand that it is not within their prerogative to give up the power even if their natural inclinations were to do so.

3. *Additional Content to Social System*

Sometimes the question is raised as to whether the society ought to have some assigned content (e.g., should it be a production factory or a school or a simulated community?). To provide such additional content might in fact provide a certain face validity to the experience and thus make it more immediately palatable to some participants. This would also, however, heighten the role-play quality of the experience thus masking the more powerful realities of dealing with pure power and inclusion issues. Additional content is certainly not needed as an added source of energy to carry the experience. If the initial structuring is done properly, the process will carry itself.

4. *Processing the Experience and Staff Roles*

A frequent design question is: Should we process as we go or wait until the end? This depends on whether you are processing in sub-systems or in the system as a whole. With regard to mid-stream processing for the entire system, there is no choice but to wait until the end. While the game is on, there is little chance of antagonistic groups openly sharing anything of much value with one another. There appears to be relatively little loss in waiting until the end since significant feelings, events and reactions tend to remain fresh throughout and are easily recoverable at a post-game briefing session.

Ongoing processing can be accomplished to good effect *within* the various sub-systems of the lab. This is likely to be most effective if the staff person has been functioning as an ongoing member/consultant of that sub-system. (It is often quite difficult for staff to establish such member/consultant roles in the Powerless Outs group where staff credibility and trustworthiness are likely to be more subject to question.)

In addition to having staff serve as member/consultant in the three sub-systems, it is also functional to have one or more staff who are outside any system and who are free to:

a. handle administrative matters,

b. coordinate staff,

c. serve as anthropologists getting the feel for the total system,

d. calling an end to the game at the appropriate time, and

e. planning and coordinating the final review activities.

5. *Ending the Game*

Only the staff can end the game and the end point should be decided before the game begins. Factors here include the amount of time required for post-game processing (anywhere from three to six hours seems to be adequate) and other planned activities (e.g., back-home planning, organizational work).

The Powerful Ins might at any time decide to call it quits and return all goods and restore all privilegese. It should be clear that this does not end the game. All that will have happened is that the Powerful Ins will have made a major intervention in the system. It is all part of the game to see what happens to this system when power and class differences have been removed.

6. *How Long Should a Power Lab Be?*

One day? Three days? A week? Here we face the same issues and trade-offs as in parallel decisions for Human Interaction Labs. However long the lab, it is critical that the Powerful Ins have a half-day with the staff before the other participants arrive, and that the staff have a full day with the facilities management before anyone arrives.

7. *Pre-Assignment to Class*

If sufficient time can be assured for pre-work with the Powerful Ins, then the issue of assignment to class is less critical than otherwise. Two matters are relevant.

a. Assignment can be based in part on your assumptions as to specific learning needs of individuals or groups. For example, people who you feel, either through previous experience with them or through knowledge of the nature of their work, "need" to develop greater empathy for the Powerless or the Outs, could be assigned to the Powerless Outs. People who you feel need to develop "muscle" around facing up to and using their power could be assigned to the Powerful Ins.

b. *With adequate pre-work,* most groups are willing and able to play the role of Powerful Ins well. Where conditions make it difficult to provide for such pre-work, however, the selection process for this group assumes added significance. Since the power of this lab rests heavily on how well the Powerful Ins create and maintain the conditions of Inness/Outness and Power/Powerlessness, it is important to select those people most likely (1) to recognize the importance of such a role, and (2) to be able to play it without guilt. As one rule of thumb, politically liberal types are considerably worse bets than either politically conservative or radical types. A second rule of thumb is to look for people who, in the general course of their lives, have experienced the pangs of Outness—e.g., certain Blacks, women and youth.

E. Variations

There are many possible variations in Power Lab design. The following are illustrative:

1. *Power Lab As a Team Development Activity*

The experiences of the Powerful Ins and the Powerless Outs are similar in that both are confronted with an adversary with power to affect their lives negatively. I suspect that the person-to-person glue resulting from such a condition is more quickly produced and more durable than that arising from helping them identify and work through their work and interpersonal issues. One approach to team development would be to take an intact work team and have them go through the Powerful Ins or Powerless Outs experience together.

2. *Providing Concrete Assignments to Particular Sub-Systems*

When dealing with a particular client group, it may be useful to assign concrete tasks which have a certain face validity for that client group. In dealing with a university population, for example, one could make the Powerless Outs the students, the Powerless Ins the faculty with the assignment of producing a learning environment for the students, and the Powerful Ins as the trustees and administration. For a state mental health client, the Powerless Outs could be the community; the Powerless Ins, the community mental health agents with the assignment of providing for the psychological and social needs of the community; and the Powerful Ins as the state mental health establishment.

IV. SUMMARY

The Power Lab is designed to help participants recognize, deal with, and break through the various "games" people play with regard to power. A colleague recently criticized the design as focusing too much on power as the "manipulation of *things*" and not enough on the internal psychological conditions and dilemmas of power. It is our belief that only through this caricaturizing and concretizing process—tying power to black and white, real life decisions about matters such as if and how well others are to eat, the conditions in which others will live, the mobility others shall have within the system, and so forth—can these relevant psychological dilemmas be raised in a relatively inescapable fashion. Each segment of this total lab culture confronts the participant with at least one piece of the power jig saw puzzle. That part of the person which bemoans his powerless state ("What do you want from me? I'm powerless.") cannot run from the totality of the power in the Powerful In group. Through the design, you are saying to him, "All right, wise guy, *now* tell us you have no power!" He is confronted with the reality and totality of his power and all the feelings associated with that.

A parallel condition exists for the Powerless Outs. That part of the person which fails to face and deal with his anger at being encroached upon and abused by power ("Believe me, if things were really bad, then I'd let *them* know about it.) can no longer run so easily from that anger. In this case, it is as if the design is saying, "Well? Are things bad enough yet?"

And the Powerless Ins are confronted with what is probably the most puzzling part of the power enigma. ("What do you want from me? I am but the hapless servant of some higher unassailable power. *They* and not me are responsible for your dilemmas.) And, for him too, the design raises numerous troublesome personal questions, not the least of which is: "Just how big a price are you willing to pay for remaining In?"

Beyond this potential for powerful and significant personal learning, there is another, possibly more important, learning potential. The Power Lab *is* a laboratory in the older experimental meaning of the term. Many of the starting ingredients are fixed; many of the dilemmas to be faced by participants and the system as a whole are predictable; but the outcomes are unknown. The Power Lab can be a laboratory for true experimentation with very significant social processes. If together lab practitioners and "clients" can successfully resist the temptation to which many of us are prone, for producing uniform and predictable outcomes, we all just might learn about some processes which surpass in importance the learning of any individual about himself. We just might learn some things about power in social systems; we might learn some things about creative aggression, creative competition, and the creative uses of human power. Who knows?

Managing for Creativity in Organizations: Problems and Issues in Training and OD

WILLIAM G. DYER

The area of creativity has been given a great deal of attention over the past twenty years. Most of the effort, however, has been centered on identifying the forces within an individual that are related to creative output and endeavor. Much research has been going on which is designed to discover those factors that are related to creativity and to look at ways of measuring creativity in individuals. There has been less effort to investigate the area of organizational conditions that tend to foster and release creative behavior in those employees in organizations and there has been even less attention paid to the management process—namely how do you go about managing people in a way that either releases or inhibits the creative effort in subordinates. And, finally, the whole change process regarding changing conditions in organizations that would facilitate creative ouput has not been dealt with to any great extent.

CREATIVENESS AND O. D.

The organization problem regarding creativeness has to do with solid profit and loss for profit-making organizations. It is concerned with the matter of generating new products in order to compete in the market place. To deal with this need for a consistent flow of new products, most organizations have moved to the solution of establishing special R & D units with the specific function of generating new product ideas. This has been a major feature in most organizations for many years. The management of the R & D unit, however, is just now coming under investigation. The question here is: does a manager of an R & D organization function in the same way that would apply to a sales, manufacturing, marketing or financial unit? To what extent do different kinds of activities require different management styles and orientations? Does an R & D unit respond equally as well to a 9,9 system of management or a system four or a Theory Y as the authors of those orientations seem to suggest will occur in the other areas of the organization? To what extent do creative persons require new and different styles of management in their superiors?

In addition to the R & D solution to the need for creative prdducts, almost all organizations find themselves faced with a range of decisions and actions that would seem to benefit from more imagination and creativity in their functioning and operation. For example, it would seem that most business organizations could benefit from imaginative activities in developing new markets, new sales methods, new uses of equipment, and imaginative solutions to personnel and administrative problems.

All areas of an organization could benefit from some type of action that generates more creative solutions to problem solving. This then leads to one of the major dilemmas in the O. D. field. It is highly possible that current O. D. efforts may be antithetical to releasing creativity in organizations. In most O. D. efforts a common beginning place is to take working units and to engage in an extensive team building process. The emphasis in team building centers on building a climate of trust and openness where people can begin to relate more authentically with each other, where a sense of cohesion and identity can be developed in the work unit. Often team training will include such things as decision making by consensus and there seems to be an emphasis on achieving interdependence in the work unit where people are working and supporting each other in effective team efforts. This raises the important issue: If we emphasize collaboration, consensus decision making, cohesion, interdependence, and building work units where people's social needs for inclusion, warmth, and connectiveness are responded to, to what extent do we mitigate against the developing of organizations that will maximize creative effort? It seems that too little attention has been given to looking at the other side effects of the current O. D. developments. As the literature on creativity is examined, there seems to be ample evidence that there is much non-conformity in the highly creative person. To what extent would current O. D. efforts, which seem to have an emphasis on integration and to some extent conformity and cohesion, restrict and inhibit individualistic, somewhat unorthodox, and deviant creative person? If we maximize the cohesive work unit, do we at the same time reduce the imaginative creative process that might unleash the innovative potential in the work unit members?

THE CREATIVE ORGANIZATION AND THE MANAGEMENT

There has really been very little hard research looking at those conditions that are characteristic of a highly creative organization. It is hard to identify an organization that would be generally accepted as being consistently creative. However, some thinking has been done in this area, and Table 1 indicates some of the parallel conditions between the creative individual and the creative organization.

TABLE 1

Comparing The Creative Individual and The Creative Organization

I. What does all this have to do with organization? What are the characteristics of the creative organization; and what are the implications of individual creativity if any?

The Creative Individual	*The Creative Organization*

Conceptual fluency . . . is able to produce a large number of ideas quickly	Has idea men
	Open channels of communication
	Ad hoc devices:
	    Suggestion systems
	    Brain-storming
	    Idea units absolved of other responsibilities
	Encourages contact with outside sources

Originality . . . generates unusual ideas	Heterogenous personnel policy Includes marginal, unusual types Assigns non-specialists to problems Allows eccentricity

Separates source from content in evaluating information . . . is motivated by interest in problem . . . follows wherever it leads	Has an objective, fact-founded approach
	Ideas evaluated on their merits, not status of originator
	Ad hoc approaches:
	    Anonymous communications
	    Blind votes
	Selects and promotes on merit only

TABLE 1 Continued

TABLE 1 Continued

The Creative Individual	The Creative Organization
Suspends judgment . . . avoids early commitment . . . spends more time in analysis, exploration	Lack of financial, material commitment to products. policies Invests in basic research: flexible, long-range planning Experiments with new ideas rather than prejudging on "rational" grounds; everything gets a chance
Less authoritarian . . . has relativistic view of life	More decentralized; diversified Administrative slack; time and resources to absorb errors Risk-taking ethos . . . tolerates and expects taking chances
Accepts own impulses . . . playful, undisciplined exploration	Not run as "tight ship" Employees have fun Allows freedom to choose and pursue problems Freedom to discuss ideas
Independence of judgment, less conformity	Organizationally autonomous
Deviant, sees self as different	Original and different objectives, not trying to be another "X"
Rich, "bizarre" fantasy life and superior reality orientation; controls	Security of routine . . . allows innovation . . ., "Philistines" provide stable, secure environment that allows "creators" to roam

II. What, specifically, can management do—beyond selecting creative participants—to foster creativity within and on the part of the organization?

A. Values and Rewards. First the creative organization in fact prizes and rewards creativity. A management philosophy that stresses creativity as an organizational goal, that encourages and expects it at all levels, will increase the chances of its occurrence.

B. Compensation. It is probably this simple: Where creativity and not productivity is in fact the goal, then creativity and not productivity should in fact be measured and rewarded.

C. Channels for Advancement. To the extent, possible, there would be formal channels for advancement and status within the area of creativity.

D. Freedom. Within rather broad limits, creativity is increased by giving creators freedom in choice of problem and method of pursuit.

E. Communication. Many observations point to the importance of free and open channels of communication, both vertical and horizontal.

Gary A. Steiner. *The Creative Organization* (Chicago: University of Chicago Press, 1965), pp. 16-22.

This table shows that certain of the conditions that are common in the current O. D. framework are also apparently present in the creative organization. However, there are some additional conditions that appear to be present in the creative organization that, up to now, at least, have not been generally thought of as an important part of an O. D. effort. For example, the creative organization seems to encourage marginal and unusual types of people. It allows eccentricity. It has a range of unique ad hoc devices which would encourage free thinking and new ideas. It would try to set up norms for risk taking and a toleration of the new and the unexpected. It would emphasize a more fun loving kind of atmosphere with freedom to pursue ideas that don't seem to be in the main stream of the organization. And there appears to be an encouragement of the different and the bizarre and freedom to roam and to engage in pursuits that are not an ordinary part of the organization routine.

If these are characteristics of the creative organizations, how do we begin to train managers to create these conditions rather than other kinds of conditions that seem at present to pay off more in the organizational system? Most managers are often rewarded if they can create a smooth working, functioning unit that works efficiently and effectively. The highly creative unit in the organization might not be seen as smooth working and efficient. It might appear jagged and uneven and kind of kooky or crazy to an ouside or inside observer. Can the organization tolerate that and can we train and reward managers who can produce conditions that seem to be out of the mainstream of current organization thinking?

Table 2 identifies the characteristics of people who have seemed to be particularly effective in the General Electric creativity course. This list points out a number of behavioral characteristics that seem not to have been emphasized to a great extent in the current O. D. literature.

A question raises itself—Do creative people also become effective managers? Does a person who has abilities to produce creative ideas also become an effective manager? Should we look for a creative manager in a creative person or do we look for a manager who has the ability to manage creative people even though he may not be a particularly creative person? When we examine current training methods, it is dubious that there is a great deal of

TABLE 2

General Electric's Creative Courses

Class members are generally selected from recent college graduates in the fields of engineering or physics. It is not possible to measure the innate creativity of these individuals by consideration of their academic record. Observation of men who have done particularly well in the course has shown several attributes that are important. These criteria are used in making the selections of course members.

1. A Constructive Discontent with things as they are. From this comes an inherent desire to improve or develop those things with which he comes in contact.
2. An Ability to Observe and understand the meaning of the observations.
3. An Active Curiosity that keeps the mind delving into the functioning of old and new devices and phenomena. The man is not content just to see something work; he must find out why, and reason cause and effect through to a logical conclusion.
4. A Well-Organized Mind that is able to file and catalog observed information for future reference. This is the source from which the individual can recall devices, ideas, etc., from everyday experiences. This material forms the basis for problem synthesis.
5. Good Reasoning Power based upon firm understanding of engineering fundamentals. This is more than the ability to solve problems by manipulation or formulae; it is the understanding of the physical significance of the basic scientific laws. It is also the ability to see through the superfluous clutter found in all engineering problems in order to find the core of the problem.
6. A Practical and Creative Imagination able to call upon past experience and present knowledge to bring about new ideas.
7. A Sense of Proportion in orders of magnitude involved in any experiment or series of calculations. This might be said to be a natural feel for a particular subject, or common sense when it comes to use of judgment in engineering problems.
8. An "I'll Show You" Attitude. This is characterized by a willingness to pitch in and find out what's wrong, or to make a model to illustrate one's idea.
9. Outside Creative Interests and activities usually give some indication of a man's creative potential in engineering. Often hobbies are good clues. The fact that he has a hobby is not the important item; it is what he had done with it. Has he contributed by original work? Or, is he satisfied with repetition of what others have done?

Also, experience has shown that an engineer entering the program must rank high in motivation and initiative, and should be at least average in his ability to get along with people.

The actual selection process consists of two parts, an entrance problem and interview. The entrance problem is made up of one or more actual Company engineering problems which need a creative solution. The prospective class members spend approximately 20 hours of their own time during one week working on this entrance problem.

After all of the solutions have been reviewed, each man is given a personal interview. This allows the man to explain the ramifications of his solutions. It also gives the interviewer an opportunity to compare the man's aptitudes with the crietria previously cited.

George I. Samstad, *A Source Book for Creative Thinking*, p. 335.

emphasis or reward given to the highly individualistic, non-conforming, creative person, and very little emphasis has been given toward developing the ability to guide and stimulate the creative efforts of others. In a typical T-group centered laboratory a very common experience is to see the non-conformist, the rebellious, the individualistically-oriented person with deviant behaviors and peculiar idiosyncracies as often the butt of a great deal of initial negative reaction and negative feedback. It would seem that a person would learn in a T-group kind of training experience that the way he best gets along with others is to conform to their expectations. If he can identify those group norms that operate implicitly and can modify his behavior to fit in adequately to those norms, then he experiences the warmth, acceptance and rewards of the group. Perhaps these are not the conditions that should be emphasized in training if we are to encourage the creative person. If we are to train managers to work effectively with creative people or to release the creative potential of others, then perhaps the T-group mode is not the most appropriate way of functioning. It is also possible, however, to create a T-group process that emphasizes an entirely different set of norms than the ones mentioned above. Here, using the same methodology, a whole new set of behaviors could be identified and encouraged in the T-group process.

TRAINING FOR THE MANAGEMENT OF CREATIVITY

We shift now to the problem of training. Specifically, how do you go about training managers to identify the creative person, to release the creative potential that is present in most people and to create those conditions in the organization that will foster and encourage creative ouput? This is a very interesting and challenging problem in training.

Table 3 identifies the learning objectives as they were set up in an initial training laboratory in creativity in organizations. The design was to try to create that training experience that would help achieve these kinds of learning goals. The laboratory design was as follows:

TABLE 3

**NTL Institute Creativity in Organizations Laboratory
Program Objectives**

1. What is the nature of the creative process both within an individual and in groups or larger systems?
2. How can we identify and assess the creative potential in individuals?
3. How can we determine the conditions in a system that facilitate or block the creative output of individuals and groups?
4. How does a manager manage in order to release the creative potential of the people in his organization?
5. How can a change agent influence managers to be more effective in their managing for creativity?

Phase I—Examining the Creative Process

The process on this first portion on the first day was to both get participants connected with the staff and each other, and to become involved in the training program (both content and process). Individuals and groups were given a series of short creativity exercises that had fun elements. After working on these tasks, the participants reported on the processes they went through in arriving at creative solutions. This introduced them to each other and also the creative process they were being trained to manage.

Phase II—Identifying Creative Talent

One of the important tasks in managing for creativity is to be able to identify and thus encourage the creative person. The second part of the training program continued the emphasis on the creative process and added the dimension of identifying and utilizing the creative person. A series of group tasks were initiated that required a creative solution (this included a case around the use of a creative employee [See Appendix 1], and a TAT picture that required a creative story).

As the group worked on these tasks, they made assessments of their own creative potential and that of the other members. Data were shared as participants filled out a creativity profile on each other (See Table 4). Feedback sessions were held as people discussed their performance on the tasks and their reactions to each other and the ratings.

TABLE 4

The Creative Individual
by
Philip B. Daniels and William G. Dyer

1. Conventional conforming	1 2 3 4 5 6 7	Unconventional, nonconforming, deviant
2. Conscientious about time, appointments, etc.	1 2 3 4 5 6 7	Time not too important often tardy, forgets time when involved in activities
3. Socializer, prefers to be in groups.	1 2 3 4 5 6 7	A lone, prefers solitary individualistic activities
4. Concerned about social amenities	1 2 3 4 5 6 7	Unconcerned about social amenities
5. Inhibited, controlled	1 2 3 4 5 6 7	Uninhibited, impulsive
6. Cannot tolerate ambiguity, needs structure	1 2 3 4 5 6 7	Can tolerate ambiguity, lack of strength
7. Has difficulty with abstractions	1 2 3 4 5 6 7	Enjoys dealing in abstractions
8. Cannot bring order from chaos	1 2 3 4 5 6 7	Can bring order and meaning out of chaos and confusion
9. Accepts things as they are	1 2 3 4 5 6 7	Curious, questioning, even about "obvious"
10. Satisfied with present system, no push to invent better ways	1 2 3 4 5 6 7	Strong conviction that there is always a "better way to do it," drive to find it
11. Cautious, conservative, hesitant	1 2 3 4 5 6 7	Bold, daring, adventurous with ideas, a risk taker
12. Easily bored with ideas	1 2 3 4 5 6 7	Playful, easily entertained with ideas
13. Anxiety about being wrong	1 2 3 4 5 6 7	Low anxiety about being wrong
14. Low self esteem, lack of confidence low ego strength	1 2 3 4 5 6 7	High self esteem, self confidence, and ego strength
15. Not reflective, introspective, or contemplative	1 2 3 4 5 6 7	Introspective, reflective contemplative
16. Not intelligent or "bright"	1 2 3 4 5 6 7	Highly intelligent and "bright"
17. Inability to concentrate, lacks self-discipline	1 2 3 4 5 6 7	Abiliy to concentrate, self-disciplined

TABLE 4 Continued

18. No aesthetic interests or inclinations	1 2 3 4 5 6 7	High aesthetic interests and inclinations
19. Not resourceful or ingenious	1 2 3 4 5 6 7	Very resourceful, ingenious
20. Not stimulating to others. and never threatening	1 2 3 4 5 6 7	Stimulating to others, and even threatening
21. Not self-critical	1 2 3 4 5 6 7	Self-critical
22. Not opinionated, confidence in the ideas of others	1 2 3 4 5 6 7	Opinionated, fond of his own ideas
23. Accepts "no" as an answer	1 2 3 4 5 6 7	Won't take "no" for an answer
24. Has impoverished fantasy and imagination	1 2 3 4 5 6 7	Has rich fantasy and imagination
25. Low capacity to integrate and synthesize	1 2 3 4 5 6 7	Great capacity to integrate and synthesize to organize into wholes
26. No use of metaphor or analogy in speech	1 2 3 4 5 6 7	Uses metaphore and analogy in speech
27. No particular need to "do his own thing"	1 2 3 4 5 6 7	Enjoys freedom to "do his own thing"
28. Not flexible and adaptive	1 2 3 4 5 6 7	Flexible and adaptive
29. Generates no new ideas and plans	1 2 3 4 5 6 7	Generates new ideas and plans
30. Beholden to the printed word	1 2 3 4 5 6 7	Not overly impressed by the printed word
31. When given a problem also wants an answer	1 2 3 4 5 6 7	When given a problem he wants to figure the answer himself

Phase III—Assessing The Creative Potential in an Organization

The design called for helping managers first understand the creative process as it applies to individuals and then as it applies to organizations. The basic question was: How can we identify the creativity level in an organization and then keep improving it?

The task of the participants now was to develop a method for arriving at the creative potential in a work system. It was arranged with the Inn where the conference was held to gather data about the creativity potential in that organization and to feed the data back into the system.

Instruments (See Tables 5 and 6) and procedures were developed for assessing the work system in the Inn.

TABLE 5

Managing For Creativity
by
Philip B. Daniels and William G. Dyer

1.	Doesn't listen	1 2 3 4 5 6 7	Listens very well
2.	Cuts people off in conversation	1 2 3 4 5 6 7	Lets people finish their statements
3.	Evaluates prematurely	1 2 3 4 5 6 7	Evaluates at appropriate time
4.	Nonverbal cues of disapproval	1 2 3 4 5 6 7	Nonverbal support and approval
5.	Never shows excitement at new ideas	1 2 3 4 5 6 7	Shows great excitement at new ideas
6.	Pushes too soon for solution	1 2 3 4 5 6 7	Delays adequately the push for solution
7.	Has low concern for the task of the group	1 2 3 4 5 6 7	Has high concern for the task of the group
8.	Discourages diversity of opinion	1 2 3 4 5 6 7	Encourages diversity of opinion
9.	Never shows admiration for new ideas	1 2 3 4 5 6 7	Shows great admiration for new ideas
10.	Low concern for people and their feelings	1 2 3 4 5 6 7	High concern for people and their feelings
11.	Not willing to tolerate playfulness in others	1 2 3 4 5 6 7	Very willing to tolerate playfulness in others
12.	Unwilling to support ideas not his own	1 2 3 4 5 6 7	Willingness to support ideas of others
13.	Cannot tolerate confusion and chaos	1 2 3 4 5 6 7	Can tolerate confusion and chaos

TABLE 6

Creativity in Management and Organization
by
Philip B. Daniels and William G. Dyer

Please be as honest as you can in filling out this anonymous questionnaire. Your responses will be added in the responses of others to make an average. You are to rate how you see your boss or your organization.

The numbers 1 through 7 are intended to reflect various degrees of the characteristics. The 1 and the 7 are extremes while the numbers between represent various degrees between these extremes. Circle the number that best represents your judgment on each item.

1. My ideas or suggestions never get a fair hearing   1 2 3 4 5 6 7   My ideas or suggestions get a fair hearing

2. I feel like my boss is not interested in my ideas   1 2 3 4 5 6 7   I feel like my boss is very interested in my ideas

3. I receive no encouragement to innovate on my job   1 2 3 4 5 6 7   I am encouraged to innovate on my job

4. There is no reward for innovating or improving things on my job   1 2 3 4 5 6 7   I am rewarded for innovating and improving on my job

5. There is no encouragement for diverse opinions among subordinates   1 2 3 4 5 6 7   There is encouragement of diversity of opinion among subordinates

6. I'm very reluctant to tell him about mistakes I make   1 2 3 4 5 6 7   I feel comfortable enough with my boss to tell him about mistakes I make

7. I'm not given enough responsibility for me to do my job right   1 2 3 4 5 6 7   I am given enough responsibility for me to do my job right

8. To really succeed in this organization one needs to be a friend or relative of the boss   1 2 3 4 5 6 7   There is no favoritism in the organization

9. There are other jobs in this organization that I would prefer to have   1 2 3 4 5 6 7   I have the job in this organization that I think I do best

10. They keep close watch over me too much of the time   1 2 3 4 5 6 7   They trust me to do my job without always checking on me

TABLE 6 Continued

11. They would not let me try other jobs in the organization   1 2 3 4 5 6 7   I could try other kinds of jobs in the organization if I wanted to.

12. The management gets very uptight by confusion, disorder, and chaos   1 2 3 4 5 6 7   The management deals easily with confusion, disorder and chaos

13. There is a low standard of excellence on the job   1 2 3 4 5 6 7   There is a high standard of excellence for me on the job

14. My boss is not open to receive my opinion of how he might improve his own performance on the job   1 2 3 4 5 6 7   My boss is very open to suggestions on how he might improve his own performance

15. My boss has a very low standard for judging his own performance   1 2 3 4 5 6 7   My boss has a very high standard of excellence for judging his own performance

16. I am not asked for suggestions on how to improve service to the customers   1 2 3 4 5 6 7   The management actively solicits my suggestions and ideas on how to improve the service to customers

17. My boss shows me no enthusiasm for the work we are engaged in   1 2 3 4 5 6 7   My boss exhibits lots of enthusiasm for the work we are engaged in

18. Mistakes get you in trouble; they aren't to learn from   1 2 3 4 5 6 7   Around here mistakes are to learn from and not to penalize you

19. Someone else dictates how much I should accomplish on my job   1 2 3 4 5 6 7   I'm allowed to set my own goals for my job

20. I am very dissatisfied on my job   1 2 3 4 5 6 7   I am very satisfied on my job

21. My boss never lets me know how I stand with him   1 2 3 4 5 6 7   My boss keeps me informed on how I stand with him

22. My boss does not communicate clearly what I am to do   1 2 3 4 5 6 7   My boss communicates clearly what I am supposed to do

23. The organization has too many rules and regulations for me   1 2 3 4 5 6 7   The organization has adequate rules and regulations for me

Phase IV—Data Gathering and Analysis in the Work System

In this part of the training program, participants interviewed members of the Inn work force, gathered questionnaire data and organization information about the structure and functioning of the Inn. After the data were collected, it was tabulated and a general analysis of the creativity level of the Inn and its management was determined.

Following this a plan was developed for feeding the data back into the system in a way that would optimize the probability of its being utilized.

Phase V—Feedback to the Organization

During this phase, a team of participants met with the management of the Inn to review the findings of the assessment process. Participants were very anxious during this task but the management was receptive and accepted the data with interest, although the shortness of the program precluded any attempt to follow up on any change that might take place.

Phase VI—Critique of the Experience

In this phase, the whole system analysis program was reviewed.

Phase VII—Planning for Back Home Application

Based on the experiences of the week, the participants were asked to make an assessment of the creative potential in their own organization (or the Unit in which they were located) and to devise a creative plan for improving the creativity level of that organization. These plans were then presented to the total group for discussion and critique.

EVALUATION OF THE PROGRAM

In this first attempt to train managers for managing for creativity, a number of both positive and negative factors were identified. Negative factors were:

1. A lack of clear assessment and training of the manager's own skill in managing for creativity. We need more experience letting the manager actually try out managing a group with the purpose of trying to develop those conditions that would facilitate innovation.

2. The experiences with the Inn were too dissimilar to most of the back home situations. The field work experience was helpful, but it was not related clearly enough to the large scale industrial organization from which most participants came, hence, a lack of relevance.
3. Lack of specific follow through and consultation in the back home setting. This is a constant problem in most training programs. Follow up letters were sent out to each participant asking for a summary of their utilization of their back home plans.

On the positive side:

1. The general orientation that managing for creativity involves different norms, organizational conditions, different awareness and insight was a new and challenging direction for the participants.
2. These managers were unfamiliar with any sophisticated frame of reference regarding the creativity process, factors related to individual and group creativity, and organizations conditions important in supporting creativeness. Exposure to these orientations was the strongest part of the program.
3. The program also introduced the participants to the field of measuring an organization regarding its creativity level and also helped them begin a process of planning and implementing change in this area.

SUMMARY

Many organizations are interested in some form of O. D. effort that will help in re-vitalizing or renewing the organization. Much of the current practice in O. D. is geared toward improving the organization that is troubled by low trust, closed communications, non-collaboration, ineffective decision making and planning. However, there are many other organizations that have problems in other areas: they have low excitement, innovation is minimal, decision making is routine, the general atmosphere is one of plodding and acceptance of the given daily schedule. These organizations need to be improved with excitement, higher levels of imagination and creative ouput. To improve this quality of organizational life, an attempt was made to train managers to manage for creativity, to locate and develop creative people and to produce the organizational conditions that release the creative potential of all.

Psychological Climate: An Exercise for Teaching Consultants and Managers

CHARLES K. FERGUSON

UNDERLYING THEORY OR ASSUMPTIONS

Nothing is less tangible nor more important in organizational life and in interpersonal transactions than psychological climate. Its existence is as real and as subject to change as physical climate, although the components that make it up, while equally identifiable, are not nearly as concrete.

Everyone knows that physical climate is the result of a combination of temperature, humidity, cloud formation, wind conditions, vegetation, geographic situation, etc. Many people have never thought directly about psychological climate nor about the ingredients that make it up.

What are the ingredients? They are attitudes and the implementation of those attitudes as expressed in behavior by one person toward another or others. We each help make a psychological climate for others by the attitudes we radiate toward them; psychological climate is the result of attitudinal radiation.

No single variable is more important in interpersonal affairs because the set of attitudes perceived by an observer determines whether he will resist or cooperate, compete or collaborate, fight or join. I hold out my hand to you as a stranger, you take it or not depending not alone on social convention but what you quickly discern my attitude to be. Trust or lack of it flows from the reading of attitude.

If threat is perceived, a human system will mobilize its energy to defend against the threat, to hold it off, avoid it, withdraw from it or fight it. The perception of threat hardens the attitudinal boundaries of a human system, makes them less adaptable, less permeable, less flexible. If I want to penetrate, examine, change, alter, modify, adapt or join another system, I must create conditions that reduce threat. A precondition for managers or consultants who want to work successfully with human beings is the creation of a climate that reduces threat.

Threat is manageable, it can be increased or reduced. I can manage my stance toward you by producing threat or by reducing threat and working to induce trust. I know how to do that. So do you. We can snarl, accuse, ignore, demean, insult, abuse, condemn, slight, object, deny, offend, embarrass, hate, dislike, and threaten in various ways. We all learn to do these things in one form or another with more or less skill.

We also can charm, flatter, indulge, accept, praise, flirt, attend, agree, inflate, be warm, hospitable, courteous, kind, straight, open, helpful, decent, likeable, understanding, respectful, loving and trustworthy. We all learn to do these things in one form or another with more or less skill.

We mostly all have the basic training through simply growing up to influence the kind of psychological climate, positive or negative, that we need or wish to have. But managers and consultants do not always see the direct cause and effect relationship between the kinds of attitudes they choose to mobilize and express and the psychological climate, with its inevitable results, that they thereby produce.

WHAT THE EXERCISE IS DESIGNED TO ACCOMPLISH

It is desirable for managers and consultants to know that they can control their influence upon psychological climate. It is important for people to appreciate that there is a cause and effect relationship between the climate they create and consequences in the behavior of others. The exercise is designed to give managers and consultants (a) a more conscious understanding of the attitudinal ingredients of positive and negative psychological climates, (b) a sense that they individually can mobilize and express different component parts of their repertoire of available attitudes and thereby significantly influence climate around them, (c) the heightened realization that the climate they succeed in generating shapes the response they will get from others and (d) to provide an opportunity for some skill practice at consciously generating the kind of psychological climate they desire.

PROCEDURE

The procedure is best employed with a group or class of managers or consultants in a training situation. It involves the following steps:

1. Introduction to the concept of psychological climate and its importance in interpersonal affairs and organizational life.
2. Ask for four volunteers from the group to simulate a subordinate (or client)—dispatch these four from the room to agree on a common premise for dialogue with a supervisor (consultant)—caution that each of the four will begin discussion with the same premise/problem but will be called back into the room one at a time.
3. While the four volunteers are out of the room on a blackboard or on newsprint construct a continuum of psychological climate with positive (+) at one end and negative (−) at the other. Get the members of the audience to call out attitudinal ingredients of a positive psychological climate (i.e. treat him warmly, listen to him, be interested, etc. etc.) and also get them to suggest or call out attitudinal ingredients for a negative psychological climate (i.e. ignore him, be in a hurry, interrupt, etc. etc.). Print this list of suggestions under a + column and a − column on the blackboard or on newsprint.
4. Ask for four volunteers to simulate a superior or a consultant. Have two of these four agree to make the positive climate operational in conversation with two of the volunteer subordinates and the other two to implement the negative climate.
5. State for all remaining, that whichever of the volunteers comes back into the room 1st and 3rd will be treated with a positive climate and whichever comes 2nd and 4th will be treated with the negative climate. Ask observers (whose suggestions constructed the lists) to observe verbal and non-verbal cues carefully for impact and cause and effect consequence of the differing climates.
6. Proceed without comment or discussion through brief but contrasting conversations stemming from the uniform pre-

mise selected and agreed outside the room by the original four volunteers.

7. Publicly interview in turn subordinate 1, 2, 3, and 4, for reactions, solicit comments by observers, and discussion.

8. Recapitulate the whole process orally, present additional theory regarding psychological climate relative to what the group has just seen and emphasize (with theory) that everyone has the capacity to influence psychological climate and that the consequences he gets (as has just been witnessed) will have a cause and effect relationship to the climate he has provided—any person can provide either positive or negative climate—the demonstration will document that we each have choice.

9. Discussion, reaction, comment.

10. Divide the group into arbitrary clusters of three. Ask one to be consultant, one to be consultee, and one to be observer. Invite these trios to practice—to consciously try to create a positive, and then in turn a negative climate. Allow approximately five minutes for one (positive) climate to develop and then give a signal signifying time for immediate change to an attempt to implement the opposite (negative) climate. If there is sufficient time available allow each of the three in the cluster an opportunity for positive and negative skill practice.

CASE EXAMPLE AND ADVANTAGE/DISADVANTAGES OF THE EXERCISE

The procedure described has been found useful in in-service training programs for personnel people in industry and for consultants in training in university and/or professional development programs. It is also useful for managers involved in management development programs. The advantages of the procedure described are that they mobilize a high degree of audience attention, they provide an active learning situation, they involve all members of the group, they draw on the experience of members of the group, they rely on internal motivations for participation and learning of members of the group, they relate theory immediately to observed behavior, they give all members opportunity for skill practice directly following relevant observation and theory thus imprinting learning.

The disadvantages are those of any situation that involves role playing or simulation, i.e., that you may occasionally get volunteers who are incapable of assuming the roles expected of them. In the experience of the writer after using the exercise many times this disadvantage has never been bad enough to spoil the exercise but it is always a risk.

VALUE SYSTEM REPRESENTED BY THE EXERCISE

The process of the exercise itself is heavily rooted in the assumption that the only real learning regarding human relations comes from an analysis of one's own experience. Procedures in the exercise are designed to mobilize immediate personal experience which can be observed and from which people can generalize.

The substance of the exercise attests to the values (a) that human beings respond most favorably in a positive psychological climate, (b) that human intelligence can describe the attitudinal ingredients of positive psychological climate and (c) that human beings can control their behavior so that it influences the development of positive psychological climate.

APPENDIX 1

Dan Johnson and His Winning Suggestion

In August of 1957, B. A. Warner, personnel director of the Irwin Manufacturing Company, was trying to decide what action he sholud take with regard to Dan Johnson, an employee of the company. Dan had submitted an acceptable suggestion but, before submitting the idea, had given it a trial run, thus violating a long-standing rule that no change could be put into effect without the prior approval of the engineering department.

Irwin Manufacturing Company was a manufacturer of electrical equipment and was located in a large city in the midwest. It was formed in 1919 by Mr. A. B. Baker, father of the present president and grandfather of two of the vice-presidents. The company organization is shown in Exhibit I. The company had no union and had a reputation as being a "good place to work." Most of the company's products were mass-produced to very close tolerances. They were sold in all 48 states by a sales force numbering almost 400. These salesmen worked out of the 53 company-owned branches and sold on commission. Home office employment was in the neighborhood of 1300 during August.

Dan Johnson had started with Irwin as a drill press operator in 1946 shortly after arriving in Chicago from his former home and birthplace. Kentucky. Irwin was the first place to which he had applied and he was offered the job on the spot. During his time with Irwin he had received frequent pay increases. Exhibit 2 contains a record of Dan's wage progress.

In 1951, five years after Dan joined Irwin, he was promoted to set-up man in the newly formed spring department. This department came about as a result of a large government contract. After the conract expired, the volume of Irwin's regular products had expanded enough to make it unnecessary to transfer Johnson back to his job as drill press operator. As a set-up man, he was responsible for the setting up of the automatic equipment in his department as well as the supervision of the 10 female "spring loopers" who also worked in the department. After the springs were automatically formed by machine, they were moved to benches where the spring loopers then formed the ends by using special pliers. Another job of Dan's was to run an engine lathe especially designed to manufacture heavy duty springs. While runs of this nature were infrequent, they were usually scheduled as reasonably long runs.

In reviewing Dan's personnel folder, Warner noticed that this was the third time he had violated the same rule. Other details concerning Johnson are reproduced in Exhibit 3. Dan's latest violation was a serious one according to the company's engineers. If it had not been detected, serious damage might have resulted.

Dan's idea concerned eliminating one entire job element in the forming operation of a certain heavy duty spring, performing it in one step rather than two. He designed a special tool bit to accomplish the form. Before submitting this suggestion, Dan decided to try out his idea. He ran 10,000 of these heavy duty springs. After inspecting them and seeing nothing wrong with the results he sent them to the assembly area where they would eventually become an integral part of machines which sold for $250.

In the assembly area they sat unnoticed for almost a week, until it came time to use them in the final assembly of the machines. At this point, an inspector noticed the difference and placed a stop order on the parts, pending investigation. Product engineers were called in and they immediately called for Joe Poppy, Johnson's immediate supervisor. When Joe expressed ignorance of the situation, Dan was called in. He readily admitted making the change and commented, "Why only yesterday I mailed in the suggestion form." This occurred on the 18th of the month. Dan was told to return to his department until disposition of his case had been determined. He was worried that he might be discharged.

Company engineers explained to Warner they could not be sure at the time if Dan's idea was a good one. They feared that his form job set up a stress concentration that might fail under repeated loadings. They further explained that if this were so, it was fortunate that the inspector had caught the mistake. Otherwise, the springs would have been assembled into some 10,000 machines, all of which might develop trouble in the field and require expensive servicing.

The afternoon of the 18th Warner instructed Bill Kay, a personnel assistant, to interview Johnson to learn more about his background. Bill Kay's comments follow:

"A very likeable, sincerely-motivated worker . . . realizes he did wrong. When reminded that he had previously been warned about trying ideas out without approval, he expressed regrets and could offer no explanation. He said he was only sorry he didn't have more of an education as he would like to study spring engineering and design. He also related an unhappy experience that happened to him about a month ago. As one of the engineers was walking through the Department, Dan had stopped him and inquired if there were any books Dan could borrow that would explain the theory of spring design. The engineer replied 'What would a hillbilly like you want with a book. Stick to your comic books and leave the technical publications alone.' Dan said he didn't mention the incident to anyone, but he thought the girls in the department had overheard the engineer's remarks. He would not give the name of the engineer. Dan said his home life was fine. He spent two evenings a week in boy scout activities and bowled on another night in the company league. When asked he had refused to attend foremanship training classes, he said he hated to spend another evening away from his family. Dan ended the interview with the hope that he would be given another chance."

Late in the next day Bill interviewed Joe Poppy. Joe said he was in favor of firing Johnson. He explained that only this morning his boss, Karl Metz, had "chewed him out" about Dan for it seems that Neal Baker, Sales Manager, had heard about the incident and called Karl in on the carpet. Neal had expressed horror at the thought that 10,000 defective machines might have been built. Joe also said Dan did a fairly good job as supervisor of women but that he could no longer tolerate Dan's constant experimenting.

Warner was reviewing the case on the afternoon of the 19th, in preparation for a meeting between Joe and Karl to decide on the fate of Dan, when the phone rang. It was Ralph Brown, product engineer, who reported that Dan's idea was thoroughly sound and that based on this evidence, he was recommending a $50 suggestion award.

Warner hung up the phone wondering what effect this should have on his decision. Company policy provided that even if Dan were discharged he would still be in line for the award.

THE GEORGE BROWN COLLEGE
OF APPLIED ARTS AND TECHNOLOGY
LIBRARY